Shakespeare's Histories on Screen

SHAKESPEARE AND ADAPTATION

Shakespeare and Adaptation provides in-depth discussions of a dynamic field and showcases the ways in which, with each act of adaptation, a new Shakespeare is generated. The series addresses the phenomenon of Shakespeare and adaptation in all its guises and explores how Shakespeare continues as a reference-point in a generically diverse body of representations and forms, including fiction, film, drama, theatre, performance and mass media. Including sole authored books as well as edited collections, the series embraces a mix of methodologies and espouses a global perspective that brings into conversation adaptations from different nations, languages and cultures.

Series Editor:
Mark Thornton Burnett (Queen's University Belfast, UK)

Advisory Board:
Dr Ariane M. Balizet (Texas Christian University, USA)
Professor Sarah Hatchuel (Université Paul-Valéry Montpellier, 3, France)
Dr Peter Kirwan ((Mary Baldwin University, USA)
Professor Douglas Lanier (University of New Hampshire, USA)
Professor Adele Lee (Emerson College, USA)
Dr Stephen O'Neill (Maynooth University, Ireland)
Professor Shormishtha Panja (University of Delhi, India)
Professor Lisa Starks (University of South Florida)
Professor Nathalie Vienne-Guerrin (Université Paul-Valéry Montpellier 3, France)
Professor Sandra Young (University of Cape Town, South Africa)

Published Titles:
Lockdown Shakespeare
Gemma Allred, Benjamin Broadribb and Erin Sullivan

Women and Indian Shakespeares
Edited by Thea Buckley, Mark Thornton Burnett, Sangeeta Datta and Rosa García-Periago
Adapting Macbeth
William C. Carroll
Liberating Shakespeare
Edited by Jennifer Flaherty and Deborah Uman
Romeo and Juliet, Adaptation and the Arts
Edited by Julia Reinhard Lupton and Ariane Helou

Forthcoming Titles:

Shakespeare, Ecology and Adaptation: A Practical Guide
Alys Daroy and Paul Prescott
Shakespeare and Ballet
David Fuller
Shakespearean Biofiction on the Contemporary Stage and Screen
Edited by Ronan Hatfull and Edel Semple

Shakespeare's Histories on Screen

Adaptation, Race and Intersectionality

Jennie M. Votava

THE ARDEN SHAKESPEARE
LONDON • NEW YORK • OXFORD • NEW DELHI • SYDNEY

THE ARDEN SHAKESPEARE
Bloomsbury Publishing Plc
50 Bedford Square, London, WC1B 3DP, UK
1385 Broadway, New York, NY 10018, USA
29 Earlsfort Terrace, Dublin 2, Ireland

BLOOMSBURY, THE ARDEN SHAKESPEARE and the Arden Shakespeare logo are trademarks of Bloomsbury Publishing Plc

First published in Great Britain 2023
This paperback edition published in 2025

Copyright © Jennie M. Votava, 2023

Jennie M. Votava has asserted her right under the Copyright, Designs and Patents Act, 1988, to be identified as author of this work.

For legal purposes the Acknowledgements on p. xi constitute an extension of this copyright page.

Cover image: THE HOLLOW CROWN, (from left): Ben Miles, Sophie Okonedo, 'Richard III'.
Photo by Robert Viglasky / ©PBS/BBC/Carnival Film & Television
Everett Collection Inc / Alamy Stock Photo

All rights reserved. No part of this publication may be reproduced or transmitted in any form or by any means, electronic or mechanical, including photocopying, recording, or any information storage or retrieval system, without prior permission in writing from the publishers.

Bloomsbury Publishing Plc does not have any control over, or responsibility for, any third-party websites referred to or in this book. All internet addresses given in this book were correct at the time of going to press. The author and publisher regret any inconvenience caused if addresses have changed or sites have ceased to exist, but can accept no responsibility for any such changes.

A catalogue record for this book is available from the British Library.

A catalog record for this book is available from the Library of Congress.

Names: Votava, Jennie M., author.
Title: Shakespeare's histories on screen : adaptation, race and intersectionality / Jennie M. Votava.
Description: London ; New York : The Arden Shakespeare, 2023. | Series: Shakespeare and adaptation | Includes bibliographical references and index.
Identifiers: LCCN 2022060170 | ISBN 9781350326644 (hardback) | ISBN 9781350326682 (paperback) | ISBN 9781350326651 (epub) | ISBN 9781350326668 (ebook)
Subjects: LCSH: Shakespeare, William, 1564-1616–Film adaptations–History and criticism. | Shakespeare, William, 1564-1616–Histories–Adaptations–History and criticism. | Race in motion pictures. | Identity (Psychology) in motion pictures.
Classification: LCC PR3093 .V68 2023 | DDC 822.3/3–dc23/eng/20230309
LC record available at https://lccn.loc.gov/2022060170

ISBN: HB: 978-1-3503-2664-4
PB: 978-1-3503-2668-2
ePDF: 978-1-3503-2666-8
eBook: 978-1-3503-2665-1

Series: Shakespeare and Adaptation

Typeset by Deanta Global Publishing Services, Chennai, India

To find out more about our authors and books visit www.bloomsbury.com and sign up for our newsletters.

For Harper and Eleanor

CONTENTS

List of figures x
Acknowledgements xi

Introduction: From Rodney King to Netflix's *The King*: Adaptation and/as intersectionality in Shakespeare's histories, 1991–2019 1

1 Through a glass darkly: Race, gender, disability and Sophie Okonedo's Margaret of Anjou in *The Hollow Crown: The Wars of the Roses* 21

2 Two Yorks, the Boy and the King of Pop: Colour-conscious casting and queer seriality in *The Hollow Crown*, Season One 55

3 The fat knight in black and white: Race, disability, gender, nation, Falstaff 87

4 Straight outta Shakespeare: *H4, My Own Private Idaho* and the universality conundrum 119

5 Film Noir, *White Heat*, 'Top of the World': Loncraine's *Richard III* in Nazi-face 149

Conclusion: Swinging the lens: *Bridgerton* as Shakespearean history in digital cultures 177

Notes 201
Select bibliography 237
Index 247

FIGURES

1. Queen Margaret after the Battle of Bosworth Field. *Richard III*, directed by Dominic Cooke 28
2. York and the Boy at Agincourt. *Henry V*, directed by Thea Sharrock 67
3. Richard II and the Bishop of Carlisle. *Richard II*, directed by Rupert Goold 77
4. Falstaff and Mistress Quickly as tragic figures. *Henry IV, Part 2*, directed by Richard Eyre 106
5. Falstaff and company at the coronation. *H4*, directed by Paul Quinn 116
6. Henry V kneels to the Chief Justice. *H4*, directed by Paul Quinn 132
7. 'The Coming of the White Man'. *My Own Private Idaho*, directed by Gus Van Sant 138
8. Two villains in extreme close-up. *Richard III*, directed by Richard Loncraine (top). *Young and Innocent*, directed by Alfred Hitchcock (bottom) 160
9. *Bridgerton* meets Shakespeare: Adjoa Andoh on Twitter 182
10. Queen Charlotte and her court. *Bridgerton*, Season 1, Ep. 1 187

ACKNOWLEDGEMENTS

This book would not have been possible without multiple intersecting inspirations, influences and means of support from family, friends, colleagues, students and institutions. My primary motivation for writing about Shakespeare and race comes from my daughters, Harper and Eleanor Forts, who over the course of the work's evolution have grown from preschoolers to second graders, with their own ever-evolving understanding of both the beauties and injustices of our world. Along with them I thank their dad and my spouse, Frank Forts, whose knowledge of history and belief in me mean more to me than I think he knows. I also can't leave out my parents, Jan and Hank Votava, who have been there in ways too numerous to list – including seeing me through my career transition from medical doctor to English literature professor and always embracing the value of the latter.

My wonderful colleagues in the literary profession have also been instrumental to this project. For his ongoing encouragement, unflagging willingness to provide insightful feedback on my drafts, and enviable dexterity with a pun as well as a pen I thank my friend and mentor Jim Bulman, aka Ancient Pistol – may he always have 'a killing tongue and a quiet sword'. I am also grateful to Alexis Hart for her sage advice on a draft of the article that became Chapter 1, to both Jim Bulman and Jennifer Hellwarth for writing last-minute letters of reference towards funding that helped me complete the final manuscript, and, throughout the process, for the support, kindness and overall awesomeness of everyone in the English Department at Allegheny College – where I've had the pleasure and privilege of teaching since the fall of 2013.

On the topic of awesomeness, I also must highlight the inspiring enthusiasm, curiosity and open-mindedness of the Allegheny students who have joined me in exploring connections among Shakespeare adaptation, race and intersectionality – especially

Jamir Wilson, KiaJah Rhodes, Devin Gaffney and Kyle DiPofi, whose work I reference in Chapter 4. For financial assistance that has supported various stages of my project, I thank the Academic Support Committee and Dean's Endowed Fund at Allegheny College. I also received much-needed funding and time-to-write support in the form of a Folger Shakespeare Library non-residential research fellowship during the summer of 2022, for which I am immensely grateful; I additionally appreciate the Folger's efforts to create scholarly community even with the library itself under construction and amidst the ongoing challenges of the Covid-19 pandemic. And I would be remiss if I didn't thank Ayanna Thompson, whose 2018 visit to Allegheny as a Phi Beta Kappa Visiting Scholar first sparked my interest in nontraditional casting, and who was so gracious when I missed our turn on the drive from Meadville to the Pittsburgh International Airport afterward.

Including such unexpected twists, the journey towards completing this book has been an immensely enriching experience that has taken me and my work to various places, geographical and conceptual, along the way. I presented my initial vision of the project in a workshop on book publishing at the Shakespeare Association of America's annual meeting in Washington, DC in April 2019, while parts of my conclusion began as a seminar paper at the same event in Jacksonville, Florida, in April 2022. I thank my seminar and workshop leaders, respondents and fellow participants for their helpful comments and stimulating conversation both at the start and towards the finish of this adventure. As mentioned earlier, parts of Chapter 1 were previously published as an article in *Shakespeare Survey 73* (Cambridge University Press, 2020): 170–83. I am grateful for the *Survey*'s interest in my work; the publisher and I thankfully acknowledge the permission granted to reproduce this copyright material. Finally, I extend my deepest gratitude to the following individuals from The Arden Shakespeare: the three anonymous peer reviewers, whose remarkably thorough and thoughtful input on my proposal proved invaluable to the revision process; Mark Dudgeon, Arden's Publisher of Theatre and Shakespeare Studies, and his excellent assistants, Lara Bateman and Ella Wilson; and Mark Thornton Burnett, the editor of the Shakespeare and Adaptation series, whose scholarship on global Shakespeare has helped define the ground on which this book stands.

Introduction

From Rodney King to Netflix's *The King*: Adaptation and/as intersectionality in Shakespeare's histories, 1991–2019

The 1991 police beating of African American Rodney King and the 2019 release of Netflix's *The King* demarcate three decades of tumultuous race relations and shifts in media technology that together have transformed the role of race in the Shakespeare history adaptation. On 3 March 1991, two years before the world wide web entered the public domain, Los Angeles plumber George Holliday produced what popular media has dubbed the 'world's first viral video' on his brand-new handheld Sony camcorder. Ninety seconds of Holliday's footage of the now infamous assault on King aired on news networks across the United States.[1] The video made indelibly visible the systemic racism of the Los Angeles Police Department, resulting in immediate public outrage and, a year later, a series of uprisings when the officers responsible for the beatings were acquitted of all charges. In part via their direct link to the Black Lives Matter movement,[2] these events would influence the self-described 'first black Shakespeare film ever done': a conflation of the *Henry IV* plays titled *H4* and set in contemporary Los Angeles.[3]

On 1 November 2019, *The King*, a multinational movie adaptation of Shakespeare's Henriad, was released on Netflix. At the time the subscription streaming video service had over 167 million subscribers in 190 countries worldwide.[4] As of this writing, *The King* has only begun to receive consideration in Shakespeare scholarship, where its all-white cast and global distribution have provoked concerns about its apparent validation of whiteness in Shakespeare as a privileged, invisible norm – the opposite, that is, of what Holliday's video accomplished with respect to the LAPD.[5] However, as I argue here, the historical and cultural contexts in which *The King* emerged – and which include that video and its aftermath – render such invisibility untenable in a way that it was not only thirty years earlier.

Central to that change are two adaptations of Shakespeare's English histories: *H4* and the BBC's two-season miniseries *The Hollow Crown*. Both productions were released in 2012 – the same year the Black Lives Matter movement began in the United States and the year in which, in the United Kingdom, a coalition of over one hundred Tory Members of Parliament called for a referendum 'on the nature of our relationship with the European Union'.[6] Eventually that call would result in the withdrawal of Britain from the EU now generally referred to as 'Brexit', which has become a cultural touchstone in ongoing, multifaceted debates about British national identity. While official pro-Brexit discourse often strategically avoided the 'language of race', subsequent analysis has found both explicit and implicit, 'post-racial' racisms underlying the eventual 'Leave' vote.[7] Just as the Los Angeles Uprising and the Black Lives Matter movement inform *H4*, these concerns permeate both seasons of *The Hollow Crown* and, as I discuss later in this introduction, *The King*.

Taking *The Hollow Crown* and *H4* as defining points of reference, throughout this book I contend that over the past three decades, race has become a necessarily visible as well as a central and constitutive part of the Anglo-American Shakespeare history play adaptation. Although I briefly address several earlier films, my chief concern is with Anglophone cinematic and televisual productions of Shakespeare's histories since Branagh's *Henry V* (1989) inaugurated a renaissance of Shakespeare movies in both the United Kingdom and the United States.[8] Except for the conclusion, the chapters that follow proceed backwards in time to show how these recent screen adaptations provide not only an open yet contested site for negotiating race in relation to gender, sexuality, class, disability, ethnicity and nation in today's world but also a means of apprehending these concerns both in prior adaptations and in their source texts. Via widely available digital media, the history adaptation has become a means of interrogating the dialectic between Shakespeare's cultural capital and racial reckonings on both sides of the Atlantic and across time.

While in *Henry V*, Branagh adopted what Courtney Lehmann has characterized as a 'classless' approach to Shakespeare, wooing a mass audience, including Americans, with references to various pop cultural works, the film used an all-white, all-British cast.[9] By the mid-1990s, however, 'the exigencies of market capitalism' pushed cinematic Shakespeare into more inclusive casting practices, spearheaded by Branagh himself, which opened up this terrain to American performers.[10] The history play adaptations that appeared during this period and that I address, respectively, in Chapters 4 and 5 – Gus Van Sant's *My Own Private Idaho* (1991) and Richard Loncraine's *Richard III* (1995) – also include only white or white-presenting actors in major roles. Nevertheless, race and its intersections with other marginalized identity valences, especially queer sexuality, are important concerns in these films and materialize in ways that can be more readily appreciated in the aftermath of twenty-first-century developments.

Emerging out of the twenty-first-century cultural milieux that produced Brexit in the United Kingdom and Black Lives Matter in the United States, both *The Hollow Crown* and *H4* directly engage with the problem of race. The former is 'one of the most important Shakespeare productions of recent times' as well as 'the largest-scale investment in Shakespeare production ever undertaken for television', and, moreover, the first version of the first and second tetralogies 'to be designed specifically for the [televisual] medium'.[11] Following a BBC mandate to produce high-quality television dedicated to 'representing and reflecting all the communities of the UK', producers of *The Hollow Crown* made a visible – if, to critics, insufficient – effort to cast actors of diverse racial backgrounds in several key roles, most notably Afro-British actors Lucian Msamati as the Bishop of Carlisle in *Richard II* and Paterson Joseph in the considerably expanded role of the Duke of York in *Henry V*.[12] In the second season, which premiered in 2016, Jewish-Nigerian-

British actress Sophie Okonedo played Queen Margaret of Anjou in Shakespeare's first tetralogy. Much more sweepingly, if to a far smaller audience, the low-budget independent film *H4*, produced by and starring African American actor Harry Lennix, directed by white American director Paul Quinn and with a screenplay adapted by African American Shakespeare scholar Ayanna Thompson, aimed 'to explore various aspects of African American politics in the 20th and 21st century'.[13] In 2015, *H4* was revised to more directly incorporate LA's relationship with a quarter century of racial conflict captured, in part, on 'viral' video.

A brief word on terminology is necessary here. In the United States, the word 'race' in its association with skin colour tends to dominate discussions of human difference, as typified by the acronym BIPOC (Black, indigenous and people of colour). This usage is opposed to the more frequent usage of 'ethnicity' in the UK, where the acronym BAME (Black, Asian and minority ethnic) holds sway. In this book I use the word 'race' more often than 'ethnicity'– both because I am writing from the cultural perspective of an American and for reasons connected to the historical dimensions and resultant political valences of the former term. The scholarly consensus on what was once considered to be the anachronism of discussing race in early modern studies has over the past twenty-five years undergone a sea change. This change is not a matter of semantics only. To insist that race existed in the Renaissance is to recognize that racism also existed in the Renaissance. Moreover, as Urvashi Chakravarty and Ayanna Thompson articulate in their introduction to a 2021 special issue of *New Literary History* on race and periodization, 'the oft-posed question of "whether race exists" in earlier periods' itself reinforces racist ideologies, 'as race is disarticulated from the contexts of its production in earlier periods and becomes something that must be "discovered"'.[14]

Following in the footsteps of pioneers in the field, in the 1990s and early 2000s scholars including Margo Hendricks, Kim F. Hall, Dympna Callaghan, Arthur L. Little, Jr, Ania Loomba, Joyce Green MacDonald, Francesca Royster and Ian Smith – and I recognize I have left many off this list – brought these concerns to the forefront of early modern literary studies. In fact, it is now understood that the formation of race as an ideological category took place prior to the Renaissance. Geraldine Heng has persuasively shown how race was invented in the Middle Ages, starting with the religious crusades of the eleventh century that brought Europeans into contact with various other nations, cultures and peoples.[15] In addition, Cord J. Whitaker has explained how medieval rhetoric helped create the modern 'mirage' of race through metaphors that linked blackness with sin and whiteness with its opposite.[16]

In this context, the theatres of early modern London actively contributed to the ongoing construction of race, both rhetorically and through the embodied presentation of racial others on stage.[17] Shakespeare's English histories were central to this process. As demonstrated by foundational new historicist and cultural materialist critics such as Richard Helgerson, Jean E. Howard and Phyllis Rackin, Claire McEachern and Graham Holderness, Shakespeare's first and second tetralogies stage origin stories in support of emergent English and British nationalisms. In the eight plays I examine in this volume, those origins involve the medieval events – from the deposition of Richard II through the Wars of the Roses – which led to the establishment of the Tudor line that culminated in the reign of Elizabeth I. Since their 1590s' composition, the histories repeatedly have been performed at moments of crisis in Britain's national identity.

In the wake of Britain's formal exit from the European Union in January 2020, the present is clearly one such moment. In her recent monograph, *Shakespeare's Contested Nations: Race, Gender, and Multicultural Britain in Performances of the History Plays* (Routledge 2022), L. Monique Pittman traces the various 'contrary movements' of twenty-first-century British and global politics, which juxtapose a 'softening of borders' with a 'simultaneous hardening of nationalism'. Events from Brexit to the War on Terror are the context for what Pittman argues is the fundamentally conservative, 'limited' vision of the 'past, present, and future of Britain' in recent stage and screen performances of Shakespeare's histories, including *The Hollow Crown*.[18] In this volume, I consider how despite their various limitations, recent screen adaptations of the histories nonetheless offer new ways of seeing race and its intersections in Shakespeare in a transatlantic context. National identity crises likewise afflict the United States, as the 2016 election and 2020 ousting of President Donald Trump as well as the perennial immigration crisis at the US–Mexican border indicate. With critical race theory in institutions of higher learning as well as the voting rights of non-whites in a democratic society continually coming under assault by political reactionaries, I approach my topic both as a scholar and teacher of early modern literature and as the American mother of two biracial daughters (their father is Black and I am white), with the hope that an analysis of Shakespeare can be a cultural as well as a scholarly intervention.

As a work of performance criticism that examines representations of race in televisual and cinematic versions of these eight plays from 1991 to 2019, this book inevitably, as the late performance critic Barbara Hodgdon acknowledged about her own work, 'trades on my own history'.[19] I acknowledge my privileged status as a white scholar in the white-dominated field of Shakespeare studies and wish to underscore the importance of scholars of all backgrounds contributing to the discussion of race in this domain. In addition to following Ayanna Thompson's call to engage frankly with the 'shitting elephant in the room' that is the presence of race in Shakespeare, I embrace what Ian Smith notes are the white Shakespeare scholar's ethical obligations of 'unpacking one's white positioning to reach toward new forms of racial knowledge', fulfilling the 'mandate for coalition building toward social justice and equity', and finally, 'positioning whiteness in relation to other social identities and classes, exchanging exceptionality for the collective solidarity of coalition building'.[20]

Through my analysis of recent screen adaptations of Shakespeare's histories as well as the plays on which they are based, I endeavour to reframe the scholarly conversation about the English histories and their contribution to ideas of nationhood by connecting it with two growing bodies of work: early modern race scholarship and adaptation theory. As I theorize the central role of race and intersectional identity categories in these adaptations, I hope to reveal both the formative role played by the English histories in the early modern invention of race and their ongoing significance to constructions of embodied difference in both the United Kingdom and the United States. The role of the English histories in the latter is a function not only of Shakespeare's long-standing presence in American education and theatre but also of digital culture and the resultant globalization of audiences. While both formal and informal scholarship is already making connections between Shakespeare and Brexit, connections between Shakespeare and the long history of America's so-called 'racial reckoning' have not been as fully articulated.[21] Making such connections is part of my overarching aim of bringing the legacy established by George Holliday's landmark viral video to the field of Shakespeare adaptation studies.

Adaptation and/as intersectionality

Together, Rodney King and *The King* exemplify two aspects of the term 'intersectional' as I use it in this book: both its specific sociological definition and its broader denotation as 'of, pertaining to, or characterized by intersection' – that is, as a matter of junctures, overlaps and crossings-over in time, space and concept.[22] As a sociological idea, intersectionality refers to the interdependence among socially constructed categories of difference that together determine relationships of power and privilege. For instance, Rodney King was not solely an African American but a poor, working-class African American man with a previous criminal conviction for robbery and a significant substance abuse problem.[23] Not race alone but, rather, complex intersections among race, gender, class and disability led to the outcome of the confrontation between King and the police in a Los Angeles suburb early that March morning in 1991.

In the broader sense of intersectionality as defined earlier, the viral video resulting from King's beating has created junctures, overlaps and crossings-over of multifarious kinds. The video went on to inspire civil unrest reflected in the Black Henriad adaptation *H4*, which in terms of both timing and content crossed paths with the initial airings of *The Hollow Crown* on the BBC and PBS. The use of nontraditional casting in both works in turn contributed to an evolving perspective on race in the histories, which in the year 2019 and following continues to inform the reception of Netflix's all-white *The King*. The means by which both 'Kings' intersect, in other words, is the ever-expanding entity known as Shakespeare.

The sociological term 'intersectionality' has a history that intersects in its own way with Shakespeare studies. It was coined in 1989 by African American legal scholar Kimberlé Crenshaw 'to describe the "intersecting" or codeterminative forces of racism, sexism and classism in the lives of black women'. The term also 'stands in for the broad body of scholarship that has sought to examine and redress the oppressive forces that have constrained the lives of black women in particular and women of colour more generally'.[24] From these specific origins, intersectionality has since been widely applied across many disciplines and periods, including medieval and early modern literary studies.[25] As a result it has been both criticized as a problematic '"all-round, catch-it-all-concept"'[26] and embraced as 'an analytic tool' that 'gives people better access to the complexity of the world and of themselves'.[27] The critique raised against the widespread academic use of the term has recently been articulated by Sirma Bilge through the lens of Afropessimism: namely, that a form of inquiry 'grounded in Black women's experience and knowledge' has been 'made fungible in present-day academe, treated as an empty receptacle' and 'turned into a proxy for master narratives that erase Black women'.[28] I emphasize intersectionality's genealogy, with the racialized woman at its centre, in part to avoid replicating in my own work as a white feminist scholar the commodification and erasures that Bilge describes. By insisting upon a link between adaptation and intersectionality, moreover, I underscore what Joyce Green MacDonald has recently described as the 'spectral quality of Black women in our Shakespearean archive – physically absent, but socially present', and thus return the conversation to the Black feminist concerns of intersectionality's origins.[29] This paradox of the simultaneous symbolic presence and bodily absence of Black women in Shakespeare can be both exposed and, potentially, at least partially redressed through the means of adaptation, especially nontraditional casting practices.

For in many ways adaptation is an inherently intersectional process in both the general and the specific senses. In her field-defining theorization of adaptation, Linda Hutcheon emphasizes how it combines two intersecting processes: a 'process of creation' and a 'process of reception' that encompass '[a]n extended intertextual engagement with the adapted work'.[30] These processes are also inseparable from their contexts 'in time and space, within a particular society and a general culture. The contexts of creation and reception are material, public, and economic as much as they are cultural, personal, and aesthetic'.[31] Such contexts include discourses of gender, sexuality, class, disability and, of course, race.

While there has been considerable recent scholarly conversation on casting practices involving race, a direct connection between this conversation and the theorization of adaptation is sorely needed. For instance, 'colourblind casting', or choosing the best actor to play a given part regardless of race or ethnicity, is often opposed to 'colour-conscious casting', or casting that is attentive to the semiotic meanings produced by an actor's race or ethnicity – usually when actors of colour play nominally 'white' characters. Both terms emphasize decisions made in production. The problem with this distinction, as numerous commentators have pointed out, is the lack of control over how any given production might be experienced on the reception side, by an audience who may or may not be 'blind' to or 'conscious' of race as its creators intend.[32] Considering nontraditional casting through the lens of adaptation as defined by Hutcheon requires not only acknowledging both the creative and receptive sides of adaptation but also recognizing the lack of fixity in a given adaptation's meanings: that it is a fluid 'process' as well as a static 'product'.[33]

As I discuss further in Chapter 1, nontraditional casting – which is a phrase I will use throughout this book to describe both colourblind and colour-conscious casting, as well as the many shades in between – has its own evolving history that contributes to this lack of fixity. It has been a tradition in the theatre much longer than it has on the big or small screen. However, largely because of the historic specificity of the main characters in Shakespeare's English histories and their resultant ties to a white English national identity, even in the theatre these roles have proved more resistant than other Shakespearean roles to racial inclusivity. The much larger potential audience of the contemporary screen Shakespeare adaptation makes these issues simultaneously more complex and more urgent.

In addition to requiring intersections between production and reception that themselves shift through time, adaptation – especially Shakespearean adaptation – creates crossings-over between moments in history. In her discussion of Shakespeare's persistent, often unacknowledged but formative role in contemporary American serial drama, Elisabeth Bronfen theorizes a process she calls 'crossmapping'.[34] Bronfen draws upon multiple prior theorizations of Shakespeare's long endurance in this ever-changing world, from Graham Holderness's conceptualization of mutually modifying 'collisions' between Shakespearean and non-Shakespearean texts to Maurizio Calbi's understanding of Shakespeare's 'hauntological' presence in screen adaptations.[35] Pivotal among these influences is Douglas Lanier's understanding of the Bard as a deeply ingrained set of 'rhizomatic relations' that permeates Western culture. A rhizome is 'a horizontal, decentered multiplicity of subterranean roots which cross each other, bifurcating and recombining, breaking off and restarting', and, moreover, lacks any 'central organizing intelligence or point of origin'. This structure 'may be entered at any point, and there is no a priori path through its web of connections'.[36]

Taking Lanier's metaphor to one perhaps counterintuitive conclusion, Bronfen insists that rhizomatic nodes from the present have influence on nodes of the past. She defines crossmapping as 'a two-way hermeneutic method, predicated on the discovery of similar concerns in the historical and the contemporary text (or sets of texts)'. Calling on 'Walter Benjamin's discussion of the constitutive reciprocity at work in translation', Bronfen underscores that the original text is itself affected by this process, undergoing a '"post-ripening" [Nachreife]' or 'change in signification as well'.[37] In other words, the change effected by any given act of adaptation not only is evident in the new text but can also be seen in the old text; the act of creating the new work inevitably and irrevocably changes how we see what came before. The act of interpretation is also involved in this process: 'the meanings that are discovered – or uncovered – in the process of crossmapping are always the effect of creative reading. . . . Like the translation of Shakespeare which the contemporary serial explicitly or implicitly undertakes, this creative reading also engenders a "post-ripening"'.[38]

Bronfen's discussion of 'serial Shakespeare' is limited to dramas that engage in the 'mutable process of disseminating and reassembling the Bard's work' but that do not 'explicitly advertise their intertextual relationship to Shakespeare'. However, even in seemingly traditional Shakespeare adaptations, race is a site where the disjunctive effects typical of the unacknowledged appropriation, which 'distances us from our present', also inevitably occur.

> As a hermeneutic practice, crossmapping thus discloses the way appropriations of Shakespeare draw into focus our present experience of his historical difference. The parts and fragments of his plays that are reused in any contemporary appropriation never simply mirror or affirm the present, because they can never shed their own history.[39]

An adaptation of Shakespeare that challenges cultural expectations with respect to race not only produces an artefact that differs from the source text but also changes our apprehension both of that text and of our present moment. Adaptation creates the conditions in which historically contingent constructions of race both in the source text and in our own time become visible.

Adaptation thereby contributes to our recognition of Shakespeare's histories as what David Sterling Brown dubs Shakespeare's 'other' race plays – that is, plays without an overtly racialized character that nonetheless engage in constructions of race.[40] According to Arthur L. Little, Jr, race, especially racial whiteness, 'haunts' such Shakespearean texts as an unacknowledged signifier. One way such a haunting takes place is through the pathological process Little calls 'white melancholia': a '"condition of endless self-impoverishment"' characterized by the longing for 'whiteness . . . that's at once immanent, intimate, and out of reach'.[41] Through nontraditional casting and other means, adaptation illuminates this otherwise evanescent presence of race in the text – thereby disturbing what Ambereen Dadabhoy describes as 'the normative gaze . . . always already rooted in the logics and epistemologies of whiteness'.[42] For instance, as I explore in Chapter 1 on *The Hollow Crown: The War of the Roses*, Sophie Okonedo's Black Margaret calls attention to inherent contradictions in the constructions of white femininity as mediated in *Henry VI, Part 1* through the frequent use of the word 'fair'. As per the mission statement of the Racial Imaginary Institute's 2018 symposium *On Whiteness*, to 'make visible what has been intentionally presented as inevitable' is to challenge the often unquestioned dominance of whiteness.[43]

By engaging the present with and through the past, adaptation also changes how we perceive race in our own time. Another example, which I discuss in Chapter 2, is the ghostly presence of Michael Jackson as an inspiration for Ben Whishaw's Richard II in *The Hollow Crown*, Season One. This presence, along with the casting of Msamati as the Bishop of Carlisle, raises to the surface both the obvious racism of Carlisle's denigration of 'black pagans, Turks and Saracens' and the more subtle racism in his prophetic characterization of Richard's eventual deposition and murder as 'so heinous, black, obscene a deed' (*R2* 4.1.96, 132).[44] Spoken by a Black man about a king metaphorically blackened by his association with the sexually and racially ambiguous, not to mention allegedly criminal, King of Pop, these lines reveal the tensions inherent in the second tetralogy's intersecting constructions of whiteness, masculinity and nation – as well as the tensions in Western culture's assessment of race, sexuality, criminality and celebrity.

In *H4*, which I discuss in Chapters 3 and 4, the dialogue between past and present emerges not only in the film's colour-conscious use of Black actors and its transposed historical and geographical setting but also in the direct transformation of the text. One line spoken by Amad Jackson's Prince Hal at his dying father's bedside in contemporary urban America substitutes 'great Black kings' for Shakespeare's 'English kings' (*2H4* 4.3.169).[45] As well as preserving the metre of the original blank verse, the addition of 'great' positions Englishness not solely in relation to Blackness but to *great* Blackness, revising the meaning of this key colour signifier of racial identity from the potentially pejorative to the panegyric.

In creating such intersections between past and present ideas about human difference, the adaptive process necessarily involves intersectionality in both the sociological sense and the broader sense. Each chapter to follow focuses on a particular adaptation issue in a single production or set of productions with respect to both kinds of intersection. Chapter 1 examines race, gender and disability with reference to nontraditional casting in *The Hollow Crown*, Season Two, while Chapter 2 explores what I call the 'queer seriality' of the opening and closing episodes of *The Hollow Crown*, Season One – a structure that undermines the cycle's seemingly normative narratives involving both race and sexuality. Chapter 3 situates two recent screen representations of a white, disabled Falstaff (in, respectively, *The Hollow Crown* and *H4*) in the context of the fat knight's distinct stage histories in the United Kingdom, where there so far has never been a Black Falstaff, versus the United States, where there have been several.

My discussion of *H4* continues in Chapter 4, which connects this twenty-first-century American Henriad adaptation with its 1991 predecessor, Gus Van Sant's *My Own Private Idaho*. I interrogate both productions' concerns with the question of Shakespeare's supposed universality as complicated by time, space and race. Chapter 5, then, scrutinizes the many intertextual references of Loncraine's *Richard III* (1995) in order to situate the film within the long-racializing history of American cinema. Finally, returning to the present, my conclusion explores the ramifications of nontraditional casting in Shakespeare upon the reception of Netflix's historical drama, *Bridgerton*, in digital cultures. By investigating conceptualizations of race, class, gender, sexuality and disability in these works, I ultimately delve deep into the histories' presence in both the British and American cultural imaginaries. Throughout I aim to extricate the common thread of the Shakespeare history adaptation's inherently intersectional status at the junctures between past and present, production and reception, and race and other categories of difference.

Whiteness visible

This book thus strives to demonstrate how the political and cultural functions of Shakespeare's histories, combined with the demands of recent world events and the changing nature of audiences in a globalized world, have rendered race and its intersections essential components of contemporary screen adaptations of these plays. As indicated earlier, however, David Michôd and Joel Edgerton's *The King*, released on Netflix in 2019, might appear to contradict this point. While receiving mixed reviews in the popular press, the film has been generally decried by Shakespeare scholars not only due to its all-white cast but also because of its substantial liberties in adapting Shakespeare's Henriad. In my own view these problems are directly connected. In both its avoidance of nontraditional casting and its drastic alterations to both the language and plot of the plays, *The King* in fact reveals the inextricable relationship among adaptation, race and intersectionality in Shakespeare's histories on screen in the twenty-first century.

Despite its gritty medieval period setting, *The King* embraces contemporary culture in numerous ways, most notably in a modern-language script designed, according to Edgerton, as '"Game of Thrones" meets Shakespeare'. As Edgerton further explains, 'there is something that happens when even the most intelligent people watch Shakespeare. They feel stupid, because he does the kind of roundabout version of telling you simple things. So, we just wanted to let the audience understand exactly what's going on, and not just some people, but everybody.'[46] Accordingly, all of Shakespeare's language is axed; there is no witty Falstaffian banter in the *Henry IV* parts and no extravagant kingly speeches in the *Henry V* parts. Also cut from the latter are Shakespeare's incorporations of non-English voices, such as the four captains scene and Princess Katherine's language lesson with her lady Alice.

The script departs from the plays' plots and characterizations in other ways, as well. Prince Hal (Timothée Chalamet) is introduced as a disaffected pacifist who despises his father for his warmongering and has no desire to be king himself. A life of drinking to the point of vomiting, listless sex and occasional joyless dancing in drag is presented as a form of self-punishment by a tortured adolescent. After Hal reluctantly accepts the crown and sheers his shoulder-length locks to present the profile of Henry V's most familiar portrait, he accepts without affront the infamous gift of tennis balls from the Dauphin – in *The King*, a single ball – as a just allusion to 'the boy I once was'. Only what appears to be an assassination plot against his own life eventually leads him to wage war against France at the repeated urging of his advisor, William (Sean Harris).[47]

Falstaff (Joel Edgerton) undergoes even further metamorphosis. Introduced as a muscular, clean-cut, trim-bearded man's man who gleefully submits to the unanesthetized cauterization of a flesh wound, he initially provides a masculine contrast to Ben Mendelsohn's long and straggly haired, beardless, moribund King Henry IV. A battle-hardened veteran, this Falstaff accompanies the eventual King Henry V in his war against France. There he functions as Hal's moral 'conscience',[48] comes up with the plan for English victory at Agincourt and proceeds to die an arguably heroic death on the front lines. 'This is what I was built for', Falstaff tells Hal before battle in the film's most overt challenge to its Shakespearean predecessor. 'I die here or . . . I die over a bottle in Eastcheap. And I think this makes for a much better story.' While reviews of the film have generally contested the directionality of that comparison, the transformation of Falstaff does create a superficially more sympathetic Henry V. He is not burdened with the need to banish his old friend but rather is free to mourn his downfall in battle.

Following his inevitable victory, the king returns to a now jubilant, united England. There he learns from his newly affianced Princess Catherine, transformed into an assertive, even proto-feminist figure, that the entire war was based on a lie.[49] The assassination plot was William's ruse – performed ostensibly in service of promoting national unity but actually undertaken out of financial self-interest, to expand his own sheep farms in France. In response, Henry stabs

William through the neck. He then joins forces with his new queen to face his future as the film's titular 'King'.

Criticisms have been levied against *The King*'s approach to adaptation in both the United Kingdom and the United States. British blogger and performance scholar Benjamin Broadribb highlights the irony of how the film's superficially contemporary packaging conceals a stale, outdated approach to the histories – in particular its 'at best ill-conceived, at worst offensively backwards' all-white cast.[50] For American English professor and Renaissance scholar Brandi K. Adams, writing for Arizona State University's *Sundial*, the problem with *The King* is how its updated plot and language offer a Shakespeare that is supposedly for 'everybody' but really is not. The film's story of a disaffected white prince in an all-white, mostly male world in which he successfully, if reluctantly, becomes king and successfully, if unhappily, undertakes and then wins a war 'glorifies an all-too-familiar redemptive arc in which an extremely privileged white man inherits his expected wealth and political power with few obstacles and little resistance'. By packaging this narrative within the guise of making Shakespeare more accessible, Michôd and Edgerton conflate 'inclusion – which would ideally welcome a variety of people into the world of the plays – with universality, an ideology that wholly depends upon a discursive privileging of white, male British/Colonial interpretive experiences and concerns'.[51] More insidious than the exclusionary nature of the film's perspective is the lie it tells about being inclusive and the resultant erasure of perspectives that are not white, male or British/colonial.

Outside the Anglo-American context, one analyst has offered an alternative opinion on *The King*. In a 2021 article in the peer-reviewed journal *Transnational Screens*, Spanish film scholar Celestino Deleyto argues that the Netflix Henriad adaptation offers a compelling feminist, transnational reappropriation of plays that historically have been used for exclusively British, nationalist purposes. Distributed via Netflix to a multinational audience as a 'co-production by Australian, British, US, and Hungarian companies', featuring a multinational production team and cast with Australians, New Zealanders and French-Americans as well as British actors in major roles, and displaying a polyphony of native French accents, spoken French and a variety of regional English voices, for Deleyto *The King* offers its own version of diverse, global perspectives.[52]

Clearly these three scholars come to the film with varying definitions of diversity. Regarding *The King* from, respectively, the British and American points of view, Broadribb and Adams see an all-white cast as problematically exclusionary, while Deleyto, a native of Spain, emphasizes national and linguistic differences. Contributing to these differing definitions of diversity is Shakespeare's foundational presence in the construction of national culture in both the United Kingdom and the United States. Particularly relevant are historical uses of Shakespeare in the systematic exclusion of people of colour from cultural representation, as well as recent attempts, as I discuss in subsequent chapters, to rectify this inequity through nontraditional casting. While, as Deleyto argues, *The King*'s multinational cast and crew alter the scope of the source texts by extending their perspective beyond the British Isles, when considered from the standpoint of Shakespeare's continued present-day role in both British and American self-construction, *The King* evades what Pittman argues are 'the ethical responsibilities of art in a digital age' to make decisions that acknowledge the experiences and perspectives of a racially and culturally diverse audience across a global marketplace.[53]

The most insidious aspect of *The King* is an element not mentioned by Adams but praised by Deleyto: namely, its ostensibly anti-nationalist, anti-monarchical, pro-feminist agenda, which, in fact, undergirds its construction of whiteness as a seemingly invisible, privileged category. This aspect of the film can best be appreciated through what *The King* presents as its most directly Shakespearean moment: the sole wartime oration delivered by Chalamet's uncharacteristically taciturn King Henry before the Battle of Agincourt begins. According to Michôd, writing this speech was 'the only time that I felt daunted, in direct relation to the spectre of Shakespeare'. Notably, this speech is inspired by pre-battle advice from Edgerton's much-revised Falstaff: 'These men deserve your confidence. And if you cannot give them that, at least tell them a magnificent lie.' Despite Michôd's expressed desire that the oration that follows be recognized as 'kind of all bullshit', the production nonetheless presents what the author himself describes as an 'incredibly rousing speech' as one meant to persuade the film's audience as well as King Henry's soldiers.[54]

The 'magnificent lie' in question turns out to be what *The King* implicitly suggests is also the central lie of Shakespeare's St Crispin's

Day Speech: the notion of English national identity as the product of bonds forged between men in wartime. As is typical of Michôd and Edgerton's script, however, not an iamb of the original speech remains. 'I have only ever hoped for one thing: to see this kingdom united under this English crown', Chalamet's King Henry begins. Getting down from his horse, he then addresses his men face to face, from the ground:

> If your day is today, so be it. Mine will be tomorrow. Or mine today, and yours tomorrow. It matters not. What matters is that you know in your hearts that today you *are* that kingdom united. *You* are England, each and every one of you. *England* is *you*. And it is the space between you. Fight not for yourselves, fight for that space. Fill that space. Make it tissue. Make it mass. Make it impenetrable. Make it yours! Make it England! Make it England!

Although the speech opens with a singular 'you', by the end 'yours' becomes a plural possessive as Chalamet's Henry reshapes individuals into a collective: an invading army with a shared corporeal substance. In the king's final series of commands, the nature of that substance slowly loses definition. The organized form of tissue becomes the more basic property of mass – in physics, a measure of the resistance of matter to an applied force. The word 'mass' also suggests cancerous growth, the loss of differentiation through which normal tissue performs its specific functions. Yet rather than conclude with this image of dedifferentiated malignancy, the king repeatedly reinscribes the army's impenetrable mass with the defining character of nationhood: 'Make it England! Make it England!'

Unlike the original Falstaff's honour soliloquy (unsurprisingly excised in *The King*), far from debunking the lie of war's magnificence as a 'mere scutcheon' (*1H4* 5.1.140), in delivery the speech presents the notion of English national unity as genuinely magnificent, even if – or perhaps even because – it is a lie. Part of the effect comes from the self-consciously elevated language and the rest from cinematic grandeur. Tense, throbbing strings on the soundtrack reinforce Chalamet's shouting elocution. Meanwhile, wide shots of the king moving amidst his men alternate with close shots of approving expressions from Falstaff and William alike, adding both expansiveness and gravitas to the scene.

A similar paradox infuses *The King*'s representation of kingship itself. Even as Catherine reminds Henry V that, as the son of a usurper, he should know that 'all monarchy is illegitimate', the film unironically celebrates its titular 'King'. Throughout Henry's first conversation with Catherine, as well as the subsequent scene when William loses his life as the scapegoat for self-serving lies, cheers from an unseen crowd resound outside the palace windows. 'That's the sound of your peace. That is the sound of your greatness' are the silver-tongued advisor's final pleading words. But are these claims, in the film's terms, lies or truth? Subsequently Chalamet's King Henry embraces his queen-to-be as truth-teller: 'I ask nothing of you. Only that you will always speak to me clear and true. Always. Will you promise me only that?'. Catherine's response is a simple 'I will'. At this point the cheering resolves into shouts of 'Long live the King!' and then 'King Henry', which lead directly to the closing title card: 'The King' in giant white letters on a black screen. In medieval England, of course, there would have been no cheering public to greet the victorious King Henry. The closing shouts outside the palace window, Charles Mudede points out, 'are actually our crowds', the '*historically* specific' result of political movements that have also led to Brexit and the rise of Trump.[55]

In the end, although *The King* ostensibly debunks social abstractions such as English national unity and legitimate monarchy, it leaves unaddressed what it assumes to be the 'politically and socially neutral' abstraction of whiteness.[56] But as *The King* adapts Shakespeare's *Henry V*, the play that for Rubin Espinosa most straightforwardly links whiteness with Shakespeare's constructions of 'nascent Englishness', whiteness substantiates the film's representation of both nation and monarchy.[57] Whiteness is an unacknowledged lie that helps the other lies continue to ring 'true' in *The King* despite their ostensible exposure as falsehoods. Central to that lie is *The King*'s stance on Shakespeare: recreating Shakespeare in the image of a modernity with the superficial trappings of a progressive take on war, nation, monarchy and gender – and constructing that modernity as exclusively white.

That this film first aired on Netflix just months before the British Parliament ratified the Brexit withdrawal agreement is no coincidence. The central tension in *The King* between a global, forward-looking and insular, nostalgic view of Shakespeare parallels pro-Brexit rhetoric about the UK's role in a changing world. In this rhetoric, race played an unacknowledged but central role in 'two contradictory but interlocking visions': 'an imperial longing to restore Britain's place in the world' as a leading power without acknowledging the problems created by its colonialist and racist legacies, coupled with a 'narrative of island retreat from a "globalizing" world' that is 'no longer recognizably British'.[58] Not acknowledging these legacies, however, does not eliminate their relevance to Britain's eventual departure from the EU. The same logic applies to constructions of whiteness at work in *The King*. In 2019, on a global streaming platform, the monolithic whiteness of the film's cast is a significant and highly visible choice. For in the wake of changes that have taken place in Shakespeare on screen since Branagh's all-white, all-British *Henry V* of 1989, the privileged invisibility of whiteness as an unmarked racial category no longer obtains. Diversely cast or not, the twenty-first-century Shakespeare adaptation – as Adams insists – can never be 'neutral'.[59]

1

Through a glass darkly

Race, gender, disability and Sophie Okonedo's Margaret of Anjou in *The Hollow Crown: The Wars of the Roses*

The presence of a Black actress, Sophie Okonedo, as Margaret of Anjou in the second season of *The Hollow Crown* brings to mainstream television a practice that is decades old in theatrical productions of Shakespeare.[1] That is so-called 'colourblind' casting: choosing the best actor to play a given part, regardless of race or ethnicity. But how blind can or should an audience be to race? This question becomes even more compelling in the culturally loaded terrain of Shakespeare's English history plays – especially in the case of a character whose gendered and ethnic otherness has long been a central issue in her theatrical representation. By adding the visual semiotics of a marginalized race to its televisual representation of Margaret of Anjou, *The Hollow Crown* demonstrates both the pitfalls and the potentials of nontraditional casting, and at times transcends the local concerns of the English histories to produce a more global and diachronic view of the 'imagined communities' they question and call into being.[2]

Initiated by Joseph Papp's pioneering efforts in the 1950s to 'combat systemic racism' through his New York Shakespeare Festival, nontraditional casting did not enter the realm of mainstream Anglo-American cinematic Shakespeare until 1993, with Kenneth Branagh's *Much Ado about Nothing*.[3] The history plays, with their own particular relationship to English and British national identities, constituted a further 'glass ceiling' for actors of colour.[4] On stage, that ceiling was not breached in the UK until 1983, when Hugh Quarshie – to considerable opposition – replaced Tim Dalton in the role of Hotspur for the RSC (Royal Shakespeare Company). On screen, progress was even slower in coming. As Quarshie himself pointed out when David Oyelowo became the first Black actor to play a historical Shakespearean king on a British stage, in the RSC's landmark production of *Henry VI* in 2001, 'I fear we shall have to wait many more years before the cinema and television industries catch up with the classical theatre when it comes to non-traditional casting.'[5]

Yet nontraditional casting in Shakespeare has not universally been embraced as a progressive intervention. In the late 1990s, playwright August Wilson famously denounced it as 'an aberrant idea that has never had any validity other than as a tool of the Cultural Imperialists'.[6] The presumption of colourblindness itself relies on two racist formulations: the privileging of whiteness as an invisible normative category and the attempt to evade the cultural significance of Blackness. As Lisa M. Anderson asserts, the 'claim to have rendered race invisible has not made race irrelevant. Colourblindness requires that we ignore three hundred years of history, or, if not ignore them, render them meaningless'.[7] Even casting decisions that are nominally conscious of race, Ayanna Thompson notes, 'can actually replicate racial stereotypes *because* [they] have not addressed the unstable semiotics of race'.[8] Thompson further explains that the meaning of race in any production 'is completely contingent on the serial effects of the decisions made by everyone involved'. Unfortunately, in practice, 'there are very few sustained discussions between these varying constituencies about those very problems'.[9] As a result – as is certainly true in both seasons of *The Hollow Crown* – genuinely progressive uses of nontraditional casting in formal productions of Shakespeare remain the exception rather than the rule.

Nonetheless, in this chapter I contend that in taking a step towards Quarshie's goal by casting Okonedo as Queen Margaret,

The Hollow Crown: The Wars of the Roses adds to the stakes of the four-century relationship between Shakespeare's English histories and constructions of political identity by making race clearly visible. I thus depart somewhat from the current scholarly conversation's emphasis on *The Hollow Crown*'s purported aim of representing a multicultural British nation – an effort, several scholars assert, that has largely failed.[10] While I agree with these authors that *The Wars of the Roses* participates in the replication of racist stereotypes, especially by placing the burden of representation on a single actor of colour, I address these concerns within a broader frame of reference.

Although *The Hollow Crown* initially aired on BBC television, it is, as Ramona Wray has argued, neither simply a TV show nor solely a BBC production. Over the course of two seasons that present seven sophisticatedly styled, feature-film-length versions of the English histories, the series blurs the boundary between TV and cinema. It is thus a prime example of what Jason Mittell calls '"complex TV"', a 'medium within which the most creative, serious, and compelling kinds of storytelling can unfold'.[11] *The Hollow Crown* is, moreover, 'a collaborative venture involving the BBC, NBC Universal, Neal Street Productions, and WNET 13'. Alongside other productions involving streaming subscription services like Netflix, Disney+, and Amazon Prime, it is not exclusively 'centred on bolstering national culture and consciousness' but, rather, focused on 'secur[ing] global consumers and spectators' in a manner that 'draw[s] purposefully on "national meanings and brandings" as part of its international appeal'.[12]

With this larger audience in mind, I examine what the successes and failures of nontraditional casting in *The Hollow Crown: The Wars of the Roses* reveal not only about the histories' relationship to British political identities but about past and present constructions of race, gender and disability. I argue that the semiotics of race that develop in the series around Okonedo's Margaret illuminate the character's complex racialization in Shakespeare's first tetralogy, not only – as has previously been explored by 1990s feminist scholarship – as a French, female other but at the nexus of emergent ideas about whiteness, Blackness, masculinity and femininity as they intersect with constructions of nationhood. Also implicated in the process is Margaret's relationship with another famously othered body: that of her eventual nemesis, Richard III.

The process of adaptation creates additional intersections among these many enmeshed constructions of otherness across past and present. While at times *The Hollow Crown* reproduces stereotypes of race, gender and disability that can be traced to Shakespeare's plays, rendering these constructions visible in their original contexts in turn complicates their implications in today's world. In the end, *The Hollow Crown: The Wars of the Roses* epitomizes why an adaptation of Shakespeare's histories can never be truly 'colourblind'.

'Who we are as a society'

From their initial performances up through the present, Shakespeare's English history plays have actively fashioned the ever-shifting landscape of political and cultural identity. In their original contexts, these plays helped formulate the distinction among English, Irish, Welsh and Scottish peoples; the invention of Great Britain as a unified state; and the gender-based division between the public and private spheres.[13] We see in these plays the 'gradual and at times contradictory' process of constructing a 'white English identity still in flux', absorbing 'those "others" who might support the English cause . . . and casting out those who threaten the stability of the nation'.[14]

It is thus no coincidence that *The Hollow Crown* appeared during a period of tumult over the definitions and borders of British national identity, as exemplified by the unfolding Brexit controversy. The first season, which presented the plays of Shakespeare's second tetralogy in four episodes helmed by three different directors and which I discuss further in Chapter 2, was released on the BBC as a celebratory expression of British culture as part of the 'Cultural Olympiad' of 2012, corresponding with the London 2012 Summer Olympics. The second season condensed Shakespeare's first tetralogy into three episodes, all directed by Dominic Cooke. Subtitled *The Wars of the Roses*, it initially aired on the BBC in May of 2016 – just one month before the referendum through which the UK voted by a narrow majority to leave the European Union. It also aired at a time of global crisis, as exemplified by the War on Terror initiated by the 9/11 attacks in the United States in 2001, with combat ongoing in Afghanistan until 2021.

In both past and present contexts, the character Queen Margaret stands out for her otherness. The historical Margaret of Anjou was the daughter of two northern European nobles of what today would be considered French and German descent. She became, by marriage at the age of fifteen, Queen Consort of England. In this period, as Arthur L. Little, Jr notes, '"race" ... works less as a stable identity category than as a semiotic field, one as infinitely varying as the cultural discourses constituting what we have come to identify as the early modern era or Renaissance'.[15] Moreover, despite the persistent polar opposition between Blackness and whiteness and the Petrarchan idealization of 'fair female beauty', in this culture the female was 'not opposed to blackness and monstrosity', as white is to black, 'but identified with the monstrous'. From the Dark Lady of the sonnets to Desdemona's 'blackened whiteness' in *Othello*, femininity, and, especially, feminine sexuality, was always already a place of racialized darkness.[16] Thus in Shakespeare's lexicon, as a Frenchwoman and as a woman, Margaret did indeed belong to a different race – as defined by both national origin and gender.

Born over five centuries later, Okonedo describes her own national and ethnic identity, 'Jewish Nigerian Brit', with a phrase that encapsulates the insufficiency of the modern Black-and-white binary to capture the differences among individuals of various ancestries at this moment in the early twenty-first century.[17] The initial public response when the BBC announced Okonedo's role as Margaret in *The Hollow Crown*'s long-awaited second season, in turn, exemplifies both the inadequacy of the concept of 'colourblind casting' and the contentious nature of 2016's local and global political milieu. UK Independence Party councillor Christopher Wood notoriously tweeted his opposition to a Black Margaret: 'So the @BBC has given up on any kind of historical accuracy. How can Margaret of Anjou be played by Sophie Okonedo?'[18] On the opposite end of the political spectrum came a headline from an *okayafrica.com* post by columnist Alyssa Klein: 'Sophie Okonedo Looks Absolutely Boss as Queen Margaret in "The Hollow Crown: The Wars of the Roses".' The post presented the same image of Okonedo as Margaret in battle gear that so outraged Wood.[19]

Former Royal Court Theatre director Cooke, who took on all three episodes of the second season as his first foray into directing film or television, explained the casting of Okonedo as a purely merit-based decision. 'I think Sophie is the best person in this country to play that part, I really do', he remarked in one interview. But he also made a comment suggesting a motive not entirely blind to colour: 'I don't think that you can do a piece of work that is about who we are as a society and just have white people doing it.'[20] While this comment accords with the BBC's official strategy of diverse and inclusive hiring practices, it also speaks to the special place occupied by Shakespeare's histories in the British cultural imaginary: as a reflection of the nation not only as it was but as it currently is.

Yet even so, British theatre has only slowly moved towards the casting of actors of colour as Shakespeare's titular monarchs, starting, as stated earlier, in the early 2000s. The 2001 RSC *Henry VI* trilogy was celebrated for its diverse cast and was successfully revived in 2006 with another Black actor, Chuk Iwuji, in the title role. In 2003, Adrian Lester played Henry V in a production directed by Nicholas Hytner for the National Theatre. But up until very recently,[21] subsequent actors of colour in these roles have, especially in the UK, been few and far between. The overall 'omission of BAME actors from these leading roles in Shakespearean history plays', Urvashi Chakravatry writes, 'troublingly situates actors of colour outside the dramatic imaginings and reconceptualizations of English history and genealogy'.[22]

Given the particular paucity of women in Shakespeare's histories, alongside the lack of physical representation for Black women across Shakespeare's corpus, the situation for women of colour in such roles is especially pronounced – with interventions such as the Globe's 2019 all-women-of-colour *Richard II* (which I discuss further in Chapter 3 and in the Conclusion) designed to redress this gap. *The Hollow Crown*, it should be noted, presents a white male British actor as every single one of its kings: Ben Whishaw as Richard II, Rory Kinnear and Jeremy Irons as Henry IV, Tom Hiddleston as Henry V, Tom Sturridge as Henry VI, Geoffrey Streatfeild as Edward IV, Caspar Morley as the boy Edward V and Benedict Cumberbatch as Richard III. Sophie Okonedo's presence as a Black queen thus stands out even further.

By adapting Shakespeare's *Henry VI* plays, moreover, *The Hollow Crown*'s second season takes on an especially difficult task. These plays are often seen as 'unplayable because unintelligible' and lacking such seeming literary basics as 'a central character' and 'a linear narrative'.[23] Trimming down the three *Henry VI* plays plus

Richard III to a three-episode TV miniseries with a clear narrative arc involved not only a condensation of plot but also an imposition of focus. According to Cooke, that focus is the rise of Richard III: 'The question was, how many bad decisions does it take to put a psychopath in power?'[24] But since the series' big-name star, Benedict Cumberbatch as Richard, does not enter until the second of the three episodes, Margaret becomes another anchor of the cycle's narrative. Cooke and his co-adapter, screenwriter Ben Power, omitted most of the combat scenes in *1 Henry VI* as well as, more surprisingly, Cade's Rebellion in *2 Henry VI* – an erasure that has clear and problematic implications for the series' representation of class diversity. The script instead emphasizes the role played by the queen and her lover, Somerset – a composite of the characters Somerset and Suffolk in the plays.

Although the casting of Sophie Okonedo as Margaret in this streamlined narrative produces various, at times contradictory, political frames of reference, those clashes are themselves revealing. It is precisely in its status as an uneven and ideologically unstable production, derived from an uneven, ideologically unstable quartet of plays, that *The Hollow Crown: The Wars of the Roses* demonstrates the instability and complexity of constructions of race, gender and disability in both Shakespeare's time and our own.

Season Two of *The Hollow Crown* begins with a vertiginous bird's-eye view of blue-green water. The shot moves in on the white cliffs of Dover, and a man on horseback takes the viewer leaping over a hedge of red and white roses. This is the messenger bringing bad news from France to the advisors of the new infant king, Henry VI, while the body of his father, Henry V, lies in state.[25] The opening visual reference to the English Channel calls attention to the ongoing Anglo-French conflict and connects it directly to the titular Wars of the Roses. The disorienting camerawork provides a kinesthetic and visceral reminder of how, in his histories, Shakespeare consistently treats Frenchness as otherness: 'quintessentially different with respect to religion, warfare, government, gender, sexuality, and personal ethics'.[26] The ultimate boundary-crosser in this series is Margaret of Anjou, French-princess-turned-scheming-English-queen, whom the chronicle histories blamed for instigating those wars, leading Shakespeare to follow suit – and who, in the age of Brexit and the War on Terror, also stands poised to represent both 'immigrant' and 'terrorist'.[27]

Meanwhile the authoritative and familiar voice of Dame Judi Dench recites a pared-down version of Ulysses's famous speech on degree from *Troilus and Cressida*. The speech concludes, 'Take but degree away, untune that string, / And hark what discord follows' (1.3.109–10). The use of Dench's cultural capital as an 'English heritage' actor gives weight to this interpolated prologue, which reads like 'a message to "respect your betters"'.[28] Although she appears later in Episode Three as the Duchess of York, a character with her own complicity in rebellion, here Dench's extradiegetic voice is the voice of the establishment. In *1 Henry VI*, the primal crime against degree has already taken place: the 1399 deposing of the hereditary monarch, Richard II, by Henry Bolingbroke. The first tetralogy is often seen as Shakespeare upholding a conservative political orthodoxy via the so-called 'Tudor myth'. According to this view, the plays present the defeat of a demonized Richard III and the end of bloodshed through the uniting of York and Lancaster in Henry Tudor's marriage with Elizabeth of York as divinely sanctioned. The Tudor dynasty, therefore, represents the return to divine right kingship.

If this point of view persisted throughout the series, the final episode should end, as does Shakespeare's *Richard III*, with a speech

FIGURE 1 *Queen Margaret after the Battle of Bosworth Field*. Richard III, directed by Dominic Cooke. © Carnival Film & Television Ltd 2015. All rights reserved. Screen grab.

by the newly crowned Henry VII, forecasting the union of 'the white rose and the red' (5.5.19). Instead, the cycle culminates with another bird's-eye view: this one of a post-apocalyptic Bosworth Field littered with unburied corpses, at the centre of which stands the dispossessed, dishevelled, yet almost deified Margaret (Figure 1). Phyllis Rackin finds Margaret's voice in *Richard III*, chiming in with other disempowered female voices, to be 'subsumed in the hegemonic discourse' in support of the Tudor myth's 'desired conclusion' – that is, Elizabeth I's reign in Shakespeare's England.[29] But in the year 2016 and beyond, on a potentially global 'stage'/ screen, does Okonedo's Margaret and her representation of 'who we are' fulfil this historical, nation-building role? In this case, who 'we' are and, especially, how 'we' see race very much makes a difference.

'Who's the fairest of them all?'

Scholars have long discussed the problem Margaret represents as a woman, queen and foreigner within the masculinist, nationalist genre of the English history play. Her depiction as a gendered and ethnic other begins in *1 Henry VI* with her parallels to other foreign, female characters who 'represent threats to the English protagonists and to the heroic values associated with history as the preserver of masculine fame and glory'.[30] As the only Frenchwoman to outlast the play and make the journey from France to England, there to marry England's king, Margaret is by far the most significant danger. She exemplifies, for Katherine Schwarz, 'a movement of monstrous female agency from margin to center'.[31] By *3 Henry VI*, she has taken control of both the English court and the Lancastrian army.

Many productions of *1 Henry VI* emphasize the shared military prowess and femme fatale wiles of Margaret and Joan Puzel, commonly known as Joan of Arc. Margaret often makes her first entrance at the same moment Joan is captured by the English and effectively takes over her role: 'as one femme fatale exits to be burnt as a witch, another appears, her double, who practises, as it turns out, even more potent witchcraft.'[32] Highlighting this parallel but taking a somewhat different approach to Joan's character, *The Wars of the Roses* additionally draws upon racializations of the two figures in Shakespeare's *1 Henry VI* to construct the complex intersectional identity of Okonedo's othered queen.

The word play inherent to Joan's Shakespearean name epitomizes both her and, by extension, Margaret's many conflicting dualities. 'Puzel' anglicizes the French word *'pucelle'*, or maid, which is also an English slang word for whore. It additionally sounds like both 'pizzle', or penis, and 'puzzle'. As Edward Burns notes, 'The woman in man's clothes wielding a sword is a pucelle with a pizzle, and therefore a puzzle'. The extended pun 'create[s] in one role a summation of binary categories normally seen as discrete – saint/witch, peasant/gentry, villain/hero, man/woman, virgin/whore'[33] and, I would add, white/black.

In Episode One, Power and Cooke's streamlined narrative reduces Shakespeare's lengthy and multiple depictions of the wars in France to two key scenes. The first scene introduces Joan of Arc (Laura Morgan) and establishes her bifurcated character. A low-angle shot foregrounds Joan's stance atop the fortress of Rouen, which she is prepared to defend for the newly declared Charles VII of France. Her armour and cropped hair code her as militantly androgynous, anticipating Margaret's own, similar transformation in Episode Two.[34] Joan's subsequent oration to her troops is intercut with that of the English warrior Talbot as he leads his own men to the fight. However, before she begins the speech, whispered voices lead into a brief flashback of a younger, more vulnerable Joan. While the hands of an unseen adult woman caress her face, the child Joan, lying supine on the floor, stares transfixed at blood streaming from the eye of a statue of the Virgin Mary.

Although Power and Cooke eliminate Joan's Shakespearean portrayal as a seductress, this interpolated speech – much of which comes from her Act 1 introduction to the Dauphin – ostensibly confirms Joan's status as the film's primary symbol of antagonistic French Catholic otherness. She identifies herself as 'a shepherd's daughter, / My wit untrained in any kind of art' and goes on to describe the divine visitation glimpsed in the flashback: 'God's mother deigned to appear to me / And in a vision full of majesty, / Willed me to leave my base vocation / And free my country from calamity' (*1H6* 1.2.72–3, 76–81). In Morgan's delivery this speech becomes a statement of nationalistic religious zealotry to which her troops respond by crossing themselves, producing an audible chorus of clanks from their metal armour.

The Hollow Crown elides a key moment in this speech – one that demarcates Joan's otherness in a way that is especially relevant to her relationship to Okonedo's Margaret. In *1 Henry VI*, Joan's divine elevation from her 'base' vocation also involves a whitening process:

> Lo, whilst I waited on my tender lambs
> And to sun's parching heat displayed my cheeks,
> God's mother deigned to appear to me . . .
> Her aid she promised, and assured success.
> In complete glory she revealed herself.
> And, whereas I was black and swart before,
> With those clear rays which she infused on me
> That beauty am I blessed with, which you may see.
>
> (1.2.76–8, 82–6)

As Little observes, out of all the material in Shakespeare's histories, this passage presents one of the clearest uses of racializing tropes. It describes 'racial blackness . . . as originating from heliosis' and 'whiteness as signifying purity, saintliness, innocence, and so forth'. The miracle of Joan's holy vision is quite literally a transformation in her 'racial character'.[35]

That Joan achieves her whiteness as a Frenchwoman and adversary to England, however, belies this apparent relationship between whiteness and purity. As Schwarz points out, her '"assur'd success" is the defeat of England'. Moreover, the miracle of Joan's whitening takes place by means of what to Protestants would have been perceived as the 'heretical iconography' of Mariolatry. Joan thus exposes both the tenuousness and the 'dangerous efficacy' of white feminine beauty, which claims holiness and purity for a figure who in English eyes is both a heretic and a whore.[36] As a woman – especially as a French woman – Joan is always already sexually and racially suspect, with a whiteness that is primed to be revealed as its dark other.

In *The Hollow Crown*, nontraditional casting transfers aspects of Joan's textual racialization onto Margaret. The parallel between the two women climaxes during the second English attack upon the French. As the English storm the French stronghold, the Duke of York and Earl of Somerset embark on parallel journeys to seize their respective female prizes. The setting of Joan's capture is thus relocated from the masculine space of the battlefield to the more enclosed, feminine space of the fortress's interior. There Margaret is likewise apprehended in a series of intercut scenes that highlight the two women's mutual treatment as spoils of war.

Neither is a willing victim. The invasion awakens Joan from sleep. Seeing the chaos outside her bedroom window, she briefly brandishes a sword before the whispers of another holy vision lead her to a room further inside the castle. Kneeling before the same statue of the Virgin that appeared in her childhood flashback, she turns to York with her hands raised to reveal what appears to be freshly bleeding stigmata as she hails him with curses. York, shouting his own choice epithets, lifts Joan bodily and carries the shrieking woman off screen. Similarly, the first part of Okonedo's Margaret to enter the screen frame in her encounter with Somerset is a hand clutching a dagger. Margaret's subsequent conversation with Somerset, although less overtly violent, likewise reveals her victimization by the patriarchal traditions of medieval warfare. Cut are the play's comical asides that demonstrate Margaret's wiles as she manipulates Suffolk for her own ends. Okonedo's Margaret is no coy seductress but, rather, a self-possessed woman in a no-win situation, prepared to defend herself with violence. In contemporary parlance, she is a 'frightened war refugee' as well as an 'at risk object of violent desires'.[37] To further emphasize the parallels between Margaret and Joan, both wear white shifts that mark their common feminine vulnerability.

Other creative choices, however, underscore Joan's and Margaret's differences. As Eleanor Rycroft observes, Margaret's hair is 'long and slightly curly', identifying her as 'the archetypal medieval maiden', while Joan's 'short crop singles her out as transgressive to femininity'. Similarly, Joan speaks with what is in this Received Pronunciation-dominated series an isolated Yorkshire accent that 'displac[es] Joan's "Frenchness" onto her "northern-ness"', while Margaret's 'RP accent indicates her gentility in spite of her Frenchness'.[38] Despite Margaret's darker skin, both hair and accent suggest Joan is the greater outsider. In fact, by emphasizing Joan's lower-class status as evinced in *1 Henry VI* by the reference to her 'base vocation', *The Hollow Crown* backhandedly participates in her original racialization. 'Base' is a word that resonates throughout Shakespeare's more obvious race plays to mark the linked discourses of race and class, from Aaron's famous rhetorical question, 'is black so base a hue?', to Othello's self-comparison to the 'base Indian' who 'threw a pearl away / Richer than all his tribe' (*Tit* 4.2.73, *Oth* 5.2.145–6).

Rather than revealing Margaret as Joan's substitute, one French femme fatale to replace another, this episode's joint representation of these two characters ultimately constructs Margaret as an other whose likenesses to and differences from Joan, as well as those to and from the society she is about to join, are almost impossible to parse. The contradictions embedded in the racial semiotics surrounding Margaret in these moments inhere in the frequent use of a word in Shakespeare's *1 Henry VI* which is preserved in *The Hollow Crown*. That is the slippery and near-ubiquitous early modern term 'fair'. 'Fair', Kim F. Hall points out, is far from 'a stable and pure linguistic and social quality'. Rather, by simultaneously evoking at times incompatible qualities of beauty, whiteness, virtuousness and high social rank, the word 'avoids particularity, and, like whiteness, it is represented as "plain", obvious, and curiously opaque'.[39] The very evasiveness of this term, Hall suggests, is central to its insidious racializing work.

In both *The Wars of the Roses*, Episode One and Shakespeare's *Henry VI, Part 1*, Margaret's initial appearance provokes the repetition of this overdetermined signifier. Somerset/Suffolk discovers her in the French stronghold and addresses her as follows: 'O fairest [woman], do not fear nor fly, / For I will touch thee but with reverent hands' (*1H6* 5.2.67–8). The alliterative linkage of 'fair' with 'fear' and 'fly' underscores the princess's female beauty as a risk factor for being raped. Later, as the Duke of Anjou and Somerset bargain over the arrangement of Margaret's marriage to Henry, Margaret's father questions her suitor's veracity: 'Speaks he as he thinks?' Although the question is directed to Margaret, Somerset replies, 'Fair Margaret knows / [The Earl of Somerset] doth not flatter . . . or feign' (162–3). Rather than either allowing Margaret to answer her father or answering in his own right, Somerset steps in and takes over his captive's position as a speaking subject, avowing that 'fair Margaret knows' that he is trustworthy. Here again alliteration is important, linking fairness with lack of flattery or feigning.

Margaret's seemingly transparent fairness, in other words, speaks for the seemingly equally transparent virtue of a man supposedly incapable of deceit. In reality, of course, there is a good deal of equivocating both on the part of Margaret's captor, who cannot possibly speak for what his prisoner 'knows', and in the word 'fair' itself, the labour of which is to make seem transparent what is almost entirely opaque. Meanwhile, the now silenced Margaret reveals her true feelings through Okonedo's eloquent use of facial expressions and body language that mingle fear, sorrow, stubbornness and – most prominently – anger at Somerset and her father alike.

As the Duke of Anjou, Patrick Troughton's demeanour towards Margaret in this scene is not at all paternal, which makes the concrete fact that two white men are negotiating over the disposition of a Black woman's body even more disconcerting. The camerawork highlights this troubling arrangement, situating the mute woman being exchanged for land amidst other voiceless objects of loot being gathered by English soldiers. Two separate shots frame Margaret's standing form, one brown shoulder exposed by her dishevelled white gown, between two seated white men at either side of the literal bargaining table. For Kirsten Mendoza, 'Margaret's silence' in this scene 'is deafening'.[40]

Back in Henry's English court, when the king's councillors – all middle-aged white noblemen – debate, as in the play, the relative worth of Margaret's 'fairness' versus the more substantial dower of the daughter of the Earl of Armagnac to whom the king is already betrothed, this power imbalance grows. During these negotiations, Somerset excludes Margaret's less 'fair' attributes of Frenchness and lack of wealth in favour of her 'fair' qualities of beauty, virginity and – somewhat dangerously – her 'valiant courage and undaunted spirit', which will ensure Henry VI a successor: 'For Henry, son unto a conqueror, / Is likely to beget more conquerors, / If with a lady of so high resolve / As is fair Margaret he be linked in love' (*1H6* 5.4.70, 73–6). However, the very features that make Margaret attractive as a breeder of English kings also make her dangerous as a French enemy on English soil, where her fairness, like Joan's, later threatens to morph from feminine beauty into problematically masculine valour. Moreover, Margaret's implicit associations with Joan call attention to the potential 'black and swart' substrate of her ostensible whiteness.

Throughout this sequence in Episode One of *The Wars of the Roses*, a conspicuous gap opens between, on the one hand, a late sixteenth-century text that deploys the term 'fair' to manage contradictions in its constructions of race, nationality and gender and, on the other, an early twenty-first-century performance that is blind to the word's colour bias and at least nominally blind to the colour of the actress playing Margaret. Although the word 'fair' here highlights the mechanisms of patriarchy, the erasure of its racial implications reinforces white privilege in much the same way as asking an audience not to 'see' Sophie Okonedo's Blackness: by making, or attempting to make, the category of whiteness invisible.[41]

Yet Okonedo's skin colour is not invisible. As a result, the presence of a Black Margaret necessarily calls attention to intersections of race and gender in both the adaptation and the source text. In a moment in 2 *Henry VI* omitted in Cooke and Power's script, a more experienced Margaret reflects on her arrival at Dover as she upbraids her royal husband for disloyalty. She describes how a long-ago near-shipwreck forecast their current marital discord:

> As far as I could ken thy chalky cliffs,
> When from thy shore the tempest beat us back,
> I stood upon the hatches in the storm,
> And when the dusky sky began to rob
> My earnest-gaping sight of thy land's view,
> I took a costly jewel from my neck –
> A heart it was, bound in with diamonds –
> And threw it towards thy land. The sea received it,
> And so I wished thy body might my heart.
> And even with this I lost fair England's view,
> And bid mine eyes be packing with my heart,
> And called them blind and dusky spectacles
> For losing ken of Albion's wished coast.
>
> (3.2.101–13)

Her description of Dover as 'thy chalky cliffs' substantiates the whiteness encoded in the phrase 'fair England' as well as 'Albion' – from the Latin *albus*, or 'white'. The pronoun 'thy', by attributing possession of those cliffs to England's king, separates both whiteness and Englishness from Margaret's 'I'. Meanwhile the phrase 'earnest-gaping sight' implicitly sexualizes Margaret's virginal and visual longing. Her desire is less for the king's body than for his white land – of which the 'dusky sky' deprives her of view.

By the end of this description, Margaret has internalized that exterior darkness. She curses her own eyes as 'blind and dusky spectacles' and longs for 'Albion's wishèd coast'. She then compares herself to 'madding Dido', who was '[be]witched' into falling in love with Aenaes (3.2.117, 119). As Joyce Green MacDonald asserts, the legendary Carthaginian queen was a site of early modern England's formation of racial otherness.[42] For Margaret, the whiteness of Dover's cliffs lurks tantalizingly beyond her grasp on account of both her Frenchness, which marks her body as existing just outside the borders of the emergent category of English racial whiteness, and, moreover her femaleness, which simultaneously casts her as a 'dark' figure and one necessary for the propagation of white English kings.

And yet at the same time Shakespeare's Margaret herself is white – both in the modern racial sense and in the early modern sense of her movement towards being England's queen. Her longing for an 'at once immanent, intimate, and out of reach' whiteness exemplifies Little's notion of Renaissance 'white melancholia'.[43] The instability and interdependence of the seemingly opposite terms 'black' and 'white' also reflect Cord Whitaker's analysis of these 'shimmering contraries' in medieval, and Renaissance, race-thinking: 'Black and white are two of Nature's essential building blocks, and since antithesis requires duality, they are interminably bound to one another.'[44] Okonedo's Black Margaret not only reveals how these racializing constructions of colour are implicit in Shakespeare's text but carries them forward into the twenty-first-century Western cultural imaginary. The famously white cliffs of Dover evoked in the season's opening image not only mark England's border with the channel, and, by extension, France, but both the limits and limitations of whiteness.

'Between the red rose and the white'

The Black-and-white binary is further disturbed by the addition of a key third colour term that directly engages constructions of gender. Okonedo's Margaret doesn't wear white for long; when she arrives in England, she exchanges her white shift for a dark-red gown. As costume designer Nigel Egerton explains, 'in contrast to Henry's neutrality and sort of shapeless garb, she comes in dynamic and sort of red'.[45] 'Dynamic' here is a euphemism for Margaret's sexuality in contrast to her husband's monkish naiveté. Margaret's lover,

Somerset, also wears red; the change in costume simultaneously encodes the awakening of her sexual power and both characters' association with the red Lancastrian rose. At this point, the series abandons its representation of Margaret's innocence and instead embraces her role as a femme fatale. Blindness to race moves from passively reinforcing white privilege to actively embracing negative stereotypes of Black female sexuality. In the process, *The Hollow Crown: The War of the Roses* implicates itself in the legacy of racial constructions embedded in the colour imagery of its subtitle.

This symbolism of the red and white roses participates in the *Henry VI* plays' constructions of race by drawing on the same humoral theories that informed early modern understandings of gendered and racial differences. As Mary Floyd-Wilson argues, humoral understandings of the body and its emotions are central to emergent sixteenth-century English constructions of the superiority of light skin colour, which contemporary Western culture has since so problematically naturalized. The classical view held that the sanguine temperament of light-skinned northern men made them physically strong but also 'reckless, rash, overly amorous, and slow-witted'. Later English authors would revise this less-than-flattering portrayal of sanguinity and describe it, instead, as the ideal disposition: 'merry, light-hearted, good tempered' and, furthermore, '"deckt with beautie which consists in a sweete mixture of those two colours white and redde"'.[46] Via the red and white Lancastrian and Yorkist roses, the *Henry VI* plays symbolically project factional conflict onto the gendered and racialized English body politic, simultaneously participating in the construction of white privilege and revealing its inherent contradictions.

In *2 Henry VI*'s seminal garden scene, Richard Plantagenet declares his claim to both the title Duke of York and, through that title, to the English throne by symbolically plucking a white rose and proclaiming, 'Let him that is a true-born gentleman / And stands upon the honour of his birth, / If he suppose that I have pleaded truth, / From off this briar pluck a white rose with me' (2.4.27–30). The nobles who ally themselves with Plantagenet further the implied association between whiteness and truth. For Warwick, whiteness signifies the integrity that underlies the false 'colour' of performance: 'I love no colours, and, without all colour / Of base insinuating flattery, / I pluck this white rose with Plantagenet' (34–6). Vernon connects such 'truth and plainness' with the virginal female body: 'I pluck this pale and maiden blossom here, / Giving my verdict on the white rose side' (46–8). Somerset, however, turns the tables by threatening a penetrative assault on the 'maiden' flower: 'Prick not your finger as you pluck it off, / Lest, bleeding, you do paint the white rose red / And fall on my side so, against your will' (49–51). If the white rose stands for virtuous (and implicitly feminized) truth, the Lancastrian red rose stands for the 'fall' of that truth into sexuality by means of penetrative violence.

Verbal play about blushing further develops the idea of the interchangeability between red and white. Plantagenet calls attention to his enemy's pallor, in 'counterfeit' of the white rose, as a sign of 'fear' (2.4.62–3). Somerset retorts that Plantagenet's red cheeks are the actual counterfeit: ''Tis not for fear, but anger, that thy cheeks / Blush for pure shame to counterfeit our roses' (65–6). In a later scene, the Yorkist Vernon is accused of likewise calling Somerset out for 'blushing . . . When stubbornly he did repugn the truth' about Plantagenet's claim to the throne (4.1.93–4). The blush, as Sujata Iyengar has argued, was a site of early modern racializing science linking the physiology of skin colour to the moral condition of shame. People with light skin were believed to blush as a sign of being 'capable of experiencing remorse', while those with dark skin were believed to be incapable of blushing and hence also incapable of shame. However, expressions of these beliefs on the Renaissance stage functioned as not 'fundamental bodily truth but its literary or hermeneutic breakdown'. Blackface could be applied to conceal the natural blush, or cosmetics could be used to fake a blush and thus falsify the appearance of female virtue.[47] In the rose garden scene this breakdown occurs on the level of rhetoric, regarding both the ability to 'counterfeit' red and white and the shifting interpretations of these colours' meanings.

The Hollow Crown: The Wars of the Roses foregrounds the rose garden scene, placing it early in Episode One's first act. Although a twenty-first-century audience is not attuned to historically specific meanings surrounding the blush, the humoral body and early modern humoral racialism, certain key colour associations persist. For instance, the respective red and white colours of the factional roses visually and thematically correspond to the colours of the St George flag. Widely visible across both seasons of *The Hollow Crown* for presumably historical reasons, the flag inevitably also invokes contemporary politics, having become a symbol of the far right in debates surrounding Brexit, British citizenship and multiculturalism. Although later in the series single-coloured roses replace St George's cross on Yorkist and Lancastrian flags, the country's unification under the red-and-white Tudor rose implicitly invokes imagery of red and white as fundamentally English.

Moreover, by turning the Lancastrian noble, Somerset, into Margaret's romantic partner as well as the scene's most obvious champion of the red rose, the series emphasizes Margaret's association with the colour red as a matter of her illicit sexual relations rather than a function of her legitimate marriage to a Lancastrian monarch. This emphasis on the sexuality of a character played by a singular Black actress in a mostly white cast resonates with the contemporary 'Jezebel' stereotype of Black female promiscuity.[48] The problem is exacerbated by the desexualized portrayal of Joan, who is so closely linked with Margaret but played by a white actress.

Margaret's racially loaded sexualization begins with the character's first appearance in Episode One. As discussed earlier, when Somerset drags Margaret before her father to bargain for her hand on behalf of King Henry, both costuming and camerawork highlight her victimization. However, once the bargain is sealed, Cooke delivers the first of many scenes featuring Margaret in a dark hallway communing secretly with her eventual lover before disappearing behind a closed door. When Somerset initiates a goodbye kiss, ostensibly as a 'loving token to his majesty', she is far from unwilling (*1H6* 5.2.202). After the kiss, her parting words are uttered with a restrained but clearly flirtatious edge. A close-up of Margaret's expression as she stands a step above Somerset invites the audience to speculate on her thoughts. Is it this man's body Margaret desires, or being queen, or both? Or is she a disempowered woman making the best of a bad situation?

The next time we see Margaret in a dark hallway, it will be to wordlessly solve the open question of her degree of agency. For Sandra Logan, the Frenchwoman Margaret in the male-dominated English court of *2 Henry VI* is 'a pawn of Suffolk, despite her desire for authority'.[49] In contrast, Okonedo's Margaret punctuates her complaints about her husband's lack of kingly power by firmly refusing sex with Somerset/Suffolk in this second hallway scene. After the two jointly plot the downfall of both the Duchess and Duke of Gloucester, the third and final hallway assignation takes place as Gloucester, himself now stripped down to a telltale white shirt, slumbers in his tower cell, oblivious to the approach of his murderers. The cries of the Duke as he is slain are cross-cut with the cries of Margaret's orgasm as she finally gives Somerset what he's been asking for. In place of Warwick's graphic speech that dwells on the appearance of Gloucester's corpse – 'But see, his face is black and full of blood, / His eyeballs further out than when he lived, / Staring full ghastly like a strangled man' – all we see of the Duke's earthly remains is a single pale leg through a dungeon doorway (*2H6* 3.2.168–70). The camera instead lingers on the climaxing face and clenching hands of Okonedo as Margaret. Hers, too, is a 'black' face in a way that can't help but register on the viewer's eye, not least in visual contrast to the whiteness of that dead leg. Whiteness and the innocence it signifies are now the sole province of the Duke of Gloucester – played by 'Downton Abbey favorite, Hugh Bonneville' – while Margaret, in her red dress and with her Black body, has become the villain.[50]

Like the rose garden scene, this moment in Shakespeare's *2 Henry VI* presents moral, gendered and racial associations of colour that can best be understood with reference to Galenic humoralism. Warwick's speech as a whole – entirely cut in *The Hollow Crown* – describes Gloucester's appearance in death as an extreme and unusual one. He posits the engorged blackness of the dead man's face as evidence of Gloucester's violent death, as opposed to the whiter appearance of the 'timely-parted ghost / Of ashy semblance, meagre, pale and bloodless' (3.2.161–6). He goes on to explain the physiology behind this difference. With a more peaceful demise, the blood will not have 'settled in the face', but instead will have 'descended to the labouring heart / Who, in the conflict that it holds with death, / Attracts the same for aidance 'gainst the enemy' (160, 163–5). Now fighting spiritual battles in the heart rather than earthly battles in the body's periphery, there the blood 'cools, and ne'er returneth / To blush and beautify the cheek again' (166–7).

Whiteness here represents neither truth nor fear but, rather, a peaceful passage into death where spiritual rather than bodily concerns are paramount. In contrast, with a violent death, an excess of blood appears as blackness in the face. Gloucester's black face is, in other words, a post-mortem blush – a blush that signifies not Gloucester's shame but the guilt of his unknown assailant. It is also a sign of his final struggle to cling to life, resulting in a full-body tumescence of which his black face is one component: 'His hair upreared, his nostrils stretched with struggling / His hands abroad displayed, as one that grasped / And tugged for life and was by strength subdued' (171–3). Although Gloucester is not the guilty party, the sexualized violence of Warwick's description and the blackness of Gloucester's face suggest that by dying in this way, with his final resources expended towards bodily survival rather than spiritual salvation, Gloucester has been morally comprised, and hence blackened, by his own murder.

In *The Hollow Crown* the sexualized energy of this description is transferred into Margaret and Somerset's bedroom, while Gloucester is reduced to the faceless, impotent whiteness of a single lifeless limb. The play's focus on Blackness versus whiteness in relation to the problem of masculine violence within the Christian spirit–body binary becomes, in the film, an emphasis on a Black woman's violent sexuality. Okonedo's Margaret at this point becomes the textbook definition of a femme fatale. It is a status she will carry through the end of the episode, in which Power extensively rewrites Shakespeare's plot, making Margaret's impassioned plea to King Henry for the repeal of her lover's banishment successful. In turn, this repeal becomes York's chief pretext to wage his war to gain the crown. The result is not only Somerset's death but also that of the king, of the young prince and all the other casualties of the civil wars to follow.

The demonization of Margaret reaches its pinnacle in the battle when the queen tortures and kills the Duke of York. This scene ranks as '"one of the most violent in all Shakespeare's plays"' and, like the affair with Suffolk/Somerset itself, is largely the playwright's invention.[51] In several ways Cooke and Power raise the stakes of Shakespeare's already vilifying portrayal of Margaret. They move the scene from the battleground of Wakefield into York's own home, where Margaret's forces disrupt a family dinner. Margaret sweeps through wearing a crown over a black-hooded cloak that makes her look incongruously like the evil queen in *Snow White*. The black head covering also 'aligns her visually with the Muslim minority in the UK', presenting what follows as 'an act of domestic terrorism'.[52] Margaret sends food and dishes crashing to the floor and sets a hanging tapestry of the Yorkist white rose ablaze. The camera lingers briefly on the furious queen's face – slightly agape and aglow in the flames as she stands spellbound by her destructive handiwork – and then on the tapestry's conflagration, which concludes as the flaming white rose rips from its seams, crumples and dramatically falls. The white/Black imagery is stark, reductive and disturbingly racist.

And it only gets worse. When Margaret finally confronts a wounded York in the courtyard while his family residence burns behind them, Okonedo plays her as gleeful and especially wicked. Rather than taunting her enemy with a paper crown, she uses a full-blown crown of thorns which she directs to be made from a white rose bush. The result is an image of a blond Christ figure incongruously adorned with white roses, with streams of blood running down his face. Instead of merely wiping York's tears with a cloth drenched in his youngest son's blood, Margaret stuffs it in his mouth, all the while licking her lips in sensual anticipation. She then leans in so close to York's face she could be about to kiss him – except, instead, she thrusts the knife into his heart.

Before his demise, Adrian Dunbar's York delivers a brief speech that highlights the two most oft-quoted one-liners on the queen's ethnic and gendered alterity:[53] 'She-wolf of France . . . / O, tiger's heart wrapped in woman's hide' (*3H6* 1.4.111, 137). In a script replete with similar epithets, these references to predatory animals present Margaret as an inhuman other by virtue both of her Frenchness and her deviant femininity as well as, the scene suggests, her Blackness. Their juxtaposition and foregrounding in Dunbar's delivery of this speech (in the source text they are twenty-six lines apart) put Margaret's foreignness front and centre with respect to her perceived inhumanity. In addition to continuing the problematic light/dark binary, the use of the rose in this moment also draws upon Shakespeare's symbolism from the rose garden scene, placing York himself in the position of the victimized 'pale and maiden blossom' violently painted red.

Yet even at this moment, Margaret is not fully villainized. For an early modern English audience, Margaret's 'unfeminine' actions in *3 Henry VI*, all with the goal of defending her disinherited son's right to the kingship, place her 'in a contradictory position' within her society and make her 'a vehicle for exposing the ideological nature of many patriarchal claims'.[54] *The Hollow Crown* presents a somewhat different set of contradictions. In a preceding scene, Suffolk's beheading in exile by pirates becomes Somerset's slaying in the Battle of St Albans by York's servant, Vernon. Vernon then plays a horrific practical joke on the queen. When a desperate Margaret, exhausted from seeking her lover, sits down right in front of the watching Vernon's hiding place behind a low wooden barrier, he reaches over her shoulder and drops Somerset's bloody head directly in her lap.

Thus, with York's slaying we are asked to sympathize with Margaret, but as an avenging lover rather than a preserver of the patriarchy. Margaret's last words to York are revised from 'And here's to right our gentle-hearted King!' (1.4.176) to 'Here's to avenge beloved Somerset!'. The concluding close-up shows tears in her eyes. The instability of the viewer's perspective on Margaret in this scene is underscored here, as well, by an on-screen act of viewing: Vernon's spectatorship from behind a smouldering wagon, a reprise of his earlier voyeuristic role with Somerset's head. Together these moments expose the constructed and self-contradictory nature of the queen's gendered and racial representations in both the original play and its adaptation, as the audience must struggle to decide if she is a hero or a villain.

Not at all coincidentally, this second episode's shift towards a sympathetic Margaret is combined with what appears to be a more colour-conscious use of her character. In the latter half of the series the racial otherness of Okonedo's queen itself becomes a call for the viewer's compassion, to the point that by the end of *Richard III* she stands for historical injustices well beyond the scope of four English history plays from the 1590s. The already unstable imagery of the red and white roses in relation to the racialized white English body is further destabilized by exhibiting the sufferings of Margaret's Black body at English hands.

Making Okonedo's Margaret emblematic of racialized suffering is a move that has its own problems, however, as it too often depends upon sacrificing Margaret's voice and agency. This change is most graphically demonstrated in the aftermath of Margaret's defeat at Tewkesbury, where she takes York's place as the tortured, grieving parent. The play presents the defeated queen as 'swooning, lamenting, begging for death at her captors' hands, but unable to taunt them into doing the deed'. While Cooke and Power's version of this scene does perform what Howard and Rackin describe as the translocation of this 'tigerish hero queen' to a definitively 'feminine subject position', it does so using a different set of signifiers involving Okonedo's race as well as her gender.[55] At this moment, as Rycroft notes, 'the wild and disordered hair that signifies distress and madness emerges'.[56] Along with this symbol of gendered emotionality, I suggest that we are also meant at this moment to see Okonedo's Blackness.

When her son is suddenly stabbed in the back by a furious and semi-crazed Richard, Okonedo's Margaret does not swoon. Instead, she delivers the wild, anguished shriek of a mother watching her own son die before her eyes. Following Richard's lead, the soldiers laugh mockingly, even those restraining Margaret on either side. The devastated mother continues to sob and scream while Richard cuts the prince's throat *at* her: that is, while staring gleefully straight at Margaret. There is something squeamishly self-conscious about this display of visceral maternal grief as a spectacle for mass consumption, in which the episode's audience is also implicated. A brief point-of-view shot from the most sensitive of the three brothers, the Duke of Clarence, as Margaret weeps over her son's dead body demonstrates an uncomfortable empathy mingled with responsibility for the queen's suffering that is simultaneously his, and ours.

Margaret's nonverbal utterances become especially important since her speaking lines are almost entirely cut. In addition to calling out her son's nickname, 'Ned!', the only words she speaks are twice to beg for her own death. These changes make Richard's curious question to his brother yet more peculiar: 'Why should she live to fill the world with words?' (3H6 5.5.44). *The Hollow Crown*'s score, however, connects the line to Margaret's role in the episode to follow, in which she and her curses acquire a musical leitmotif. The motif begins with a tremulous, ominous chord that suggests a supernatural presence. When Richard asks his question as if seeing his own unhappy future, we hear this music for the first time.

In a setting of imbalanced power, this performance of grief, which so heavily relies on nonverbal cues, makes Okonedo's race a key visual signifier. The connotations of a dark-skinned woman dragged away by two armed and grinning white men resonate with unhappily iconic images from subsequent world history, particularly the transatlantic slave trade that was already underway when this play was originally performed. Margaret returns to the screen one more time in this episode. The final scene takes the viewer from the royal court to a dark, dank dungeon where Margaret droops in the background. When a jailer comes by to toss her an unappetizing meal, she rises, revealing wrists shackled by heavy chains to the floor. 'Listen to me', she cries with increasing desperation as her sole addressee departs. 'I am the queen! I am the QUEEN!'

Her shackled body speaks to the viewer even more than her words. E. Patrick Jonson argues that the proverbial elephant in the room, the fact that 'the black body has historically been the site of violence and trauma', renders blindness to an actor's race in performance a simultaneous blindness to 'these consequential aspects of bodily harm'.[57] Given the subsequent centuries of slavery and its legacy in the Western world, the implications in the twenty-first century of a Black body in chains cannot be overlooked.

'Mirror, mirror'

By *The Hollow Crown*'s final instalment, the deposed queen is no longer in chains – and her presence alone, regardless of race, is no longer 'historically accurate'. The historical Margaret of Anjou was not in England during the events represented in the final play of Shakespeare's first tetralogy. For this and other reasons, the choice to include Queen Margaret in *Richard III* is by no means a given. Both standalone big-screen productions of the play from the twentieth century – Olivier's technicolour version from 1955 and Loncraine's historically transposed adaptation from forty years later (which I discuss in Chapter 5) – excise a character who speaks a great deal but ostensibly contributes little to the plot.

In the long arc of Cooke's *War of the Roses*, however, Margaret's role is pivotal. By acknowledging the marginalizing effect of the defeated queen's Blackness and presenting her character as increasingly sympathetic and ultimately heroic *as* a marginalized figure, the third and final episode of the trilogy broadens the scope of the English histories to offer a more inclusive vision. Notably, in contrast to the previous two episodes, in which faces of colour other than Margaret's appear only among unbilled extras, the final episode features several darker-skinned actors in speaking parts: most importantly, Ugandan-born British actor Ivanno Jeremiah as Blunt. In Power's script, Blunt is the soldier who slays Richard's horse – thereby sealing the tyrant's fate, not to mention leading to some of the most famous last words in English literature.

Yet at the same time, the episode's concomitant uncritical representation of Richard III's evil in terms of his intertwined deformity and metaphorical blackness undercuts its evolving representation of Margaret's Blackness as an affirmative quality, especially given what both text and film present as the two characters' similarity. Beginning with her opening appearance at which Rivers marvels, 'I muse why she's at liberty' (*R3* 1.4.304), a small round hand mirror becomes a recurrent symbol of Margaret's role as prophetess as well as a meditation on the problems of seeing. So often used in Shakespeare's plays to interrogate the power of theatre, mirrors in Cooke's *Richard III* reveal the increasingly acknowledged problem of race in this series as it connects both to the multiple significations of Richard's deformity and to the nation-building project of *The Hollow Crown* as a whole.

In Cooke's *Richard III*, Margaret first picks up her mirror to hold her enemies spellbound as she utters her infamous curses. In it each enemy sees her or his reflection, followed by excerpts from other moments in the show's run. Queen Elizabeth's reflection gives way to flash-forwards of the young princes heading for their doom. Richard sees, among other things, a flashback of the white rose tapestry in flames from Episode Two and his own fallen form on a muddy battlefield from this episode's foregone conclusion. Later, when Richard receives the unwelcome news that Buckingham has defected, curse music heralds the reappearance of that same mirror, grasped by a disembodied brown hand. The prop returns again in Richard's dreams the night before the Battle of Bosworth Field. Margaret appears at his bedside with the mirror, in which he sees the face of the murdered Henry VI. After cursing him one by one, his victims gather, laughing tauntingly as Margaret holds out the mirror once more. Richard looks for his reflection, even waves his hand before the glass, but anticipating his pre-battle soliloquy – 'Is there a murderer here? No. Yes, I am' – there is no one there (5.3.185).

Whether as a supernatural presence, a hallucination or something in between, Margaret continues to wield that mirror until her final appearance on the battlefield, where it becomes the direct means by which she appears to take Richard down. Richard and Richmond are locked in combat to the death, wrestling in the mud. Richmond is on top, but Richard fights back until he is distracted by a vision of Margaret, who blinds him with the mirror. We see two reflections of Richard as he receives his death blows: the first while he is still alive, the second after he is dead.

The most explicit function of the mirror is, as seen earlier, to register visually the power of Margaret's curses and her role as an Old Testament-style prophet in what on some level functions as a morality play – as it additionally contributes to the long-standing association of Blackness with witchcraft. But the mirror also alludes to the play's perspective on Richard III's physical and moral deformity and his underlying connection to Okonedo's queen. In a key scene after Richard's coronation, when Margaret first appears as a vision in his dungeon study, Richard sees both of their reflections simultaneously in his dagger. The moment mimics an image from the series' previous episode in which the three Plantagenet brothers see their individual reflections coalesce in their father's sword. As in Shakespeare's *3 Henry VI*, this heavenly vision of '[t]hree glorious suns' which 'join, embrace and seem to kiss' until they become 'one lamp, one light, one sun' erroneously forecasts the brothers' unity under their father as king (2.1.26, 29, 31). In Cooke's *Richard III*, instead of falsely expressing the power of unified masculine light/whiteness, Richard and Margaret's joint reflection indicates Richard's true darkness and effeminacy – and forecasts his inevitable doom.

Those qualities are, in turn, directly implicated in Richard III's physicality. His body is one not 'made to court an amorous looking-glass' (*R3* 1.1.15). He is also the 'false glass' that reveals and punishes his mother's, and his society's, 'shame' (2.2.53–4). As Elizabeth Tavares notes, Cumberbatch's Richard 'is routinely surrounded by mirrors that wobble and fracture alongside his sense of (and his actual) power . . . [R]efracting his body back to him in these moments of political failure inherently links the two: a broken body so therefore a broken politics'.[58] In the terms of the early modern binary linking blackness with evil and whiteness with holiness, Richard's deformed body is also a Black body. His appearance as a 'foul bunch-backed toad' overlaps with his identification as 'hell's black intelligencer' and a 'fiend' conjured up by a 'black magician' (4.4.81, 71; 1.2.34). These descriptions, for Urvashi Chakravarty, 'affirm his place within the dramatic lineage of the Vice figure, rehearsing the semiotics of bodily markers as signifiers of sin'.[59] Tellingly, several such epithets are Margaret's own coinages. In uttering them, Okonedo's Margaret effectively 'breathe[s] [her] curse against [her]self', just as Richard attempts to trick her into doing in Act 1 (1.2.239). Margaret is simultaneously the hero who takes Richard down, a reflection of his evil and a participant in her own blackening.

The camera's obsession with Richard's deformity builds across *The Wars of the Roses*' three episodes. At the conclusion of the first episode, the enticing silhouette of his lurching adolescent form provides the cliffhanger into Episode Two, where we first meet Richard as a young man. In a long-delayed pay-off, the extended opening shot of Episode Three then begins with a close-up of a chess board in a dim cavernous room. A ringed hand first appears as Richard moves a black chess piece to take a white one. As our view moves outward from Richard's strong right arm, an arc shot reveals his prosthetically crafted spinal deformity: a humped left shoulder and upper thorax with starkly demarcated ribs. Meanwhile, curse music – Margaret's music – plays, this time sung by an eerie, distant chorus of human voices. The music links Richard's deformity to the unseen dispossessed queen. Although we never again see Richard unclothed, the final shot of the tyrant's mirrored face in death represents the culmination of this long arc of repellant fascination as well as of Richard's connection to Margaret.

This opening shot also develops a visual motif that connects Richard to the colour black. The hue of his controlling chess piece is, of course, significant. Following his brother Edward's coronation towards the end of *The Wars of the Roses*, Episode Two all the way through Richard's own coronation in Episode Three, Richard's all-black outfits showcase his moral evil, as they also link Richard to the Renaissance performance tradition in which white actors mimicked black skin via the colour of their clothing.[60] Similarly, the empty mirror into which Richard stares in his pre-Bosworth dream reflects to him not only moral absence but also internal blackness. In this context it is telling that Richard's most loyal follower, Catesby, is played by one of the episode's actors of colour, South Asian performer Paul Bazely. Such an uncritical perspective on blackness as evil both taints the film's representation of Margaret as a heroic character and amplifies its equally troubling representation of Richard's disability.

Yet complicating both the play's and the film's ableist vision of Richard's atypical body/deviant morals is Cumberbatch's status as a popular cultural icon and sex symbol. Online interviews with the actor emphasized this factor. Although one declared its own headliner image 'a topless picture of Benedict Cumberbatch that won't set pulses racing', a commenter on the same page posted, 'I know I sound desperate, but even with a hunch back I would date him'.[61] Cumberbatch/Richard's shirtless torso, revealed at the same time that it is prosthetically concealed, operates at the nexus of desire and revulsion. It becomes what Rosemarie Garland-Thomson in her work on freak shows and photography calls an 'extraordinary body', which, on display, becomes 'a text written in bold face to be deciphered according to the needs and desires of onlookers'.[62]

Although the history of the disabled body in the Western culture of exhibition is one in which, Garland-Thomson elsewhere observes, that body is made 'visually conspicuous while politically and socially erased', the historicity, celebrity and frank reverence attached to the disabled body of a historical English monarch – and/or his cinematic representation by a famous actor – modify the degree and scope of such an erasure.[63] Adding to the puzzle in the case of the display of Richard III's disability in *The Hollow Crown* was the 2012 discovery of the historical king's skeletal remains under a Leicester parking lot, images of which have been extensively reproduced both in photography and video documentary.[64] Two years later, mitochondrial DNA analysis revealed Cumberbatch himself to be the real King Richard's 'third cousin sixteen times removed'.[65] Although genetically speaking this is essentially a meaningless connection,[66] it was nonetheless played up in promotional media for *The Hollow Crown*, to the point that Cumberbatch – in a 'professional capacity', but also in the bizarre capacity of ersatz next of kin – was asked to read a eulogizing poem at the 2015 ceremonial reinterment of the real Richard III's remains.[67]

This largely fabricated link between the actor's body and the actual Richard's body elevated Cumberbatch himself, on the one hand, to a royal, even mythic status of originary Englishness: not only hailing from the prestigious Harrow school but also genetically linked to a medieval royal line.[68] On the other hand, the extraordinary nature of this particular king's body – made doubly extraordinary by its deadness – adds layers to how we are asked to view Cumberbatch as Richard in both senses, as an actor playing the part of Shakespeare's infamous character and as a descendent of the historical man. Over and above his prosthetic deformity, through this connection Cumberbatch's own body becomes an 'extraordinary' body, simultaneously venerated and compromised.

Black bodies in Western culture, and more particularly in Western theatre, also have an important tragic history of being marginalized and deprived of agency through exhibition.[69] The use of the mirror in *The Hollow Crown*'s final episode to link Cumberbatch's Richard and Okonedo's Margaret's bodies enters into this history. As it visually demonstrates the connection often postulated between Richard and Margaret as two villainous rhetorical virtuosos, the mirror also places their differently marginalized and extraordinary bodies on display. The connection between Margaret and Richard, however, destabilizes the power relationships that might otherwise be seen as unequivocally disempowering both. A Black Queen Margaret becomes the agent of the downfall of a Richard who is simultaneously extraordinarily English (and therefore white) and extraordinarily villainous/deformed (and therefore Black).

The episode's representation of Margaret, moreover, evidences what Rachel O'Connell argues is the 'radically unstable and ambivalent' nature of the relationship between onlooker and extraordinary body.[70] Such a relationship is visualized on screen in Crooke's version of the 'three queens' scene, in which Margaret joins a chorus of avenging, mournful female voices along with her rivals Queen Elizabeth and the Duchess of York. After Elizabeth begs, 'O thou, well skilled in curses, stay awhile / And teach me how to curse mine enemies', the Duchess gestures for the other women to join hands – first Elizabeth and then, after a brief hesitation, Margaret (4.4.116–17). In a close-up, Margaret's brown hand conspicuously joins with the Duchess's white one. Margaret then offers her hand to Elizabeth, who regards her tentatively both before and after taking it. The camera lingers briefly on the clasped hands of the latter two. Unlike that of the Duchess, Elizabeth's white hand is obscured by the material of a forest green velvet glove, and her arms, moreover, are blackened by the lace of her sleeves.

In early modern discourse, as David Sterling Brown observes, the lady's 'white hand' is a central synecdoche in which whiteness emerges as a privileged racial category.[71] Elizabeth, in this parlance, has been 'blackened' by both mourning and witchcraft. When the women join hands, curse music plays once more. It continues to do so in the subsequent scene featuring an increasingly beleaguered

Richard. This colour palette of hands exemplifies how the relationship between onlooker (Elizabeth) and extraordinary body (Margaret) 'carries a cost for its agent as well as its object'. In desiring to possess Margaret's extraordinary and embodied power of cursing, Queen Elizabeth quite willingly 'risks losing possession of herself'.[72] Accordingly Elizabeth's own hand – itself no longer visually white and clasped in the brown hand of her former enemy – now becomes the object of the spectatorial fantasies of *The Hollow Crown*'s unseen viewers. At the same time, the Black/white binary is at least partially undone, demonstrating in a modern context the medieval idea of slippage between these 'shimmering contraries'.

A similar slippage occurs in the series' final scenes. Following Queen Margaret's supernatural wartime assist to Richmond and the resulting death of Richard III, the new King Henry VII's final battlefield speech in which he announces the union of 'the white rose and the red' cuts away to his formal coronation (5.5.19). There, as Henry concludes the speech and presents his marriage to Elizabeth as 'God's fair ordinance' of peace between the warring houses, he takes her hand in view of all his court (5.5.31).[73] In contrast to the mix of actors on the battlefield, the faces here are uniformly white; in contrast to the joining of Elizabeth's and Margaret's hands in the three queens scene, the hands that join here are both fair in complexion. The division between white and black is made yet more flagrant as the camera pans down to Richard's cavernous study below. All that remains, illuminated by a shaft of light from above, is a single overturned chess piece on the floor: the black king.

This blunt contrast between opposing colours is not the last word on the matter, however. With the shot of the fallen chess piece, a brief fade to black then returns us to the battlefield where foot soldiers fill a pit with corpses. The camera pans upward to a low-angle view of a cloaked, dishevelled, grey-haired Margaret looking away from us into a clearing sky. Her exhausted, despairing face then looks upward as if searching for the God of the God's-eye shot that follows. Margaret is simultaneously Richard's double, the Black queen to his black king, and the adversary that takes him down.

The film's score further complicates the significance of this final shot. Note for note, the music that begins with the new King Henry VII's announcement of his betrothal to Elizabeth of York reprises the sombre epic tune that accompanies two other climactic moments in the series: the intercut scenes of Duke Humphrey's murder and Margaret and Somerset's carnal embrace at the end of Episode One, and the enactment of Henry VI's deposition in Episode Two. The same sonorous theme in the strings that follows the murderers to Humphrey's cell and accompanies York's brief ascendancy to the throne takes us down to the depths of Richard's dungeon, while the resolving minor chord that laments over Humphrey's dead white leg and the pallid King Henry VI's abdication lands, at the conclusion of *Richard III*, on a Black Margaret's upward-gazing face. The repeated motif positions the 'fair conjunction' of white rose and red through lawful marriage as no more redemptive than Somerset and Margaret's 'black' adultery (5.5.20). It also makes a specific visual link between Humphrey's whiteness and Margaret's Blackness as emblems of their tragic arcs. The result is a troubling of the early modern Black/white binary so often uncritically reflected in both Cooke's cinematography and Power's script.

This final interpolated scene is ultimately incompatible with either the conservative message of the series opener – in which a battlefield strewn with the unburied dead represents nothing more than the cost in English lives of failing to adhere to 'degree' – or the upholding of a whitewashed Tudor myth as exemplified by King Henry's final speech. Also incompatible with the veneration of the Tudor dynasty are the broader symbolic resonances of Margaret's mirror. In addition to reflecting the corrupt mind and extraordinary body of Richard III, Margaret's mirror recalls the mirror another Richard, Richard II, asks for in that primal deposition scene: 'That it may show me what a face I have, / Since it is bankrupt of his majesty' (*R2* 4.1.266–7). Although the earlier Richard 'seems with this narcissistic image to be looking at himself', he's actually 'looking at the whole of society'.[74] In Cooke's *Richard III*, Margaret's mirror is likewise held up to Britain as a whole, as well as to a much larger audience.

With this larger audience in mind, the final aerial shot of the episode deconstructs and transcends both the Tudor myth and the narrow view of British nationalism for which the red and white colours of the St George flag have been appropriated to stand. It also zooms out to a more global purview. One reviewer writes, 'The brutality was tantamount to a holocaust. . . . Queen Margaret presides over the war dead as their bodies are tipped into huge open graves. . . . Sophie Okonedo's warrior queen is transmuted into an angel of despair – at this massacre and all its successors still to come.'[75] One such successor is the Holocaust of the Second World War, the culturally pervasive images of which this final panorama references with visceral intent. The word 'holocaust' with its connotations of genocide – etymologically, race-murder – also conjures up more recent events. Among them stands the mass slaughter of the Tutsi during the Rwandan Civil War: the massacre represented in the 2004 film *Hotel Rwanda*, in which Okonedo played an acclaimed starring role as an African humanitarian. The actress's Jewishness must also be acknowledged, although this aspect of her identity doesn't visually signify.

In this moment of contemporary intertextuality not imaginable to Shakespeare, the screen image of Okonedo as Margaret, surrounded by tangled corpses, links the Battle of Bosworth Field and the dawn of the British nation state under the Tudors with these far bleaker moments of twentieth- and twenty-first-century history. In a series invested in what is so often an unsuccessful attempt to construct a unified yet multicultural, multiethnic British nation, it belatedly but powerfully yields centre stage to the ever-shifting semantic and semiotic field of race, and how human differences of all types have been constructed and upheld as justifications for the unjustifiable. This final shot thus opens the door for a critique not only of Western history writ large, as well as of the entirety of this two-season miniseries, but for what I will undertake in the remainder of this book: an interrogation of the unstable dialectic between Shakespeare and race in the two tetralogies' recent on-screen history.

2

Two Yorks, the Boy and the King of Pop

Colour-conscious casting and queer seriality in *The Hollow Crown*, Season One

Considering questions of adaptation, race and intersectionality in the complex work that constitutes *The Hollow Crown*'s initial season requires accounting for both continuities across and disruptions within its serial presentation of Shakespeare's second tetralogy. Unlike the second season, which presents the artistic vision of a single director and screenwriter, in the first season three different directors offer three distinct visions across four episodes. Royal Shakespeare Company associate director Rupert Goold, whose prior TV directing experience consisted of his acclaimed Soviet-inspired adaptation of *Macbeth* for the BBC in 2010, directed *Richard II*; former National Theatre director Richard Eyre brought his expertise directing film and television as well as theatre to both parts of *Henry IV*; and English theatre director and writer Thea Sharrock – the sole female director across both seasons of the series – took the helm in *Henry V*.

Nonetheless, Tomas Elliot notes, under the overarching vision of producers Sam Mendes and Pippa Harris, *The Hollow Crown*'s first season also presents itself as a cohesive whole, with continuities in casting, location and production team. In the shows themselves, intertitles and 'previously on' sequences link each episode to what came before.[1] Moreover, like Season Two, after first airing on the BBC and PBS as a miniseries, Season One has been globally marketed as a serial unit. DVDs are purchasable in a single case with a cover featuring a triptych of all three titular kings of the second tetralogy, and component movies are sold as chronologically numbered episodes on platforms such as Amazon Prime and Apple TV.[2] The trappings of modern television and streaming video thus replace the editorial and theatrical markers of seriality previously imposed upon Shakespeare's unruly histories – first in the 1623 Folio's retitling and ordering of these plays 'in an integrated linear sequence' and later in the mid-twentieth century by the tradition of staging cycles of chronologically sequential history plays.[3]

Even more than theatrical cycles, televisual seriality produces audience expectations of consistency in cast, content and style. *The Hollow Crown*, Season One, breaches such expectations in several ways, key elements of which involve race. While the middle episodes, Eyre's two parts of *Henry IV*, completely eschew nontraditional casting – an issue I will take up in Chapter 3 – both the opening and closing episodes consciously cast actors of colour, but to remarkably different effects. Moreover, in one peculiar if heretofore largely overlooked instance of casting discontinuity, the same historical character in Goold's *Richard II* and Sharrock's *Henry V* is played by two different actors, one white and one Black. That is Richard II's and Henry IV's youthful cousin, Edward of Langley – a main supporting character in Shakespeare's *Richard II* known in that play as the Duke of Aumerle, who later in life gained his father's title, Duke of York. This individual then became one of the few men 'of name' to be slain during the Battle of Agincourt as represented in a bit part in Shakespeare's *Henry V* (4.8.104). Enacted in Goold's *Richard II* by youthful white British heartthrob Tom Hughes, the same figure is played in Sharrock's *Henry V* by Afro-British Shakespearean Paterson Joseph in a considerably expanded role.

While older editions of *Henry V* often included a footnote to document the link between Aumerle and York, by the late twentieth century such glosses largely disappeared. However, *The Hollow Crown*'s serial presentation of Shakespeare's histories along with a quirk of digital culture has caused Aumerle and York's common identity to slip back into view. Wikipedia's entry on the series features a grid that charts the actor(s) playing each character across both seasons. One box lists the 'Duke of Aumerle', and in smaller print, 'later Duke of York'.[4] The combination of digitally monitored televisual seriality and nontraditional casting has simultaneously forged a link and opened up a rift between two characters whose common historical identity was also to all appearances of no particular consequence to Shakespeare, but who became in the year 2012, on Wikipedia, the same individual played by a white man in Episode One and a Black man in Episode Four of the same TV miniseries.

Together these two Yorks epitomize the structural and thematic relationship between the first and last episodes of *The Hollow Crown*'s first season as well as between these episodes and the plays on which they are based. I am calling this relationship 'queer seriality': a term that combines the concept of queer temporality with Elisabeth Bronfen's theorization of seriality in televisual Shakespearean appropriation, as well as Elliot's specific concern with how both *The Hollow Crown* and the plays on which it is based, as 'serialized' versions of history, 'systematically disrupt' the apparent linear flow of time.[5] My definition of queer temporality follows that of Annamarie Jagose: 'a mode of inhabiting time that is attentive to the recursive eddies and back-to-the-future loops that often pass undetected or uncherished beneath the official narrations of the linear sequence that is taken to structure normative life.'[6] I also invoke Lee Edelmen's influential understanding of queer time as a repudiation of 'reproductive futurism', a heteronormative political philosophy centred on 'the Imaginary form of the Child', in favour of the queer 'death drive'.[7] Although not necessarily queer, Shakespearean seriality as explained by Bronfen inherently inhabits a recursive relationship to time. It involves both a 'large-scale process of citation' by which the text 'posits a serial relation between itself' and Shakespeare, and 'self-citation on a small scale', such as the 'use of recurring plot elements, character constellations, and dramatic actions in successive episodes'. In such a 'logic of seriality', movement forward necessarily involves a circling backward. That movement occurs both within the limits of the adapted work and all the way back to the source text, enabling the process of 'crossmapping' through which our apprehension of the source text changes through our engagement with the adapted text.[8] Such a model of seriality becomes queer when the revelation of such 'recursive eddies' or 'back-to-the-future loops' disturbs the 'official', 'linear' narratives of 'normative life' – or, in this case, of normative history.

The two Yorks in Season One of *The Hollow Crown* offer an exemplary instance of queer seriality in that they call attention to non-normative structures of race, gender, sexuality and time that underpin cross-citations between both the season's first and last episodes, as well as between the series and the plays. One cross-citation links Aumerle in Goold's *Richard II* and the Boy in Sharrock's *Henry V*. Another links York in *Henry V* to two differently racialized figures in Goold's *Richard II*: the Bishop of Carlisle, played by British-Tanzanian/Zimbabwean actor Lucian Msamati, and Richard II himself, played by white British actor Ben Whishaw with inspiration from twentieth-century pop cultural icon Michael Jackson. In both *Richard II* and *Henry V*, a white boy mediates the violent sacrifice of a metaphorically or racially Black figure of authority. Following the logic of a queer serial approach to these plays, I begin by examining the season's concluding episode before circling back to how the series premiere simultaneously forecasts and undermines that conclusion's apparent take on race and futurity.

'And take the Turk by the beard'

In Episode Four of *The Hollow Crown*, Season One, Black actor Paterson Joseph has a significant presence as the Duke of York, a character largely invented by Sharrock and co-screenwriter Ben Power. A relatively minor character from *Henry V* transforms into the loyal best friend and dependable advisor Shakespeare's isolated young monarch so desperately needs. Towards the end of the episode, York is fatally stabbed in the back by the French Constable in an interpolated scene that replaces both the off-stage death of York and his wartime comrade Suffolk, as well as the death of Falstaff's Boy. In this version of the play, not only does the Boy survive; he is revealed at the end of the film to have grown up into the Chorus (John Hurt).[9]

In part because of Joseph's York, several scholars have expressed disappointment with what they perceive as the jingoistic message of Sharrock's *Henry V*. David Livingstone condemns the episode's 'reactionary' streamlining of Shakespeare's depiction of the titular monarch in an adaptation that deliberately axes key scenes representing dissenting voices of the lower classes and non-English ethnicities.[10] Commenting on York's visual role in affirming the king's more questionable actions, L. Monique Pittman sees the nontraditionally cast character as a version of the 'Magical Negro': the late twentieth-century American cinematic trope of a 'black man who nurtures white masculinity and then willingly departs the scene once his healing power has worked its magic'. York's death, which both replaces the Boy's death and justifies the king's subsequent order to kill the French prisoners of war, for Pittman ultimately 'catalyzes the hegemonic voice of history that will deny non-Caucasians and non-English a more fully agential role in the national story – a black sacrifice underpinning white history'.[11] However, as Ramona Wray notes, in this highly masculinist drama Sharrock does take care to include and centralize perspectives of 'women and children'.[12] In my own view, Sharrock's revisions of both York's and the Boy's roles can best be understood in light of the queer serial structure of *The Hollow Crown*'s first season and its relationship to Shakespeare's *Henry V*, where the Boy functions as a chief figure in the histories' emergent, intersecting discourses of white racialization and heteronormativity.

In Livingstone's view, Sharrock's adaptation 'actually has the boy included in even more scenes than the play but inexplicably fails to provide him with his best lines'.[13] This change can be at least partly explained by *The Hollow Crown*'s attempt to soften the discords of Shakespeare's *Henry V* in order to represent a harmonious multiracial, multicultural Britain. One consequence is a shift in the Boy's role as meta-commentator. In Shakespeare's play, the Boy's role is to critique the dissenting voices of his fellow low-ranking companions and ultimately to uphold, through his own tragic sacrifice, emergent ideals of white British masculinity that teeter precariously at this play's far-from-stable ideological centre.[14] By displacing the Boy's sacrifice onto a Black York and consolidating the Boy with the Chorus, Sharrock seemingly stabilizes his status as a harbinger of patriarchal, heteronormative white supremacy. However, the queer serial structure of *The Hollow Crown*,

Season One's first and last episodes undermines any monolithic understanding of race, gender, sexuality or history.

In both Shakespeare's and Sharrock's *Henry V,* the Boy is Falstaff's otherwise unnamed servant. He initially helps report the loss that lies at the centre of the play's affective structure: Falstaff's illness and death. In the play, the potential pathos of these moments is offset by insults directed at Bardolph's notorious complexion, which include the racializing discourse of colour: 'Good Bardolph, put thy face between his sheets and do the office of a warming pan'; 'Do you not remember 'a saw a flea stick upon Bardolph's nose and 'a said it was a black soul burning in hell-fire?' (2.1.83–4; 2.3.37–9). This language marks the Boy's low-ranking companions with an 'irredeemable moral and social condition' against which the Boy's own privileged whiteness emerges, despite his similar lack of social status.[15] For Anna-Claire Simpson, the Boy exemplifies the status of childhood as a form of what Robin Bernstein calls surrogation, 'the process whereby "culture reproduces and re-creates itself"' and which is 'central to "large-scale racial projects"'.[16] Such body-based insults, in fact, make up the majority of those 'best lines' from the Boy that are missing in Sharrock's *Henry V*, thus erasing a key aspect of Shakespeare's participation in the emergent discourse of whiteness that, as I argue below, emerges elsewhere.

Likewise omitted from Power's script – which preserves Bardolph's death by hanging but eventually rehabilitates Pistol and Nym into cooperative soldiers – is the Boy's repudiation of his companions in heteronormative terms. In France he delivers a lengthy soliloquy in which he declares his intent to abandon the three scoundrels: 'I am boy to them all three, but all they three, though they would serve me, could not be man to me, for indeed three such antics do not amount to a man' (3.2.27–30). The puns in this passage not only conflate social rank and gender roles – 'boy' means both 'male child' and 'servant', and 'man' both 'male adult' and 'master' – but also include a sexual innuendo. To 'serve' also means to penetrate anally. Along with 'antics', which alludes to the world of the theatre, this diction calls attention to the boy player's culturally queer gendered and social status as a 'Ganymede'.[17] As the Boy questions his companions' identification as men by rendering them 'grotesquely subhuman',[18] he embraces his own masculinity both by vowing to eschew thievery and by rejecting the position of sodomitical sexual partner: 'They would have me as familiar with men's pockets as their gloves or their handkerchiefs, which makes much against my manhood if I should take from another's pocket to put into mine, for it is plain pocketing up of wrongs' (46–50). The language through which the Boy rejects his Ganymede status cannot be disentangled from the discourse of race and class privilege. His desire to 'cast up' his companions' 'villainy', which 'goes against [his] weak stomach', is a metaphor that captures the many intersectional valances of the Boy's self-purging of bodily corruption (51–2).[19]

Such concerns subtly underpin a later scene when the Boy helps Pistol by translating during a ransom deal with a French soldier (4.4). In *Henry V*'s original performances, Sarah Werner suggests, this scene would have resonated with the play's prior translation scene involving Princess Katherine and Alice (3.4); the same boy actor may have doubled as Katherine and the Boy. Hence the Boy's refusal to provide a gloss for Pistol on the sexually suggestive words 'fer', 'ferret' and 'firk' symbolically resists erotic availability on both his own and on Katherine's behalf. Meanwhile, Katherine's innuendo-filled itemization of her body parts in broken English calls attention to the 'male body under her female dress'.[20] Together, the two scenes simultaneously embrace and repudiate the Boy actor's queer status.

In the play's final scene, when the Boy character is technically absent but, potentially, physically present in the form of the actor playing Katherine, intersections between race and sexuality confound King Henry's own attempt to construct a white future. In a brilliant reading, Simpson links the Boy to the potential son about whom the king verbally fantasizes during his courtship of Princess Katherine as two 'surrogations' of whiteness. As the difference between French and English is erased and subsumed under the umbrella of whiteness via Henry's repetition of the keyword 'fair', a third, off-stage race, the Turk, becomes the common enemy and other: 'Shall not thou and I, between Saint Denis and Saint George, compound a boy, half French, half English, that shall go to Constantinople and take the Turk by the beard?' (5.2.202–5).[21] Following Katherine's consent, the French king ratifies this fantasy of peaceful union through common Christian '[i]ssue', vowing that never again should 'war advance / His bleeding sword 'twixt England and fair France' (5.2.339, 344–5).

As Werner points out, the boy actor's existence casts doubt upon the ease of these 'terms of procreation', which depend upon a female body.[22] Moreover, as the epilogue soon reminds us, the actual Henry and Katherine's historical offspring offered no such 'fair' future, either: 'Henry the Sixth, in infant bands crowned King / Of France and England, did this king succeed, / Whose state so many had the managing / That they lost France and made his England bleed' (5.2.373–6). The rhyme on 'succeed' and 'bleed' underscores how in this case 'succession' has generated only lack of fulfilment. Along with the boy actor's material body, the material facts of history would seem to obliterate the fantasy of a 'fair' reproductive future that the courtship scene calls into being.

In symbolically denying King Henry and, by extension, England a reproductive future, the Boy's queer status at least superficially resonates with Edelman's conception of the queer 'death drive'. The actual death of the Boy's character at the hands of the French potentially adds weight to this connection. Like Macduff's slaughtered son in *Macbeth*, whom Amanda Zoch reads as a queer figure, the Boy 'fail[s] to align with the futurity he, as a child, appears to symbolize'.[23] In fact, the Boy is, in these terms, even more queer than Macduff's son. Other than his symbolic relationship to the king, the Boy exists outside genealogy; he hence lacks reproductive futurity in the play's terms even when alive.

Both the boy actor's Ganymede status and the Boy character's lack of reproductive potential would thus seem to forestall the white futurity imagined by King Henry in the play's conclusion. However, in another way the Boy's death also enables whiteness. By differentiating him from the stigmatized bodies of his companions, Simpson asserts, the Boy's battlefield demise is essential to his elevation to white Englishness.[24] I argue that the Boy's death also paradoxically ensures his futurity – a white futurity – by non-reproductive means. Through his death the Boy achieves a symbolic whiteness propagated not through his own progeny but through his queer, theatrical status and his repeated performance on stage and on film up through our own time – *The Hollow Crown* included.

The same could be said of the imagined white progeny of Henry and Katherine's union. For although King Henry V has 'no future' in terms of biological generation, he does indeed have a future via the play that bears his name – a monument that, like several of Shakespeare's sonnets to the Fair Youth, aims to achieve futurity through memorialization rather than sexual reproduction. In Shakespeare's *Henry V*, whiteness is passed down not as a hereditary property but as a powerful fantasy, achieved in theatrical performance rather than genealogical time. In *Henry V* and especially, as I now will argue, in Sharrock's adaptation of *Henry V*, white futurity is queer futurity.

'In your fair minds let this acceptance take'

In other contemporary performances of *Henry V* in which female actors play female characters, the Boy's originally queer status is, for the most part, lost. In both major twentieth-century cinematic versions of the play, visual representations of the Boy's body become a way of managing the play's homoeroticism and providing a culturally 'safer' way than Exeter's monologue on York and Suffolk's love-death to display wartime male–male bonds. Olivier has Fluellen deliver his outraged 'Kill the poys and the luggage!' speech while cradling the bleeding body of the Boy in his arms (4.7.1).[25] In Branagh's *Henry V*, a Christ-like King Henry famously carries then-fifteen-year-old Christian Bale across the field to a mournful yet triumphant chorus of '*Non nobis*'.[26]

The link between the Boy and King Henry's imagined progeny is given a further, biological spin in Peter Babakitis's independent 2007 adaptation of *Henry V*, where it also intersects with an evolving concern with race. In a cast of largely amateur actors, Babakitis himself plays Henry V, while his adolescent son Alexander, who resembles his father, plays the Boy. Although the production's stark visualization of the Boy's dead body face down on the ground contributes to Babakitis's intended presentation of King Henry as 'a morally ambiguous character',[27] the father–son pairing implicitly casts the Boy as an embodiment of normative reproductive futurism as well as whiteness. This casting choice underscores the conservatism of the film's initially uncritical use of an all-white, mostly male cast.

Such conservatism is exacerbated by the presentation of the Chorus in the film's original cut as an 'impersonal', even 'godlike' documentary-style voiceover which, according to Sarah Hatchuel, undercuts any intended criticism of its 'heroic and "official" version' of history.[28] In the revised version of the film currently marketed on Amazon, however, the director's addition of South Asian actress Sabaa Rehmani as an embodied Chorus reads as an attempt to restore his critical take on the play on both counts. Rehmani's Chorus at times appears with dreadlocks and, on one occasion, wears a black headscarf and facial veil.[29] Such signifiers of gendered and racial otherness emphasize this Chorus's estrangement from and at times frank disapproval of the king's drive towards imperial conquest and the patriarchal, heteronormative, white supremacist future the Boy would appear to represent.

In contrast, Olivier's *Henry V* makes the unusual move of calling direct attention to the cross-dressed male actor playing Princess Katherine (if not the Boy). At the point in the film when Henry and Katherine's concluding wedding shifts back to the Renaissance stage simulacrum where the action began, the female actress playing Katherine morphs into a cross-dressed male earlier seen dressing backstage. In Olivier's eulogizing of Shakespeare's theatre as a metonym for English culture, what is at stake is not the reproductive future of the English monarchy but, rather, the continuity of a revered national past with a future now jeopardized by war.[30]

In *The Hollow Crown*, the threatened breach between the nation's past and future is, instead, a downstream result of realizing Renaissance England's imperial ambitions: the creation of what has become, by the year 2012, a nation amidst an identity crisis. At the same time, the series strives to make Shakespeare relatable and accessible to a global digital audience. The weight of these concerns falls not only on the shoulders of the sole Black cast member, Paterson Joseph, but also on his connection with those two key figures of historically emergent whiteness, King Henry and the Boy. Although not explicitly homoerotic, the homosocial bonds among these figures are crucial to the episode's structure. Four key scenes involving the King, York and the Boy interpellate the audience in a series of affective transactions. In all four scenes, the Boy's largely spectatorial presence is itself a key object for the viewers' focus, guiding them through their own *Bildungsroman* into proper white, masculine Englishness.

The first of these scenes links the three characters through a chain of symbolic St George references. A close-up of a throne-room tapestry depicting St George on horseback accompanies key lines from the Act 2 Chorus: 'O England, model to thy inward greatness,

/ Like little body with a mighty heart, / What mightst thou do, that honour would thee do, / Were all thy children kind and natural!' (2.0.16–19). St George is simultaneously an embodiment of the English 'kind' and of King Henry himself, who in Sharrock's film likewise appears riding a white horse. In the tapestry his face is the same colour as the flag's pale background, demonstrating the 'Palestinian' warrior's appropriation as a symbol of whiteness as well as nationality.[31] Later in the same sequence, while the Boy looks on, York distributes swords to soldiers wearing armbands bearing the symbol of St George's cross. Later, left alone outside the tavern after hearing the news of Falstaff's death, the Boy reaches inside his jacket and takes out a folded armband he had concealed there: a prop that, like Othello's infamous handkerchief, will return at several key moments later in the episode. The armband is, of course, white, bearing the red cross of St George.

The second triangulation among the king, York and the Boy is the execution of Bardolph, which is also a key example of what Pittman argues is York's 'Magical Negro' role.[32] An earlier interpolated scene shows York arrest Bardolph for stealing a 'pax' (3.6.39). Sharrock then presents Bardolph's execution as already accomplished, presumably by York himself. Following York's affirming nod to his king's expressed wish to 'have all such offenders so cut off', the camera takes us to the foot soldiers behind the mounted officers, several of whom hold aloft tattered St George's flags (3.6.105). At the end of that line stands the Boy. His sad but reconciled gaze is the last to linger upon his own former companions before he, too, marches on. Like the viewing audience, the Boy has learned from this interaction between his sovereign and commanding officer. The moment is played as a bittersweet coming-to-terms with adult understanding.

The third interaction occurs the night before the Battle of Agincourt. After King Henry delivers his prayer to the 'God of battles' he looks over and is surprised to realize the Boy has been watching him (4.1.281). Wrapped in a blanket and sitting on the same hill overlooking the coming day's battlefield, the Boy gets up and leaves just as York approaches behind the king and places a comradely hand on his shoulder. York's touch replaces what in the play is the recognizable voice of Henry's biological brother Gloucester as he exclaims, 'My liege!' (297). The touch of his friend York is equally familiar to Hiddleston's king, who responds in a grave but intimate tone, without turning around. The replacement of a reverent phrase with direct physical contact emphasizes the emotional connection between these men. The Boy is included as a silent participant in this family moment that translates brotherhood from the genealogical to the affective dimension.

This moment foreshadows the more extended affective triangulation among the same three characters during York's climactic death scene and its aftermath, which revise and expand the character's very brief role in the source text. Shakespeare's York has only one line in which he bravely begs 'the leading of the vaward' at the start of the Battle of Agincourt (4.3.130). Later the Duke of Exeter delivers a vivid description of York's subsequent death alongside his fellow soldier, the Duke of Suffolk, in that intensely homoerotic passage: 'and over Suffolk's neck / He threw his wounded arm and kissed his lips, / And so espoused to death, with blood he sealed / A testament of noble-ending love' (4.6.24–7). The mingling of blood on the battlefield functions metonymically as the consummation of a wartime 'marriage' between fatally wounded comrades-in-arms.

The erotic charge to this language in its original context was perfectly consistent with a masculine battlefield ethos, in which, according to Alan Sinfield, 'same-sex passion, when sufficiently committed to masculine warrior values, is admired, even at the point where it slides toward the feminine'.[33] In today's world, however, it sticks out like the proverbial bad reaction to Viagra and is cut in both major twentieth-century cinematic versions of the play. Olivier deletes it completely. Branagh cuts the role of Suffolk but includes a tableau in which York is surrounded by enemy soldiers and brought down by multiple stab-wounds. *The Hollow Crown* presents a more fully rendered adaptation of the episode than either movie in an interpolated scene that depicts the Duke of York's death not during combat but on the sidelines, in the company of the Boy.

The scene begins at the periphery of the Battle of Agincourt. The Boy is watching the action from behind a tree when he is surprised by York's friendly hand on his shoulder – a strikingly similar move to that with which York approached the king himself the night before (Figure 2). The Boy's body thus momentarily takes the place of King Henry's, demonstrating their symbolic identification as figures of white Englishness to whom York plays a similarly supporting role.

FIGURE 2 *York and the Boy at Agincourt.* Henry V, *directed by Thea Sharrock.* © *Carnival Film & Television Ltd 2012. All rights reserved. Screen grab.*

York seems about to offer kind words when he is stabbed from behind by an angry and vengeful Constable of France. A moment later he falls into the Boy's arms. Horrified to see his hand covered in his commanding officer's blood, the Boy removes his St George's cross armband and ineffectually uses it to staunch York's bleeding wound.

Without respect to considerations of race, this interaction both supplements and amplifies what in the play is Exeter's solely verbal description of the powerful bond between close male companions shedding blood and dying together in battle. In the film Exeter, accompanied by the Boy, later delivers the news of York's death to King Henry. As in the York-for-Gloucester substitution the night before battle, the intimacy of touch displaces language. With the lines, 'And so espoused to death, with blood he sealed / A testament of noble-ending love', Exeter hands the king the bloody armband as a tactile token of this love, which has been transferred from the erased Suffolk to the king himself.

The semiotics of race, however, complicate this picture. Sharrock uses the bond between the king and York to justify what is, in the text, a jarring change of mood, in which King Henry shifts from suppressing his tears to dispassionately ordering his soldiers to kill their prisoners. Hiddleston's Henry, rather, gives this order in a fit of rage and grief for his lost friend. For Pittman, this moment is the culmination of York's status as a Magical Negro: 'In death, York facilitates the full actualization of Henry V's character, a monarch deeply loyal to his people who willingly risks his life for his nation.'[34] His task complete, York disappears from the film.

He does not disappear altogether, however. Rather, he returns via the other white figure whose agency his death enables – the Boy-as-Chorus – as well as in the form of the Boy's symbolically dense armband. The dying York's red blood has been both metonymically and literally absorbed into that armband's white material, which is also marked with the red cross of that Palestinian/English martyr, St George. For Wray, the armband is a *'memento mori* not only of the wounded war body but also of the war crime' and 'makes manifest the film's memorializing strategies'.[35] With respect to race, however, I would like to suggest that embedded in those efforts to memorialize is a strong – if incompletely realized – desire to forget. Like St George's Palestinian origins, York's Black body has been subsumed into a white symbol of Englishness.

When Hiddleston's King Henry carelessly drops that armband the Boy picks it up again. The next time we see this heavily invested object is with the delivery of the epilogue, which takes place over a montage of the king's funeral intercut with previous images from the film. Eventually the camera falls on the Boy, where he gazes at Henry's dead-but-still-handsome body and clutches the armband in both hands. At this moment John Hurt's voiceover as the Chorus intones the phrase 'and made his England bleed'. The camera follows the Boy's gaze down to the red St George's cross on the armband and the young hands morph into Hurt's aged ones.

The Chorus's voice, now embodied in the Boy's vastly aged and visibly frail human form, becomes both surrogate for the king and spokesman for his absence. Hurt kisses the cross just before delivering his final line – in person rather than in voiceover in the now empty throne room, where the St George tapestry is dimly visible in the background: 'For their sake, / In your fair minds let this acceptance take' (5.2.377–8). Although much delayed, this kiss is an implicit substitute for York's battlefield kiss of Suffolk's bloody 'gashes' and the pay-off of an intricate triangulation of simultaneously erotic and patriotic energies among the Boy, the dying York and the now dead king. The Boy's bonds with both his commanding officer and his sovereign have been transferred to this armband soaked in the former's blood and marked by the symbol of the latter's reign.

By substituting York's sacrifice for the Boy's, Sharrock's *Henry V* provides Shakespeare's Boy with a future as the Chorus that concretely realizes his theatrical surrogacy as Henry's issue outside of generational time. Along with the Boy/Chorus, Sharrock presents two other interpolated child characters in the episode's framing scenes: an unnamed young child of indeterminate gender who carries a flower to Henry's funeral during the prologue and, in the epilogue, the infant Henry VI, revealed in a bundle first carried by Alice before being transferred to Queen Katherine's arms. The kiss Katherine plants on her infant son's pale, chubby forehead presents, like the Boy/Chorus's kiss of the ancient armband, as the kiss of a relic. Alongside the Boy, these supplemental children are means of showing reverence to a dead king whose futurity is, paradoxically, a matter of memorializing the past. Because of the colour-conscious casting of York, *The Hollow Crown*'s concluding memorialization of a dead white king is more starkly racializing than its source material. Instead of projecting the Boy's sacrificial, heroic whiteness onto both Henry and Katherine's imagined progeny and the memorialized fantasy of Henry himself, Sharrock's *Henry V* presents a Boy who has survived to become the play's Chorus as a direct result of a Black man's sacrifice.

The epilogue, moreover, is a Shakespearean sonnet, a form with its own racializing origins. Traditionally written to construct the speaking subject's unrequited desire, according to Kim F. Hall the Renaissance English sonnet is also often used to poetically 'whiten' a mistress initially posited as 'dark', and thus 'to refashion her into an acceptable object of Platonic love and admiration'.[36] The closing couplet, offered as an intimate exchange between the now solitary Boy/Chorus and the episode's viewers, invites those viewers to 'accept' the performance in their 'fair minds' and thereby participate in a transhistorical and communal act of mourning, nostalgic longing and whitening.[37]

As Chorus, the aged Boy now addresses the audience not from his own time – which, according to a rough calculation, would be around sixty years after the Battle of Agincourt, or around 1475 – but from ambiguous theatrical time. Much as Olivier's Chorus (Leslie Banks) recites the epilogue from a simulacrum of the Globe

Theatre's thrust stage, and Branagh's Chorus (Derek Jacobi) does the same after closing the doors on the sound stage where the wooing of Katherine has just taken place, the Boy/Chorus delivers his final lines from one of *The Hollow Crown*'s central theatrical settings, the interior of the throne room. It is a version of the same space where the season also began, with Ben Whishaw's voiceover as Richard II inviting the audience to 'sit upon the ground / And tell sad stories of the death of kings' (*R2* 3.2.135–6) as if in a 'prologue from which the rest of this television series will spring'.[38] The arc of the season has circled back both spatially and thematically to where it began. And where it began is with another pivotal sacrifice of which both Henry V's and York's death are echoes: the primal regicide of Richard II.

This is not an exact echo, however. Not entirely unlike the tangled chronologies of Shakespeare's histories as originally written and performed, the chronology of *The Hollow Crown* is not precisely linear nor precisely circular. Rather, it exhibits the features of queer seriality – the 'recursive eddies and back-to-the-future loops' that undermine the official, linear narratives not only of 'normative life' but also of normative history. In Goold's *Richard II* the murdered King Richard prefigures not only the mourned King Henry but also the sacrificed Black body of Paterson Joseph's York. Similarly, Tom Hughes's Aumerle prefigures both the Boy as the agent of that Black sacrifice and York himself, as an unacknowledged earlier version of the same historical character. In the case of the longer arc of *The Hollow Crown*'s Season One, queered time and queered race directly intersect with questions of gender and sexuality in the famously queer figure of Shakespeare's Richard II.

'Almost from another planet': King Richard II in HIStory

Shakespeare's representation of one of England's most famously deposed kings has long been intertwined with imputations of non-normative gender and sexuality.[39] Bolingbroke's accusation against the king's male followers – that they have with 'sinful hours / Made a divorce betwixt his queen and him, / Broke the possession of a royal bed' (3.1.11–13) – places Richard on the sodomitical side of what Alan Bray argues is the seemingly absolute, but in practice often slippery, early modern distinction between laudable male friendship and sinful sodomy.[40] Characterizations of Richard as homosexual go back at least as far as Laurence Olivier's description of Michael Redgrave's 1951 performance of Richard as an 'out-and-out pussy queer, with mincing gestures to match'.[41] Recent theatrical productions, at times drawing on Elizabeth I's reputed response to the play – 'I am Richard II, know ye not that?' – have emphasized the king's femininity.[42] In order to dissociate homosexuality from effeminacy, Deborah Warner's 1995 *Richard II* for the National Theatre cast a female actor, Fiona Shaw, in the title role.[43] Roughly contemporaneous with *The Hollow Crown*, Gregory Doran's production of *Richard II* as the first instalment of the RSC's tetralogy, *King and Country*, specifically highlighted the homoerotic possibilities in King Richard (David Tennant) and his first cousin Aumerle's (Oliver Rix) relationship, having them share a kiss in the middle of the Flint Castle scene.[44]

To all appearances following this trend, the first episode of *The Hollow Crown* presents a King Richard who has been described by various outside commentators as 'fey', 'effeminate', 'effeminate (if not gay)', presenting 'undertones (never made explicit) of homosexuality' and as the head of a 'gay playboy coterie'.[45] As Wray points out, the casting of Ben Whishaw as Richard underscores his character's queer presentation by invoking that actor's 'previous queer film and television roles, such as Sebastian Flyte in *Brideshead Revisited* (dir. Julian Jarrold, 2008) and Danny in *The London Spy* (dir. Jakob Verbruggen, 2015)'.[46]

Yet when it comes to *The Hollow Crown*'s portrayal of Richard II, neither 'queer' nor 'effeminate' tells the whole story. In various intersecting ways, Goold's adaptation constructs King Richard as a multiply othered figure who is not only queer and effeminate but also, in certain respects, Black. These methods of othering include a queer serial structure identifying Hughes's white, youthful Aumerle with Joseph's Black, adult York from Sharrock's *Henry V*, engagement with early modern gendered constructions of Blackness and coded references to Michael Jackson sprinkled throughout the episode.

Goold's representation of Richard as both Black and queer accords with aspects of the character's depiction in the source text. Shakespeare presents two contradictory perspectives on Henry IV's deposing of Richard II: as both the inciting crime against the English monarchy leading to rampant civil war and destruction, and as a necessary step towards the rise of the modern British nation state. Previous scholarship has emphasized how the play creates a gendered opposition that at least partially validates this transition. It encodes Richard's ritualistic exercise of medieval hereditary authority as feminine and Bolingbroke's politically minded garnering of public support as masculine.[47] What has remained largely unmarked is how racial constructions intersect with these gender concerns, especially the link between feminine sexuality and Blackness discussed in Chapter 1. As an effeminate character, Richard is also a 'Black' character. His elimination from the throne augurs not only a more masculine but also a whiter England – albeit at a considerable cost. Through its representation of King Richard as both a racial and sexual other, Goold's *Richard II* explores how these concerns translate into an early twenty-first-century British as well as global context.

Although the Michael Jackson–Richard link is not overt in *The Hollow Crown*'s final version of *Richard II*, in an interview with Derek Jacobi for *Shakespeare Uncovered* that followed the first airing of the programme on BBC2 in July 2012, Goold described having long been 'interested in Richard II as a Michael Jackson figure', explaining that both were 'sexually ambiguous ... playful, capricious divas'.[48] Moreover, in his DVD commentary, Ben Whishaw names Michael Jackson as one of the chief inspirations for his portrayal of the titular monarch: 'the way he was always performing, and his eccentricity and his love of spectacle, his otherworldliness'.[49] Officially speaking, the only explicit element of the Michael Jackson connection that remains in the episode itself is Richard's possession of an exotic pet, a macaque monkey named Rosie; Jackson was well known for his pet chimpanzee, Bubbles.[50] Yet the connection remains a crucial undercurrent of a production that combines, as did Jackson himself, sexual and racial ambiguity and otherness, and also embraces a temporally queer approach to history in which parallels between a deposed medieval English king and the so-called King of Pop are not as unexpected as one might think. Goold's *Richard II* uses the Michael Jackson motif along with the nontraditional casting of Msamati as Carlisle and imputations of a queer relationship between Richard and Aumerle to highlight the play's inherent ambivalence about the legitimacy of Richard's rule, but in terms that reflect a twenty-first-century understanding of racial, gendered and sexual difference.

Of the three contemporary models for Whishaw's performance, Oscar Wilde, Morrissey and, most prominently, Michael Jackson, the latter is a figure not only of sexual but also racial ambiguity and otherness, and adds an element of contemporary, global celebrity pop culture to an ostensibly period, British performance. A child prodigy who rose to superstar status in the 1980s, Jackson remained a widely beloved but increasingly controversial figure up through his highly publicized death from an accidental drug overdose in 2009. At the time of *The Hollow Crown*'s initial 2012 airing, the queerness of Jackson's public persona was not only about gender and sexuality but also about the resistance of *any* rigid identities, including that of race.[51] The press's preoccupation with how Jackson's lightening skin might have been the result of cosmetic interventions (versus the singer's own, generally ignored claim, verified after his death, that he suffered from vitiligo), combined with the incompatibility of his persona and music with stereotypical 'Black' behaviours and style, demonstrates both Jackson's perceived racial ambiguities and the overall tenuousness of such constructs of Blackness.[52] One ostensibly comedic media sound-bite strides across the categories of race, gender, sexuality, class and age: 'Only in America can a poor black boy grow up to be a rich white woman.'[53] Although the one-liner implies that Jackson was ashamed of his Blackness and sought to erase it, it also presents that Blackness as inextricably combined with poverty, youth and masculinity.

A decade after Jackson's death, an emotionally heated controversy that had long haunted the singer's reputation hit the popular media with the airing of the 2019 documentary *Leaving Neverland*, which presented two men's narratives of childhood sexual abuse by Jackson. It is necessary here to repudiate the malicious, stigmatizing and unfounded association of the LGTBQ+ community with paedophilia, while also recognizing the importance of these allegations to the particularities of Michael Jackson's media representation. In March 2019, the various semiotics of otherness that had long attended the celebrity's media presence became intertwined with the overt threat of erasure, as radio stations around the world banned Jackson's songs from their playlists, Transport for London stripped from public buses posters asserting Jackson's innocence, and America's long-running satirical cartoon *The Simpsons* formally shelved an early episode in which the singer guest starred.[54] Such attempts to purge Jackson's presence from all types of media have, inevitably, been largely self-defeating. As Henry Bolingbroke has been discovering on the Shakespearean stage in *Richard II* for the past four hundred and thirty years, it is not such an easy thing 'T'undeck the pompous body of a king' (*R2* 4.1.250), even when that 'king' is an alleged child molester.

Although predating the 2019 documentary, Goold's *Richard II*, along with its initial media reception, foreshadows this peculiar combination of notoriety and invisibility, teetering on the edge of erasure. In publicity material, as cited previously, Goold and Whishaw frequently mentioned Michael Jackson as a remote inspiration for Richard's character, of which Rosie the monkey ostensibly remained the sole concrete trace. Reviewers correspondingly found the celebrity's ghostly presence simultaneously repellant and fascinating. As Tim Dowling wrote for *The Guardian* after first viewing *Richard II* and then watching Jacobi's documentary, 'I knew that Ben Whishaw['s] camp, flutey and painfully self-conscious Richard put me in mind of someone, but I'm happy I didn't realise it was Michael Jackson until afterward.'[55]

Alongside the symbolism of Richard's pet macaque, the wardrobe of Whishaw's Richard also draws on the legacy of Michael Jackson's various iconic costumes, most notably the king's outfit in the emotionally charged scene at Flint Castle in which Richard visually and verbally prefigures his deposition. Dressed in dazzling golden armour, he first faces down his rival from high atop the castle battlements, flanked by two golden angels with a halo-like golden sun over his head before dramatically descending to the dusty courtyard below. The costume echoes Jackson's gold lamé bodysuit featured in promotional materials from his third and final solo concert tour, the 1996–7 HIStory World Tour. One of Jackson's spectacular uses of this costume involved his stage entrances, which began with an elaborate ten-minute prelude featuring the real-life Jackson descending 'in a gold suit' from a virtual reality space capsule floating above the earth.[56] To enhance his 'otherworldly' persona, Jackson presented himself as someone literally from another world.

Both Jackson and Whishaw's Richard don their golden outfits as parts of a 'huge theatrical trick'.[57] As Whishaw himself has explained, Michael Jackson provides a 'contemporary parallel to help us understand' the king's historical self-presentation. 'Here's a character who sees himself not really as a human being, but as a demigod – a conduit for men on the earth to experience the divine, someone who revelled in a sense of magic and mystery about themselves.' There is 'a sense that they come almost from another planet that they're so far beyond you'.[58]

The word 'almost' is key. Following his dramatic HIStory Tour entrance, the singer doffed his gold spacesuit and helmet to reveal the underlying human form. Similarly, Goold's camerawork uses extreme close-ups at disorienting angles to alternately focus on disparate aspects of Richard's self-presentation on the battlements of Flint Castle. We see the ornate details of his imposing costume – golden gauntlets, bejewelled sceptre, the gems on his crown, the hilt of his sword and individual links of his chainmail – and fragments of the king's vulnerable human body: sideways and frontal views of his quivering eye; the fissured red of his lips; the hairs of his jawline, brows and beard; and beads of sweat collecting on his temple, his features pulsing with his 'agitated breathing' as the very pores of his pale skin become subject to view.[59]

The scene's split focus echoes the medieval theory of the king's two bodies, divine and mortal, that has been so often applied to Shakespeare's *Richard II* since Ernst Kantorowicz's 1957 book on the topic.[60] It simultaneously invokes Jackson's characteristic mixing of extravagant theatrical fantasies with human vulnerability.[61] Similarly, Goold's presentation of Richard does not clearly demarcate the line between demigod and man. The fragments of Richard's body are revealed in the same piecemeal and estranging fashion as the fragments of his kingly array. Rather than be compelled to feel with the king as he sweats and trembles in his glory, the spectator is invited to view with wonderment Richard's very humanity.

'Shall kin with kin and kind with kind confound'

Notably, in very few of their publicly quoted interview comments regarding the Michael Jackson–Richard parallels do Goold or Whishaw explicitly invoke sexuality, and never do they mention race. However, Richard's otherness emerges in several additional, intersecting ways in the production itself. The film's sole acknowledged Michael Jackson reference, Richard's pet macaque, first appears on a perch in Richard's elaborately embroidered 'stately pleasure tent made up of yellow-orange drapes that flutter in the breeze',[62] where it comes across as a consciously exotic animal, at home in an orientalizing visual context reminiscent of the paintings of Jean-Léon Gerome. The show's colour scheme is also exoticizing. Richard wears and is surrounded by not only gold but also bright pastels. While ostensibly building on verbal imagery of gold and gilding in play's text, the colours also suggest effeminacy, further queering Richard and, moreover, adding to the portrayal of Richard as what Edward Said describes as the Western view of the East as 'passive' and 'feminine'.[63] Meanwhile Bolingbroke and his faction appear in 'blues, browns, and grays', a 'dun palette'[64] that marks the future Henry IV and his fellows as homespun and English. Richard's differences are also implicitly suggested through his intimate association with two key figures of otherness: the Bishop of Carlisle as performed by Lucian Msamati – one of only a few non-white cast members and the only one with an African accent – and Tom Hughes's queerly inflected Duke of Aumerle. Both characters appear at Richard's side in two climactic scenes preceding Richard's deposition and death: the king's return from Ireland in Act 3, Scene 2 and his subsequent parley with Bolingbroke's faction at Flint Castle.

Goold relocates Richard's Irish return to a beach on the coast of Wales. The king first appears in the liminal and traditionally feminized space of the water alongside the Bishop of Carlisle, who offers him physical support as they wade through the waist-high surf. Arriving from a foreign land, neither man looks stereotypically 'English'. Bearing their respective staffs of secular and sacred authority, Richard wears a white turban topped with his crown while Carlisle wears a black head-cloth (Figure 3). The characters' similar visual exoticism is thematically linked with their shared belief in divine right monarchy, although the latter's is more grounded. When Richard expresses his confidence in the earth's very stones to 'Prove armed soldiers, ere her native king / Shall falter under foul rebellion's arms', the Bishop more circumspectly invokes the Christian God as the source of the kingship's defence: 'Fear not, my lord. That Power that made you king / Hath power to keep you king in spite of all' (3.2.25–8). Particularly from a twenty-first-century perspective, both Richard and Carlisle stand outside the march towards modernity which Bolingbroke's military might, pragmatism and relative lack of imagination represent.

FIGURE 3 *Richard II and the Bishop of Carlisle*. Richard II, *directed by Rupert Goold.* © *Carnival Film & Television Ltd 2012. All rights reserved.* Screen grab.

Richard's younger cousin Aumerle is the first to greet the pair of travellers on land. Goold's queer coding of Richard and Aumerle's relationship is not a unique take on this play; as mentioned earlier, Gregory Doran's 2013 RSC production goes so far as to have the two share a kiss. Unlike Doran's production, however, Goold's emphasizes the age difference between the two. Although Tom Hughes was twenty-seven at the time of the episode's release, his Aumerle appears 'painfully young', while Whishaw, at thirty-two, comes across as a mature, if eccentric, adult.[65] Like the Boy in Sharrock's *Henry V*, Hughes's Aumerle has a largely spectatorial presence, amplified through multiple silent close-ups which position him as an audience to the king's various performances. As the younger, white prefiguration of Paterson Joseph's York, moreover, Aumerle's audience function also parallels York's status as the visual affirmer of the king's questionable actions in Sharrock's *Henry V*, albeit with an important difference: Aumerle's expressions, while at times approving, are also often ambiguous. Aumerle thus captures the audience's presumed uncertainty about how to view this flamboyant, capricious king.

On the beach in Wales, Whishaw's Richard delivers his buoyant speech of confidence in God's support of his kingship to his audience of two while standing on the stage of a solitary rock. He compares himself to the shining sun overhead, which is about to reveal and quash the 'thief' and 'traitor' attempting to steal his kingdom by night (3.2.47). Aumerle can't help but flash a brilliant, loving smile at Richard's description of how Bolingbroke's 'treasons will sit blushing in his face, / Not able to endure the sight of day' (51–2). A moment later Carlisle nods his more tight-lipped approval at the lines 'Not all the water in the rough rude sea / Can wash the balm off from an anointed king' (54–5).

While Carlisle's Blackness and accent mark the marginalization of his religious, medieval politics, Aumerle reflects another aspect of this Richard's otherness, his sexual attraction to men. Richard's physical contact with Aumerle in the beach scene follows the gamut of his cycling emotions between euphoric grandiosity and crushing despair – from taking Aumerle by the hand and raising him up to the rock at his side towards the end of his triumphant initial speech to casting his cousin violently into the surf when Richard later learns of the defection of Aumerle's father, the Duke of York, from his ranks of supporters.

In the following Flint Castle scene, between the gold-clad Richard's formal addresses to Bolingbroke, the king delivers a more personal performance as he converses with Aumerle in the fortress's interior. The two sit knee-to-knee in the claustrophobic confines of a turret where their tête-à-tête is observed by the Bishop of Carlisle and two of the king's other remaining supporters. While Richard verbally consoles himself with increasingly macabre imaginings, Aumerle, listening silently, at last dissolves into tears. Richard notices and begins to direct his consolations towards his cousin, turning them into an increasingly whimsical story. With the line 'Or shall we play the wantons with our woes', he places a hand upon Aumerle's knee (3.3.164). He then crafts a fanciful image of the cousins' hypothetical love-death in which they dig 'a pair of graves' via their mutual tears (167). Again there is brief physical contact – a moment of hand-holding. The pay-off is a shared chuckle and an assenting nod from Aumerle when Richard concludes the anecdote: 'Would not this ill do well?' (170).

The conversation is one of the most frankly homoerotic textual moments in *Richard II*. As Derrick Higginbotham notes, the line about 'wanton' woe-sharing portrays the cousins 'as unruly and unchaste' and 'enables a reading of the signs of male friendship as possibly sodomitical, as queer'.[66] Goold's choice for restrained physical contact here, versus the frank kiss at the same moment between Tennant's Richard and Rix's Aumerle in the RSC's *King and Country*, highlights the boyishness of Hughes's Aumerle versus the shared manly grief of Tennant and Rix. In contrast, Carlisle's presence in this scene is relatively understated. Richard's looming fall – distantly adumbrating Michael Jackson's posthumous exposure – is thus forecast in part by his distancing from his adult supporters and his increased intimacy with his child-like younger cousin.

The Bishop of Carlisle's most central moment comes in Richard's deposition scene, when he pronounces the prophecy of doom set to befall England if Bolingbroke is crowned. The scene takes place in the throne room. Msamati's Carlisle delivers his almost uncut monologue to Henry and his supporters while the former stands on the dais near the throne and the others congregate around Carlisle below, while alternating high and low camera angles drive home the differential in power:

> What subject can give sentence on his king?
> And who sits here that is not Richard's subject?
> [...]
> And shall the figure of God's majesty,
> His captain, steward, deputy-elect,
> Anointed, crowned, planted many years,
> Be judged by subject and inferior breath,
> And he himself not present?
>
> (4.1.123, 126–30)

As the spokesperson for divine right monarchy, Msamati himself remains the focus of the camera's attention except when he addresses the soon-to-be King Henry IV, at which point he is relegated to a blurred position in the right foreground of the screen. The cinematography foreshadows the eventual marginalization of a figure who represents both the losing side in the march towards modernity and an object of nostalgic loss.

The colour scheme of Carlisle's costume and Goold's use of darkness and light in the scene also subtly call attention to the Bishop's contradictory position. His plain black skullcap contrasts

in both colour and ornateness with his white silk pontifical gloves.
He uses those white gloves to point shamingly at both Henry and
his men as he castigates them for what he dubs, using the source
text's colour-biased metaphor, 'so heinous, black, obscene a deed!'
(132). After delivering the line 'And if you crown him, let me
prophesy' (137), the viewpoint changes once more to a low-angle
shot of Carlisle from the shoulder up, almost in silhouette against
the blurred white light coming from an overexposed shot of the
stained-glass windows in the West end of St David's Cathedral.
The shot simultaneously deifies the Bishop's perspective and, in the
process, obscures it.

In one of *Richard II*'s most frankly racializing images, Msamati's
Carlisle then delivers his prophetic coup de grâce:

> The blood of English shall manure the ground,
> And future ages groan for this foul act.
> Peace shall go sleep with Turks and infidels,
> And in this seat of peace tumultuous wars
> Shall kin with kin and kind with kind confound.
>
> (4.1.138–42)

Exhibiting the late sixteenth-century English theatre's fascination
with the Turk, Shakespeare's Bishop 'condemns Bolingbroke's
accession as an act of religious and political apostasy'.[67] The irony
of having the most prominent actor of colour in Goold's production
deliver these lines to an audience of mostly white men, in an accent
that also audibly marks him as other, underscores this moment's
self-contradictory historical construction of the white, masculine
British nation. Here the Bishop of Carlisle allies true Englishness
with feudal obedience to Richard's divine right to rule and
Bolingbroke's modern nation state with 'black' apostasy and the
Turkish other. However, by the conclusion of *Henry V*, Bolingbroke's
son will imagine his own son as an emblem of whiteness going 'to
Constantinople' to 'take the Turk by the beard'. Immediately after
his speech, the Bishop of Carlisle is perfunctorily taken prisoner –
an act that paves the way not only for Richard's deposition but for
the eventual worldwide domination of the British Empire.

Drawing on the queerness and performativity of the Michael
Jackson persona, Goold's version of the latter half of this scene

paints Richard himself as differently othered character. As a highly self-conscious Christ figure, Whishaw's gold-trimmed, white-clad Richard thespianically performs his dethroning to an audience of 'straight' men in both senses of the word, ironizing his self-abnegation as he mocks his usurping cousin's inferiorly poetic mind. Throughout the scene Kinnear's reaction shots as Bolingbroke are pricelessly deadpan. At the seriocomic climax of this one-man show, Richard lies face down on the floor and rolls the crown across its stones. A ground-level shot follows the bejewelled metallic prize as it clanks to a rest at his cousin's feet. As Bolingbroke frankly rolls his eyes, Richard stands up and lightly asks, 'What more remains?'. Here David Morrissey's menacing Northumberland gruffly intercedes, articulating the thoughts of every other man in the room: 'No more!' (4.1.222).

The interplay in this scene between the serious staging of Msamati's self-sacrificing prophecy and Whishaw's delicate dance of queerness, mockery and genuine abasement pays off further in the episode's conclusion, when Whishaw's Richard follows Msamati's Carlisle with his own 'Black' sacrifice. Intermixed with continued references to Christ, this highly stylized death scene also invokes symbolism of that patron saint of gay men, St Sebastian – who takes the baton from Michael Jackson as a latter-day icon of queerness.

'And put on sullen black incontinent'

While in interviews Goold and Whishaw have on several occasions brought up Michael Jackson as an inspiration for the Richard character, they seldom mention St Sebastian – most likely because of much more widespread public knowledge of the pop star versus the medieval saint. On the flip side, St Sebastian, as the more visible influence, has the blogosphere attuned. Numerous internet commentators note abundant allusions to the martyred icon alongside more expected Christ references in Goold's *Richard II*.[68]

The iconic status of St Sebastian has a long history. Initially a third-century 'Christian saint invoked against illness throughout medieval times', he later became an 'exquisite, beardless youth of Apollonian beauty in the Renaissance', a '"decadent" androgyne throughout the nineteenth century' and a 'self-consciously homosexual emblem in the twentieth'. For Richard Kaye, writing just past the crest of the US AIDS epidemic in 1996, St Sebastian is therefore much more than an 'inside joke' for gay men who wish 'to mock religious ecstasy as an erotic put-on'. Rather, the figure had become a problematic symbol of what for the outsider is 'the supposedly sado-masochistic nature of male same-sex eroticism' and, for the insider, a 'homosexual eros that is menacingly narcissistic and suicidal in kind'.[69]

In Goold's *Richard II*, St Sebastian first appears in an interpolated scene that simultaneously exhibits the film's metacinematic and anachronistic technique, establishes Richard's homoerotic interests and foreshadows his martyr-like demise. Following the episode's initial credits, the king is discovered in his chambers watching his retainer Bushy (Ferdinand Kingsley) painting a portrait of St Sebastian in a distinctly non-medieval style. Another male companion, Bagot, stands at his side. The camera slowly takes us from Sebastian's loincloth-covered groin up over the three arrows that pierce his bleeding naked torso and finally to his impassive, haloed face. A young male model in the identical pose and with prop arrows harnessed to his body is then revealed to the left of the frame. Richard rises from his chair and approaches the model. In a close-up we see the king palpate the fake blood from the 'wound' under the model's left nipple, inspecting it on the tip of his finger (as if checking to see if it is genuine) before his gaze moves upward to the model's face. The two exchange a brief, intimate glance. For Pittman, this is one of several moments in the film in which Goold consciously exposes the 'mechanics of representational art'.[70] The interpolation also highlights both Richard's queer sexuality and the queer temporality of a film in which Richard is all at once a Christ figure, a medieval king, a Michael Jackson prototype and a connoisseur of mid-nineteenth-century paintings of a twentieth-century gay icon.

In case the implications of this scene with respect to the 'possession' of Richard's 'royal bed' are lost on its viewers, the next cut takes us to the queen and her handmaid walking quickly through the castle corridors. She arrives in her husband's chambers moments after the audience witnesses an intimate moment between Richard and the artist: the king's lingering touch on Bushy's shoulder followed by Bushy's brief adoring smile while the king's gaze travels downward over his friend's form. The camera pulls back to reveal that Richard is surrounded by two additional male companions, Scroop and Green, before he leaves his men to take his wife's hand.

By the second half of the film, Bushy and Green have been executed for crimes both treasonous and sodomitical, Bagot and Scroop have been relegated to the sidelines, and Aumerle has taken their place as Richard's closest comrade. Erotic tension between Richard and Aumerle climaxes in their final scene together with the transformation of Aumerle into one of Richard's executioners. This alteration to the play's text also appeared in Doran's 2013 staging of *Richard II*.[71] As Higginbotham reads that performance, 'Richard's own lover' takes the king's life in an intimate moment of backstabbing.[72] In Goold's version, a similar plot twist plays out, although with important stylistic differences.

Aumerle's 'painfully young' portrayal again comes into play when his other older cousin, now Henry IV, discovers that Aumerle has conspired in a plot to slay him. The scene in which the Duchess of York (Lindsay Duncan) begs for her son's life is played seriously rather than comically, not only highlighting the Duchess's dignity and agency, as Pittman argues, but also demonstrating Aumerle's vulnerable youthfulness.[73] After Aumerle's dismissal from the king and his mother's final, withering words, the youth cowers hunch-shouldered on a bench just outside the throne room. There he is silently approached by a furtive Lord Marshall, unspeakingly bearing his executioner's summons.

In the next scene, in a dim, smoky tavern, Aumerle reluctantly accepts a silver coin from the king's agent as payment for his traitorous task, a move that underscores his role as a Judas. The scene opens, however, with a more sympathetic view of Aumerle repeatedly sticking his finger into a candle's open flame. This framing demonstrates a twenty-first-century understanding of adolescent turmoil and suggests that accepting the task of Richard's murder is also a form of deliberate self-harm. Throughout the Lord Marshall's speech, Hughes's Aumerle listens numbly. His eyes fill with tears as he realizes what he must do. If Richard is being punished for his queerness, so, this scene suggests, is Aumerle – in part via an internalized self-despising homophobia which he is being paid to project onto his cousin. In solidarity with his later incarnation as a Black Duke of York, this Aumerle is the object as well as instigator of sacrifice.

The film further divides its sympathies between Richard and his executioner in its final moments. The king's death scene visually replicates Bushy's painting of the martyrdom of St Sebastian; in the depths of his dungeon Richard likewise becomes the victim of penetrating violence. From a distance at which it is unclear whether Richard recognizes his cousin, Aumerle fires the first shot from his crossbow, striking Richard near his right shoulder. As he did the paint on Bushy's model, Richard touches the blood near the first arrow's entrance as if to check if the wound is real. Unnamed assassins then fire the second two arrows, which strike home lower in Richard's torso. In addition to the wounds' location, Richard's attire mimics that of the St Sebastian model – he is naked except for a loincloth. The lachrymose soundtrack swells as the camera lingers on Richard's staggering form. A close shot zooms in on his chest and then his face before he finally falls, blood trickling out the corner of his mouth, his eyes upturned as in Bushy's painting. His death itself is a work of art.

Along with the obvious homoeroticism, the dim lighting and use of period choral music in the scene seem deliberately to invoke the regicidal dream-sequence from Derek Jarman's *Edward II* (1991). But whereas Jarman subverts Marlowe's infamous ending – having Edward's would-be executioner toss the fatal red-hot poker down to sizzle in a pool and, instead of agonizing death, deliver to his king an equally sizzling kiss[74] – Aumerle, willingly or not, carries out his task to the end. Over the course of Richard's climactic demise, three separate close-ups highlight the youth's ambiguous reaction to each blow as he stares, stunned, mouth (characteristically) slightly agape; after the third, he lowers his eyes.

The screen goes briefly black before the final scene of the film unfolds. Intercut with close-ups of Aumerle's bloody hand, chafed by ropes as he laboriously lugs Richard's coffin to the king, we see Henry IV in his throne room. One by one his opponents' heads are irreverently tossed on the ground before him – their punishment for treachery. The final traitor to appear is Henry's sole still-living adversary, the Bishop of Carlisle. He is dragged in wearing dirty, torn and bloody white robes, one eye swollen shut. The clothing and skin on his back bear the unmistakable signs of whiplashes. As with Okonedo's Margaret, the historical resonance of images of a Black body abased and abused by a group of white men are inescapable. Yet Carlisle is also the only one of the king's enemies to leave the room alive. He groans as he rises to his knees, maintaining defiant silence as the king pronounces his exile.

The very next moment the door bangs open and a stony-faced Aumerle enters with the coffin of the former king, wood scraping ominously on the stone floor. While Kinnear's Henry IV follows the script in renouncing direct responsibility for the deed while accepting his guilt in having desired it, he significantly omits key lines punishing Richard's executioner (in the play, Exton) with exile as well. Instead, Aumerle's triumphant declaration that he has slain 'the mightiest of thy greatest enemies' is followed only by emotional rejection by his king: 'I hate the murderer, love him murdered' (5.6.32, 40). The omission implies that Aumerle has already been punished by means of the act of murdering his closest companion – a punishment bound up with both his and Richard's queer representation – and/or by losing his still-living cousin's love. Our final view of Aumerle is as a confused and dejected adolescent before an audience that includes his own father (David Suchet's Duke of York). Meanwhile King Henry wastes no time in removing the coffin's lid to expose Richard's pale, emaciated corpse – over which the camera lingers long at the episode's close, panning upward to underscore Richard's resemblance in death to the crucifix sculpture high in St David's Cathedral.

Through the sacrifice of Richard II that, in turn, allows the ascension of Henry IV, Tom Hughes's Aumerle – an unacknowledged prefiguration of Paterson Joseph's Black York – only reluctantly and incompletely ushers in a dawning white, heteronormative, masculine history. It is no coincidence that the new king begins his reign by vowing to 'put on sullen black incontinent', expressing the desire to expunge his sins with an ethnically cleansing, self-whitening 'voyage to the Holy Land' (5.6.48–9). As Ayanna Thompson notes, Henry IV's longing to 'wash this blood off from my guilty hand' demonstrates the king's essentialist anxieties about two compromised bloodlines: 'the blood that reveals the guilt of his actions *and* the blood inside of him that does not have God's gilding (annointing)' (5.6.50).[75] This king can never be white enough. In Goold's *Richard II*, Aumerle enables Henry's precarious reign only via the queer martyrdom of both himself and King Richard. Kinnear's Henry IV, moreover, implicates himself sexually as well as racially in this bloody sacrifice. After rejecting but not exiling Aumerle, he mournfully and lovingly caresses the slain Richard's face – thereby, through an act of potentially homoerotic touch, granting literal truth to his claim to have racializing blood on his hands.

Via *The Hollow Crown*'s queer serial structure, moreover, Goold's final visual emphasis on the deposed, slain king's contorted, crucifix-like pose links his body not only to Christ but also to the Black body of Joseph's York, sacrificed to save the Boy/Chorus, and the death of King Harry, whose body provides the focus of the opening and closing moments of Sharrock's *Henry V*. These bodies, in turn, bear a ghostly link to the future history of popular culture as written, in part, by the far from normative expressions of the deposed King of Pop himself. The heavy-handed visual symbolism with which Richard's last act invokes the martyrdom of both Saint Sebastian and Christ is itself a Jacksonesque move of spectacular showmanship, even in death. Obscured but not entirely forgotten as a source of Goold's *Richard II*, and hence of *The Hollow Crown*, Season One as a whole, the idea of Michael Jackson provides a conduit between these English history plays from a culturally remote age and a contemporary global audience. Not unlike the haunting presence of Okonedo's Queen Margaret at the end of the series as a whole, the shadowy persistence of Jackson's legacy refuses to allow the Black and queer bodies whose various sacrifices underlie the invention of white, heteronormative history to be entirely erased.

3

The fat knight in black and white

Race, disability, gender, nation, Falstaff

With their entirely 'traditional', all-white casts, Richard Eyre's *Henry IV, Part 1* and *Henry IV, Part 2* stand out – not only in relation to the other episodes of *The Hollow Crown*'s first season but also with respect to a conflated adaptation of the same plays released the same year. That is Lennix, Quinn and Thompson's *H4*, which deliberately goes against the grain in multiple ways. As described in my introduction, it transposes the plot of *1* and *2 Henry IV* to the setting of contemporary Los Angeles (LA) in what its creators describe as 'the first black Shakespeare film ever done'.[1] In addition, as I discuss further in Chapter 4, via a combination of archival footage, filmed stage performance and on-location shooting, *H4* deliberately pushes the boundaries of cinematic Shakespeare.

The diametric contrast between these two productions makes one seemingly small but significant similarity between them even more striking: the presence in both of a white, disabled Falstaff. While in Chapter 4 I address the broader implications of *H4*'s Black American *Henry IV*, in this chapter I explore the significance of these two white Falstaffs in the context of the role's distinct performance histories on either side of the Atlantic. In the United Kingdom and the United States alike, Falstaff has long been a political and cultural as well as theatrical icon, appropriated to service 'various visions of England'.² In both countries, moreover, a shift over the past few decades has transformed Falstaff from a comic to a tragic character. Productions have increasingly made Prince Hal's development the dominant narrative of the plays, emphasizing the politics of 'repression and expulsion' behind Falstaff's final banishment.³ Falstaff's large size has also undergone a shift in meaning, from a positive representation of a copious wit and merry lifestyle to the disabling 'disease' of obesity.⁴

When it comes to race, however, stage depictions of the fat knight have undergone a striking divergence. While to date Falstaff has remained an exclusively white role in the United Kingdom, in the United States Falstaff has become one of the most frequent Shakespearean history play roles to be assigned to Black actors. This gap applies to both the Falstaff of the *Henry IV* plays and what is usually considered that character's lesser incarnation (in status, if not in girth) in *Merry Wives of Windsor*. Meanwhile, as previous chapters have described, casting trends over the past few decades have altered the racial composition of lead roles in the English history plays in both the United Kingdom and the United States. Yet although there have been female Falstaffs in the UK, as of this writing I have been unable to discover a Falstaff of colour in a major British production – except for a Swahili *Merry Wives of Windsor* and Mexican and Argentinian *Henry IV, Parts 1 and 2* at the 2012 Globe to Globe Festival.⁵

The presence of white Scotsman Angus Macfadyen as Falstaff in the mostly Black cast of Lennix, Quinn and Thompson's *H4* is thus an especially conspicuous choice. Similarly, the lack of a Black Falstaff on the British stage and screen demands an explanation. In what follows I examine two modern screen Falstaffs – Macfadyen's white, British Falstaff in a Black American *Henry IV* and Simon Russell Beale's version of the same character in *The Hollow Crown* – with respect to both the long history of the Falstaff role and the contemporary contexts in which these two very different approaches to the *Henry IV* plays emerged. Although both productions feature disabled, white, British or English Falstaffs – Beale is English, while the Scottish Macfadyen's character speaks with a posh English accent – the implications of each character's disability, whiteness and national identity are quite distinct.

In *The Hollow Crown* Simon Russell Beale presents a Falstaff whose girth is a mark of disease rather than a symbol of festivity. Along with his diminutive height, this Falstaff's fatness designates a social dispossession that intersects in multiple ways with ideas about Englishness, masculinity, disability and class. Meanwhile, in *H4*, Macfadyen's Falstaff is a figure of the white colonization of the Black American subject as represented, in part, by Shakespeare's persistent cultural capital in the United States. By maintaining Falstaff's double-edged comedic role as a critic of his culture simultaneously implicated in that culture's worst shortcomings, *H4* demonstrates the persistent utility of appropriations of Shakespearean drama towards contemporary political ends. Together these two Falstaffs reveal a common theme: a reckoning with the historically signifying power of Shakespeare as a product of a national culture imagined as *white* culture.

'This Falstaff': Staging the fat knight in the UK

Falstaff's seemingly contradictory status as both a symbol of authentic Englishness and a figure of subversion and difference dates back to the character's origins. Despite the historical progenitor behind his initial name, Sir John Oldcastle, Falstaff is generally considered Shakespeare's own creation. The opposition between Falstaff's use as a figure of subversive merriment and the 'proto-Puritan martyr' of his first namesake is another apparent Falstaffian paradox. It positions him as the representative of both '"historical revisionism"' and '"a powerful, irresistible nostalgia"' even at his originary moment, when he stood for '"the forces that many Elizabethans held responsible for the demise of England's merry past"'.[6]

Such paradoxes, however, are a central and defining aspect of Falstaff's character. Throughout Falstaff's history, his marginality has not stood opposed to but, rather, has been an essential aspect of his traditional Englishness. Discourses of Falstaff's Englishness and of his marginalization often overlap in that the character stands for a national identity that is either already lost or under the threat of extinction. This is true of his original association with pre-Reformation festivity and also of the changes that took place in

Falstaff's relationship with England's national identity around the Second World War.

Nostalgia for a national past as epitomized by Falstaff is endemic to the latter three plays of the second tetralogy, especially *2 Henry IV*. Such nostalgia inheres in the word 'merry', forms of which, Jonathan Baldo observes, are used in this 'more sober and less festive' of the *Henry IV* plays more often than in any other Shakespearean work.[7] The word's connotations derive from religious controversies surrounding sport and festivity in and around the Elizabethan period. In the sixteenth-century 'merry' and its close cousin, 'mirth', were most 'frequently used of social pleasures and entertainments' but were also increasingly 'overlaid with nostalgic and on occasion recusant overtones'.[8] 'Merry', of course, is also a key word in *The Merry Wives of Windsor*, which transplants the historical Falstaff character to a farcical comedy set in Shakespeare's own time.

The nostalgia Falstaff evokes via his pre-Reformation roots is variously double-sided. Baldo sees Falstaff's persistent, if nominally erased, association with Lollard martyr John Oldcastle as a marker of his larger role regarding memory and forgetting in Shakespeare's histories. Although a 'trigger of divisive historical memories', Falstaff is also a 'virtual emblem of forgetfulness'. Forgetting becomes an eminently practical tool both for the usurping King Henry IV, whose enemies wield memory as 'an instrument of resistance', and for Shakespeare's own 'post-Reformation culture of rising nationalism, mercantilism, and self-invention'. Its applications include not only past and current religious conflicts but also matters of ethnic strife, such as the memory of the Welsh and Irish cultures subsumed often unwillingly into 'the forgetful political construct' of the British nation. Yet at the same time Falstaff stimulates nostalgia in his on- and off-stage audiences, he remains 'a skeptical voice corrosive to nostalgia', and thus 'permanently damages the very attitude he elicits'.[9]

A similar doubleness can be seen in Falstaff's shifting role in the twentieth century. The politics of the Second World War were the primary force behind British theatre's turn away from Falstaff, which coincided in the post-war years with a turn towards the performance of ambitious history play cycles – exemplified by Anthony Quayle and Michael Redgrave's production of the second tetralogy at Stratford Shakespeare Memorial Theatre as part of the 1951 Festival of Britain.[10] These cycles exhibited a defensive British nationalism: 'the desire to assert the continuing dominance of the nation's culture after the devastation of the German bombings'.[11] Falstaff's plot became a path towards definitive rejection by the burgeoning national leader, Henry V, while Henry himself became the centre of the narrative.

Accordingly, scholarship on Falstaff during this period underwent a reversal from romantic celebrations of the character by A. C. Bradley, Maurice Morgan and William Hazlitt to sharp condemnations by wartime critics such as J. Dover Wilson, E. M. W. Tillyard and G. Wilson Knight, who justified what had until then been viewed as King Henry's unfathomable betrayal of his friend. Yet even these critics upheld Falstaff as an essential symbol of English values.[12] Tillyard's *Shakespeare's History Plays* established these dramas' connection to England's national identity. The histories in which Falstaff played a central part offered 'a model for reconstituting a post-war culture in which "Shakespeare-history" could legitimate and validate the national self, the "character" of England'.[13] Moreover, according to Knight, Falstaff provided the young Henry V insight into key aspects of the 'national temperament' – both the native English 'sense of humor' and also 'a deeply satiric sense of the futility of military ambition – as an end in itself'.[14] Although these characteristics 'had no place in war' and therefore necessitated Falstaff's banishment, war had to be fought 'so that those values might ultimately be saved'.[15] Similarly, underneath the patriotic wartime message of Olivier's film *Henry V*, the interpolated appearance of George Robey as Falstaff acting out the old knight's death scene 'takes care to register Falstaff's death as a real and significant loss, as something as fully momentous as the death of a king'. The casting of former music hall comedian Robey as the dying old knight superimposes upon his death a nostalgia for this lost English art form.[16]

The link between Falstaff and nostalgia for an always-vanishing ideal of Englishness extends into the twenty-first century. In his recent discussion of Falstaff's performance history in the UK, Robert Shaughnessy analyses an image used to advertise the RSC's 2008 production of the two parts of *Henry IV* as 'the centerpiece of a marathon cycle of eight history plays'. In this image, David Warner's Falstaff, with his prominent midriff, 'stands for both Shakespeare's Histories and the RSC itself'.[17] In standing for theatre, Falstaff also stands for the British nation writ large, as it is continually and communally imagined and re-imagined via theatrical performance. Even more than Shakespeare's most familiar historically based monarchs, Falstaff remains a highly recognizable figure, bound up in the public imagination with what Barbara Hodgdon suggests is Britain's quintessentially theatrical culture and its persistent, if oft-contested, value: 'Each revival of the *Henrys* has marked a particular moment when, for sociopolitical and economic reasons, theatrical culture has seemed to be in jeopardy . . . Falstaff would seem to be the most organic indicator of the character of the culture: though always rejected, his figure remains ready to turn "history" into a theatrical commodity.'[18] Transformed into the infinitely reproducible digital medium of *The Hollow Crown*, that commodification would appear to be complete.

The persistence of Falstaff's whiteness on stage and screen alike in the UK cries out for an interpretation that takes account of Falstaff's status as an 'indicator of the character of the culture' in Britain.[19] The recent call for diverse casting in British Shakespeare is not only about equity in the theatrical and television job markets but also about making explicit political statements about the status of race in the British nation. As discussed in prior chapters, since Hugh Quarshie's Hotspur for the RSC in 1983, the presence of actors of colour in the history plays has been an increasingly productive if still underutilized site of these explorations. In March and April 2019, Shakespeare's Globe Theatre made waves with a landmark production of *Richard II* jointly directed by Lynette Linton and Adjoa Andoh that featured a cast and crew made up entirely of women of colour, with the aim of producing 'a post-Empire reflection on what it means to be British in the light of the Windrush anniversary and as we leave the European Union'. By invoking both Brexit and Windrush – a scandal that threatened the legal presence of UK residents who arrived from the Caribbean before 1973 – the Globe called attention to a contested definition of Britishness in the history play that is in some respects most directly 'about British national identity'.[20] Highlighting the irony of a brown-skinned, female John of Gaunt's dying speech on 'this sceptered isle . . . this little world, / This precious stone set in the silver sea, /Which serves it in the office of a wall', the production revises any truly insular understanding of 'this earth, this realm, this England' (*R2* 2.1.40, 45–7, 50).

But what about Falstaff and his role in the *Henry* plays? As Falstaff himself is first to point out, the old knight is far from 'gaunt', and is, moreover, in many ways a far-from-insular character. A 'globe of sinful continents' with a 'whole school of tongues' in his belly, he can only be banished at risk of also banishing 'all the world' (*2H4* 2.4.283, 4.2.18; *1H4* 2.4.471–2). Yet despite Falstaff's inherently 'global' nature and despite expanding nontraditional casting in the support of a broadening (so to speak!) definition of Britishness, the role of Falstaff in Britain has, as described earlier, remained white. This is true even of the Globe's continuation of their 2019 Henriad. In the summer of that year, Linton's and Andoh's *Richard II* was followed by productions of *1 Henry IV*, *2 Henry IV* and *Henry V* directed by Sarah Bedi and Federay Holmes and starring Ghanaian-British actress Sarah Amankwah as Hal/Henry V. In a cast that was diverse in terms of both race and gender, white British actress Helen Schlesinger played Falstaff. Another recent version of the *Henry IV* plays with a multiethnic cast, the Donmar Warehouse's 2014 all-female *Henry IV* directed by Phyllida Lloyd, which takes place in a women's prison, also had a white Falstaff played first by Ashley McGuire and later, on tour in the United States, by Sophie Stanton.

The trend of casting Falstaff as a woman represented in both of these recent productions is part of a longer history. Beginning with a performance of *1 Henry IV* at the Haymarket Theatre in London in 1786 and up to as late as 1862, the role of Falstaff was taken on by women at least five times in Great Britain in the eighteenth and nineteenth centuries.[21] The cross-gendered casting of Falstaff literalizes the character's textual associations with femininity, such as his enormous 'womb' and its many loquacious 'tongues' (*2H4* 4.4.1.367, 371). For both historicist and psychoanalytic scholars, Falstaff's feminine transgressiveness is a negative quality that must be eliminated for the modern, masculine British state and subject to emerge.[22] With femininity, however, comes rhetorical, theatrical power. With his ability to take down cultural 'sacred cows' such as honour and kingship, Falstaff is, according to Patricia Parker, an inherently unruly 'Shakespearean "fat lady" who is ostensibly no lady at all'.[23]

The use of female Falstaffs in twenty-first-century British productions of the *Henry IV* plays mingles contemporary political concerns about gender and race and, in the case of Lloyd's all-female *Henry IV*, also class. Lloyd's goal was 'to take the most voiceless group you might imagine-women prisoners; refugees from our culture, if you like . . . and watch them electrify an audience with nothing but Shakespeare's language'.[24] Reviews of the Donmar production frequently noted McGuire's use of a brash Cockney accent to give her Falstaff a rough working-class edge.[25] Her bullying of her fellow prisoners – especially the prisoner who played the Hostess, 'the only Muslim in the cast' – at times took on white supremacist overtones.[26] Lloyd's production thereby demonstrated a consciousness of Falstaff as a figure of reactionary white privilege, called upon in threatening circumstances to defend itself.

In contrast, Bedi and Holmes's Shakespeare's Globe Ensemble productions were officially gender-blind and colourblind, with the intent to 'portray a fair representation of modern-day Britain with all its diverse racial and cultural identity'.[27] The two parts of *Henry IV* were each subtitled to reflect the name of a chief character in that play who ultimately undergoes defeat. *Henry IV, Part 1* thus became 'Hotspur' and *Henry IV, Part 2* 'Falstaff'. Strikingly, both the slain Hotspur and the banished Falstaff were played by white women, while the ultimately victorious Henry V was played by a Black woman – a pattern that suggests a not entirely colourblind approach to these plays.

The subversive role of the white female Falstaff in the UK would thus appear to speak not only to historical issues of honour and kingship but also to historical and contemporary issues of race, including the construct of whiteness. But what happens when Shakespeare's most notorious fat white lady morphs into the racial and gendered obverse, a fat Black man – or, as has recently occurred in several US performances, into a fat Black lady? The precarious balance between memory and forgetting that Falstaff has represented since his proto-Puritan origins has, in late twentieth- and twenty-first-century America, increasingly become a matter of race as well, in terms that reflect the distinct history of this character on the other side of the pond.

'That Falstaff': Plump Jack in America

In his 1932 inaugural lecture as the first director of research at the Folger Shakespeare Library in Washington, DC, Joseph Quincy Adams described 'the clear recognition and appreciation of Shakespeare's greatness' as one of the 'bases of our national culture'.[28] The statement encapsulates the Renaissance English playwright's peculiar position as an 'American institution'. In the United States, Shakespeare's prominent presence in classrooms as well as in performance has been an important, if at times contradictory, element of the nation's self-construction since its official foundation.[29]

The performance history of the English history plays epitomizes the paradox of Shakespeare's early appropriation as 'a naturalised American poet' despite the republic's initial opposition to the 'dominant monarchist British culture of the seventeenth and eighteenth centuries'. In the early nineteenth century, *Henry V*, which was considered to be full of pro-English propaganda, was only staged at the risk of riots. Yet by 2002 *Henry V* would be one of four books provided in pocket-sized editions for US troops to carry into combat. In contrast, *Richard III*, appropriated for a 'political message that reinforced the ideology of republicanism', holds the distinction of being by far the most popular Shakespearean play on American stages from the colonies' struggle for independence through the first half of the nineteenth century. *Richard III* was also the first play to be performed by Manhattan's African American company, African Grove Theatre, in 1821, with James Hewlett in the title role.[30]

The anti-English flame of early America subsided in the later nineteenth and early twentieth centuries and was replaced by the goal of preserving 'national unity' against the perceived 'threat' of an increasing immigrant population. As Shakespeare was appropriated by the American establishment as a symbol of 'Anglo-American monoculture', his plays became a tool for promoting the superiority of the English language.[31] In this context, the *Henry IV* plays became part of America's regular stage repertoire. The beloved fat rogue Falstaff was a key to their appeal. Nineteenth-century American actor James Hackett developed such an affinity for the role, which he played in both New York and London, that 'Falstaff' became his nickname. Abraham Lincoln, who was known for carrying a volume of Shakespeare with him around the White House, wrote Hackett a letter in which he praised the actor for his performance of the fat knight.[32]

Starting in 1935, American theatre companies followed the global trend of staging full cycles of Shakespeare's histories as

Britain's 'great national epic'. As in the UK, in these cycles Falstaff was to some degree sidelined. However, even outside the playhouse he maintained a peculiar role in mainstream American culture. That role is exemplified by the story of Falstaff Beer, a product of a German-American family's St Louis brewery founded in the late nineteenth century.[33] With a marketing refrain that emphasized 'man-sized pleasure' that was 'satisfying to a man-sized thirst' but 'light enough to leave room for more', the brew's peak popularity in the 1950s and 1960s had little to do with Falstaff's actual characterization and more to do with Shakespeare's overall appropriation as an emblem of aspirational middle-class masculinity.[34] Declining sales led to the shelving of the label in 2005.[35]

Even in the aftermath of its commercial demise, the symbolism of Falstaff Beer continued to be deployed in American performance. The Orlando Shakespeare Theater promoted a 2015 staging of *The Merry Wives of Windsor* with a mock Falstaff Beer commercial featuring a sales pitch from John Ahlin in character as Falstaff, quoting from the soliloquy on sack from *Henry IV, Part 2* while drinking from the (for a certain demographic) still-familiar bottles. One nostalgic YouTube viewer posted, 'I wish they still made Falstaff beer'.[36] A Southwest Shakespeare production of the same work in the same year was presented as 'a '50s sitcom complete with commercial breaks and a catchy jingle for Falstaff beer' as part of the play itself.[37] Both productions capitalized on a nostalgia not for Shakespeare or for England but for the mid-century America this appropriation represents, and that by 2015 was already a thing of the past. John Ahlin was, it should be noted, a highly traditional Falstaff: just past middle age, large in build, heavily bearded and white. By 2015, Ahlin had already made a career of playing this character a total of eleven times, in three different plays.[38] However, by 2015 other representations of Falstaff had already gained considerable ground in the United States.

As in the UK, American directors tend to frame their nontraditional casting choices as a matter of representing national diversity and attracting a younger, more diverse audience. While colourblind casting is a frequent strategy, there have been several recent colour-conscious attempts to translate the English medieval/Renaissance interests of the *Henry IV* plays into the contemporary American political sphere, with concerns such as choosing a leader, the politics of regime change and managing a multiracial, multicultural population.

The shift towards including actors of colour in major roles in Shakespeare's English histories other than *Richard III* took place in the United States in the 1990s, a decade before these developments in the United Kingdom. Despite Joseph Papp's well-known colourblind casting practices, stagings of the histories during his New York Shakespeare Festival from the 1960s through the 1980s included actors of colour primarily in relatively minor roles. The exception was the first Black Henry V, played by Robert Hooks in 1965 and followed by T. S. Morgan in Atlanta in 1993.[39] A. Bernard Cummings was the first Black Prince Hal of which I can find record, in a modern dress *1 Henry IV* for the 1992 New Jersey Shakespeare Festival[40] – although the American Shakespeare Center touts Brandon Carter's role as Hal in its 2019 *Henry IV* as marking the same milestone.[41] In 1994, Trinidadian Peter Callender played Henry IV in the California Shakespeare Festival's *Richard II*. A Richard II of colour was longer in coming; Indian-American actor Lijesh Krishnan took on the role in a modern verse production for the African-American Shakespeare Company in 2022.[42]

Although technically outside the realm of the histories, the trend of Black Falstaffs in America began in the nation's capital with Paul Winfield's performance in a 1991 outdoor production of *Merry Wives of Windsor*.[43] Well known on both stage and screen, Winfield had played Buckingham in *Richard III* at the Lincoln Center in 1974.[44] In 1990 Papp himself reportedly asked Winfield to play Falstaff in *Henry IV*, but the actor had to turn down the offer due to the financial difficulties of relocating to Manhattan.[45] Subsequently several African American actors played Falstaff in *Merry Wives*. These include Paul Bates for The Hudson Valley Shakespeare Festival in 1993,[46] G. Valmont Thomas for the Oregon Shakespeare Festival in 2006 and John Livingston Rolle for the St Louis Shakespeare Festival in 2009.[47] In a role that was historically, at least, a stepping stone to the history plays for white actors, Thomas is the only Black actor to date to have made the jump to the same role in *Henry IV*.

The first Black American Falstaff in the *Henry IV* plays took the stage in summer 2004, when two appeared at roughly the same time. A *Henry IV* conflation by the Shenandoah Shakespeare Company (now the American Shakespeare Center) featured two

African American actors – Eric Quander as Falstaff and Rene Thornton, Jr, as Prince Hal – in the unfortunately titled, nearly three-hour-long 'Most Lamentable Comedy of Sir John Falstaff'.[48] A more traditionally structured *Henry IV* conflation starring Reg E. Cathey as Falstaff was adapted by Dakin Matthews and directed by Mladen Kiselov for the 2004 California Shakespeare Festival that same summer.

Matthews and Kiselov's production transposed the Henriad's politics to 1930s America. 'King Henry looks like a sharp-suited captain of industry', one reviewer observed. 'The upstart lords are mobsters. . . . Hal smokes cigarettes from a silver case and drinks wine straight from the bottle. Glen Miller and Duke Ellington play on the soundtrack.' Although the production featured numerous non-white actors in more minor roles, Cathey's Falstaff, as the sole African American, stood out as 'a brooding, black hepcat in a graying beard and sunglasses who plays saxophone'. As the same reviewer pointed out, contemporary political concerns coexisted with the Depression-era setting. *Henry IV*'s plot about the transition of power from father to son was subtly used to comment on the relationship between George H. W. and George W. Bush in the year in which the latter would win a second term by an exceedingly narrow margin.[49] While Cathey's Falstaff possessed a refreshingly tough and cool Black masculinity, Prince Hal, played by pale, red-headed actor Sean Dugan, presented for another reviewer as a 'debauched and callow whelp seriously in need of a smackdown . . . He is, when all's said and done, the George W. Bush of Henrys'.[50] The production thus reversed the traditional gender binary in which Prince Hal achieves properly masculine kingship in part by banishing a feminized Falstaff. Instead, a Black, masculine Falstaff accentuated the insufficiency of a white, effeminate king.

A decade later, in the aftermath of another memorable political contest, a new African American Falstaff took the stage. This Falstaff was played by G. Valmont Thomas, a fourteen-season member of the Oregon Shakespeare Festival who, as seen previously, got started in the role via *Merry Wives*.[51] In summer 2017, the OSF put on productions of both parts of *Henry IV* to fight the backlash against Obama's presidency and other civil rights' gains epitomized by the 2016 election of Donald Trump. The OSF has been singled out by Ayanna Thompson as an unusual enclave of nontraditional casting in affluent and mostly white Ashland, Oregon – where audiences, as with most Shakespearean theatre, tend to be on the even whiter (as well as wealthier and older) side.[52] Thomas's presence in the company was part of the initial surge in diverse hirings which began with the tenure of artistic director Libby Appel in 1996.[53]

In publicity interviews posted on the OSF website and YouTube, the directors of *Henry IV, Part 1* and *Henry IV, Part 2*, Lileana Blain-Cruz and Paul Cofield – both of whom identify as people of colour – emphasized how they wanted to make these productions both modern and American. The factionalization and prejudice that characterized the United States in the era of Donald Trump's presidency were reflected, for Blain-Cruz, in the similar lines of ethnicity and nationality drawn in the *Henry IV* plays.[54] In these productions, Henry IV was played by a white actor (Jeffrey King), Prince Hal and Hotspur by LatinX actors (Daniel José Molina and Alejandra Escalante) and Falstaff by a Black man. The king's 'whiteness in the diverse cast is conspicuous', reviewer and scholar Hailey Bachrach noted. 'It casts a telling shadow over his disdain for the Percys and for his own son.'[55] As a sympathetic version of the prince, Molina's Hal is torn between the white world of monarchical power represented by his father and the illegitimate tavern world represented by Thomas's African American Falstaff. The rebels, moreover, are 'an array of black and Latina actors standing up to' the white king. In slaying Hotspur, his Latina doppelgänger, Hal slays both his 'masculine-feminine foil' and his own ethnic otherness, which he follows up by his 'adoption of white cultural habitus that he eventually dons in order to rule'.[56] Accordingly in Cofield's *Part 2*, after the old king's death, Henry V banishes a Black Falstaff and aligns himself with a white Lord Chief Justice played by Robin Goodrin Nordli.

The inauspicious vision offered by Hal's rejection of ethnic alterity was partly mitigated by the production's persistently transgressive representations of gender. Although Cofield's production was 'whiter and more male' than Blain-Cruz's *Part 1*, Nordli portrayed 'a cool and confident Lord Chief Justice in a sober skirt'.[57] Further, the epilogue's promise to have Falstaff return to the stage was made good by the simultaneous staging of a white female actor, K. T. Vogt, as Falstaff in a simultaneous production of *Merry Wives of Windsor*. Publicity for the OSF's 2017 season emphasized the presence of two 'Falstaffs' on the company's combination of stages, underscoring the constructedness of both race and gender in these plays.⁵⁸ A season ticket holder could watch Thomas play Falstaff in the *Henry IV* plays and then go see *Merry Wives* – to find the character transformed from a Black man to a white woman, playing a man who on one memorable occasion dresses up as a woman.

The shift exemplifies on a metatheatrical scale the play's own concern with 'the possibilities of ongoing shape-shifting through theatrical representation'.⁵⁹ Such shapeshifting has culminated in several recent American productions featuring Black female Falstaffs, including a 2013 updated staging of *Merry Wives of Windsor* by San Francisco's African-American Shakespeare Company and a 2015 all-female production of *1 Henry IV* by the Baltimore Shakespeare Factory.⁶⁰ These Black female Falstaffs bring the character full circle, demonstrating his/her/their continued subversive potential on the twenty-first-century stage.

A not-so-'merrie' England

On screen, Falstaff's shapeshifting has taken a different path that in various ways links the role's distinct stage histories in the United States and the United Kingdom. The fat knight's most famous cinematic representation is the product of an American's creative vision: Orson Welles's *Chimes at Midnight* (1965). The two-hour adaptation starring Welles as Falstaff conflates not only both parts of *Henry IV* but also smaller portions of *Merry Wives*, *Henry V* and *Richard II*. Sidestepping what Welles saw as the commercialism of the American film industry,⁶¹ *Chimes at Midnight* was funded by Swiss and Spanish sources and shot on-location in Spain.⁶² The result, while technically a transnational production, emphasizes the director's particular understanding of Falstaff as an icon of Englishness. Welles has famously described the film as a lament for 'the death of merrie England', with 'merrie England' understood as 'a myth which has been very real to the English-speaking world . . . the age of chivalry, of simplicity of Maytime and all that'.⁶³ As an act of mourning for this always already bygone place and time, the lament is also, Kathy Howlett points out, a socially conservative gesture that highlights the director's own inner 'aristocrat' and evasion of 'historical and socioeconomic realities'. Welles's Falstaff is, correspondingly, a 'fallen' knight but still very much an aristocratic figure.⁶⁴

The two middle episodes of *The Hollow Crown*'s first season inevitably engage with, but do not entirely emulate, this monumental predecessor. In a 2016 interview, both director Richard Eyre and actor Simon Russell Beale described their Falstaff as the 'opposite' of the character's commonplace idealization as 'the icon of bucolic England'.[65] Accordingly, despite his Englishness, whiteness and classical Shakespearean pedigree, in certain ways, Beale is an atypical Falstaff. At five-foot-six, he is 'considerably shorter than other characters' in Eyre's *Henry IV*, especially lanky, six-foot-two co-star Tom Hiddleston (Welles himself was six feet tall). As a result, 'he looks like a man who is always trying to measure up to others, and failing'. This height differential showcases what becomes in Eyre's production the character's decidedly un-festive 'vulnerability', which is also 'emphasized by his limp, his being perpetually out of breath and his impotence with Doll, for which he apologizes with a self-deprecatory "I am old" (2.4.274)'.[66] The fact that Hiddleston towers over Beale is particularly noticeable in the scenes where Hal and Falstaff match wits in banter, not only making Falstaff appear the loser in these exchanges but visually underscoring the fact that Hal is Falstaff's social better.

Physical stature is not the only signifier of the social gap between the prince and the fallen knight. Beale's Falstaff provides a prime example of what Robert Shaughnessy describes as the prosthetic nature of the modern Falstaff's costume.[67] In addition to donning the typical fat suit, to perform the role the actor underwent a significant cosmetic transformation of his face. In an interview Beale described the extensive process behind this 'extraordinary piece of make-up', in which he appeared, to his own view, 'unrecognizable'.[68] To underscore the alienation he felt from his own image, Beale recalled taking a photograph of himself in his Falstaff outfit to show friends and family – something the highly experienced actor had never done before.

In the televised mode of Eyre's *Henry IV*, Beale's estrangement from his Falstaff costume takes on a different resonance from the disjunct Shaughnessy describes between theatrical and cultural practice on the British stage. In an age in which fatness is more often a mark of poverty than of wealth, for the modern stage Falstaff, 'an essentially aristocratic and potentially tragic figure . . . the belly is not only bogus but socially miscast'. But although clearly tragic, Beale's Falstaff is not exactly an 'essentially aristocratic' figure like that of actors Shaughnessy cites: Brewster Mason, Joss Ackland, Robert Stevens and David Warner.[69] The theatrical artifice of the stage prosthetic belly becomes, through cinematic magic, the visual transformation of Beale into what is presented as a genuine embodiment of obesity, with all the attendant contemporary meanings. Despite Falstaff's designation as 'Sir John' and breathless RP accent, those meanings include the insinuation of lower social rank.

The fatness of this Falstaff, that is, bears the stigma as well as the stigmata of the twenty-first century's understanding of obesity as a disease that predominantly afflicts the economically disadvantaged, with comorbidities such as osteoarthritis, obstructive sleep apnoea and other cardiorespiratory complications. Hiddleston characterizes his own character's rejection of Falstaff in *Henry IV, Part 2* in these very terms: 'Hal is shedding his skin, he's shedding this cloak of irresponsibility and becoming more of a man, becoming someone who will be king. In Falstaff, he sees a sad old man who's disabled by his weight and full of lies and deceit.'[70] The actor's choice of metaphors revises his character's self-description as 'the sun' breaking free from 'base contagious clouds' (1.2.176) to present Falstaff as excess body weight he plans to shed to make himself 'more of a man'. Falstaff, in contrast, is both physically and morally 'disabled' by those extra pounds.

Despite the source text's fascination with Falstaff's fatness, Hiddleston expresses a modern prejudice. According to Elena Levy-Navarro, the present-day tendency to accept at face value the plays' apparent privileging of the thin and denigration of the fat indicates our own interpellation into prevailing ideologies about bodyweight. Shakespeare's text, rather, invites questioning of the social constructions of the 'new bodily aesthetic that Hal uses to define himself' and 'to establish the superior virtue of his line' – the descendants of John of Gaunt – 'against the decadent, soft Richard'.[71]

In the opening of Eyre's *Henry IV, Part 1*, while a jovial fiddling tune plays on the soundtrack, establishing shots of Eastcheap focus the viewer's attention immediately on concerns of the flesh. The first thing we see is a butcher's gloved and chain-mailed hand chopping up cuts of raw meat on a board. As the shot zooms out the camera reveals a lively meat market in which a woman plucks a chicken, a vendor hands his customer a dead rabbit and a wolfhound hungrily sniffs the carcass of a pig lying on a wagon. That pig's head is visually juxtaposed with the sign hanging outside the eponymous Boar's Head tavern, into which we follow the prince on his way to visit the fat knight. As these opening shots present the consumption-oriented tavern world over which Falstaff presides as a site of violent self-interest, they also prepare the audience for a gradual revelation of the fat knight's fleshy body as a site of both moral and physical compromise.

Meanwhile the lanky, handsome Prince Hal navigates the bustle with grace and ease, both literally and figuratively a head and shoulders above it. As he enters the tavern and makes his way upstairs, the fiddling tune recedes as the sound of raucous snoring crescendos. The first of Falstaff's grotesque bodily emanations that the audience encounters, the sound also signifies obstructive sleep apnoea – as mentioned earlier, a condition often associated with obesity. The camera follows Hal into the bedroom. Before we see Falstaff, we see Hal looking at Falstaff, shaking his head with a rueful chuckle that invites us to join him in friendly disparagement. A shot from the foot of the bed then shows Falstaff's supine clothed legs and giant belly in the foreground. Next to him lie the prone legs and one visible buttock of the sex worker, Doll Tearsheet. After a playfully teasing Hal gives his friend's foot a poke, a close tracking shot takes us up Falstaff's thigh, over his mountain of a belly, to his red, puffy face, bulbous nose and bushy white beard. He wakes with a start and finally speaks in a gruff, groggy voice: 'Now, Hal, what time of day is it, lad?' (*1H4* 1.2.1).

With Falstaff's grotesque body substituting for his verbal plethora, Hal is the only character to speak at length in this scene. Meanwhile Falstaff rolls over, slaps Doll on the buttock and attempts to engage her sexually – an effort which is sleepily rebuffed as the camera takes us to the court scene of Act 1, Scene 1. When we return to the bedchamber for the remainder of Scene 2, the dialogue is accompanied by Falstaff loudly pissing into a corner chamber pot. Beale's Falstaff also turns out to be a 'close talker'; Hiddleston's demeanour registers a thinly veiled disgust with his friend's malodorous breath as well as his fresh potful of urine. Falstaff's corpulent and leaky body foretells his banishment much as Hal's trim form and handsome features foretell his success.

Yet as off-putting as his body may be, this is a Falstaff with psychological depth. Co-star Jeremy Irons, who plays a gaunt and moribund King Henry IV, recalls how the first time he saw Beale in costume he 'could hardly see him. That is, until you see the eyes, and then there he is.'[72] Close shots of Falstaff's watery, bloodshot eyes become the centre of a performance of interiority that is paradoxically enhanced by his encumbering exterior prostheses. For instance, following the 'play extemporé' scene, extended pauses while melancholy strings play on the soundtrack highlight Beale's sorrowful expression when he pleads, 'Banish plump Jack and banish all the world' only to be told by Hiddleston's downcast Hal, 'I do, I will' (*1H4* 2.4.471–3). Preceding low-angle shots of Falstaff playing king high on the tavern table forecast this outcome, displaying the elevation of his plump, gnomish form as patently ridiculous.[73]

This early dialogue bears fruit in the final coronation scene, which emphasizes both Falstaff's infirmity and his short stature as he pushes his way, limping, through a crowd of uniformly taller onlookers to catch the attention of his 'lambkin' who is now King Henry V (*2H4* 5.3.117). Beale's reddened face expresses genuine anguish as 'his' Hal admonishes him, and his lower lip quivers as the king pronounces his banishment. He stifles sobs before hobbling away. The final shot of the episode shows Falstaff being dragged off by the king's guards to prison, with a slow-motion close-up on his despairing face while familiar plaintive strings lament his final tragedy.

Even in the fat knight's least sympathetic moment, his soliloquy on his misuse of the 'king's press', *The Hollow Crown*'s viewer is encouraged nonetheless to pity Beale's Falstaff (*1H4* 4.2.11–48). Dwarfed despite his bulk by a dim and barren landscape, Falstaff marches breathlessly on foot along with his men as he delivers the speech. Afterwards the prince and Westmoreland ride comfortably up on horseback, forcing the panting old man to jog to keep pace as he declares his ragtag army 'food for powder' who will 'fill a pit as well as better' (65–7). Although he leads a troop of men whom he describes as 'scarecrows', Falstaff's corpulent body paradoxically identifies him as one of their number, marching towards his own death (38).

Falstaff's soliloquy on honour, delivered a few scenes later in a melancholy voiceover as he wanders through the army camp on the eve of battle, seemingly raises Falstaff to the ranks of film's most famous soliloquizing Shakespearean tragic heroes such as Olivier's

Hamlet and Jon Finch's Macbeth. This Falstaff represents, however, not an Aristotelian but an entirely modern tragedy. We are asked to experience on the protagonist's behalf not terror but only pity – as Anna Mollow argues, a pervasive if undertheorized element of current cultural constructions of obesity as a disease.[74]

Nearly a decade after the programme's initial airing, *The Hollow Crown*'s tragic perspective on Falstaff recently has been further reconsidered in light of the economic ramifications of the Covid-19 pandemic. In April 2021, British writer and Oxford lecturer Sally Bayley published an article on BBC.com about *Henry IV* titled 'The Shakespeare Tragedy that Truly Speaks to Us Now'. With reference to the economic downturn of the early twenty-first century up through the early pandemic years of 2020–1, Bayley describes Falstaff as 'a potent symbol of dispossession and social misfortune'. He exemplifies 'a figure for those left behind; those who have failed to find a foothold on the social ladder: specifically, men without salaries and homes; discarded men turning back into children'.[75]

The article's primary image is a large-scale still from the BBC's *Henry IV, Part 2*. Beale's Falstaff and Julie Waters' Nell Quickly stand in a street outside the Board's Head Tavern, both with sombre faces featuring prominent broken blood vessels, Nell clutching Falstaff's arm (Figure 4). Both characters are looking outward towards the viewer, their mouths slightly open as if caught in a moment of desperate pleading. In the background, as in the opening scene of *1 Henry IV*, a street butcher can be seen. His garments and hands are blood-streaked, his gaze cast firmly downward as he goes about his brutal business, far more interested in his own survival than that of either the animals whose flesh he sells or his fellow human beings.

The spirit of the still tellingly contrasts with the enacted moment it represents. That is an early, comic scene in Eyre's *Henry IV, Part 2*: a brawl that results when two sergeants attempt to arrest Falstaff 'at the suit of Mistress Quickly' for his unpaid bar tab (2.1.44). Falstaff's costume – the upscale cloak, leather gloves and maroon doublet, shirt and hat he has purchased with the proceeds from his successful performance at the Battle of Shrewsbury – presents him at his most obviously aristocratic. Yet nine years later the image was reappropriated to substantiate Falstaff's status as the poster boy for the isolation and destitution of the common man in the world of Covid-19.

FIGURE 4 *Falstaff and Mistress Quickly as tragic figures. Henry IV, Part 2, directed by Richard Eyre. © Focus Features 2012. All rights reserved. Film still from* 'The Hollow Crown *Photo Gallery*'.

These apparent contradictions demonstrate not only the ongoing dialectic between production and reception in the process of adaptation, but also how class concerns intersect in Eyre's construction of whiteness and disability in the two parts of *Henry IV*. For the whiteness of this cast, in the end, is not solely or even primarily about historical accuracy or Shakespearean tradition but also about the status of contemporary England's white population. Not only are the Hostess and Falstaff white but so are those likewise imprisoned at the end of *Part 2*: Peto, Bardolph, Pistol, Shallow and Doll. Meanwhile Falstaff's Boy remains free but jobless and alone – as emphasized by a close shot of the child soberly surveying the fate of his master and his companions before turning to beat a solitary retreat.

Played by a different child actor than in Sharrock's capstone episode, this Boy stands in his own right as a figure of 'white history', albeit a history with a strikingly different trajectory. For Eyre's *Henry IV* is not a narrative of imperial domination but a story about the social dispossession of white men – and not only those of the lower classes. Although appropriable to the narrative of working-class dispossession, in the end the whiteness and disability of Beale's incompletely aristocratic Falstaff also signify the dispossession, through contemporary history, of Welles's idea of 'merrie England'.

The relationship between Eyre's episodes and Welles's film is subtly indicated by a variety of intertextual citations. For example, Eyre's staging of the scene of impotence with Doll – with Falstaff straddled supine on a bed while Poins and Hal spy on them from the rafters above – is a direct cinematic quotation from *Chimes at Midnight*.[76] Eyre's unflinchingly violent and lengthy representation of the Battle of Shrewsbury also pays considerable homage to Welles.[77] Falstaff's level of vulnerability in the two battles, however, is notably different. While Welles's suit-of-armour-clad Falstaff at no point seems in danger, Beale's fat knight has his face exposed and wears only a chain mail vest. Eyre emphasizes Falstaff's greater vulnerability when he, like Welles, has the knight witness the climactic battle between Hal and Hotspur while hiding behind a tree. Versus Welles's unconcerned cheering on of his prince, Beale remains silent throughout the fight, his expressive eyes wide with terror. While Welles gets too close to the prince and Hotspur and is comically knocked down by their swordplay, Beale, still concealed behind the tree, falls without a clear inciting cause. Although presumably he is playing dead, it is also possible he faints with fright. To someone unfamiliar with the play, he may initially even appear to have fallen dead from a stress-induced heart attack.

By linking Beale's Falstaff to Welles's but making him smaller, weaker and more vulnerable, Eyre's *Henry IV* ties the fat knight's tragedy to Welles's lament for 'merrie England' while simultaneously undermining the notion that England was ever truly 'merrie'. In a key shift midway through *Chimes at Midnight*, the jovially imposing Welles delivers Falstaff's famous soliloquy in praise of sack from *Henry IV, Part 2* to an audience of enthusiastic soldiers after the Battle of Shrewsbury. He offers a cup to the disillusioned Hal, who declines and walks away to the castle, thereby signalling the irreparable split between them. Eyre likewise moves the speech on sack from *Part 2* to *Part 1* and provides it with an audience. But Beale's speech is transposed to Act 3, where it is delivered in the claustrophobic setting of the Boar's Head tavern to a sombre audience consisting only of the tavern crew – most of whom are not even drinking. As a solitary drinker celebrating the properties of alcohol to his surly, sober companions, Beale's subsequent attack on the Hostess for allegedly picking his pockets reads like the sudden turn of a happy drunk to an angry drunk, adding a modern pathological resonance to Falstaff's concluding advice to his hypothetical sons to 'addict themselves to sack' (2H4 4.2.121).

Through such revisions of *Chimes at Midnight*, Eyre's *Henry IV* reveals the idea of a 'merrie England' populated solely by white people who live, labour and drink in communal harmony as a fantasy that never existed. Falstaff's disabled body marks the tension between nostalgia for this always already vanished past and the consciousness that this nostalgia is misplaced. Although Falstaff's long-standing association with Englishness persists in *The Hollow Crown*, it is a morally and physically compromised Englishness that, in the play's own terms, stands in need of a 'purge' (2H4 4.1.65). As discussed in Chapter 2, in the upcoming episode of *The Hollow Crown*, Sharrock's *Henry V*, Hiddleston's King Henry receives a physically and morally healthier Black best friend to replace the degenerate fat old white knight. In anticipating this conclusion to the first season's cycle, Eyre's all-white *Henry IV* ultimately evokes both nostalgia for 'merrie old England' and a pained self-consciousness of that construction's insufficiency in twenty-first-century Britain.

A white British Falstaff in King Harold's LA

Lennix, Quinn and Thompson's *H4* also struggles with Falstaff's complex relationship to England and Englishness as it simultaneously wrestles with Shakespeare's deep-rooted appropriation as an American cultural icon. Unlike the widely broadcast *The Hollow Crown*, *H4* premiered in limited venues in 2012 and was only released to the general public in a re-edited version on streaming video and DVD in 2020. With the express intent 'to explore various aspects of African-American politics in the 20th and 21st centuries' and 'contribute a unique and original statement on Shakespearean performance and on the modern American socio/political landscape', *H4* combines both parts of *Henry IV* into a single ninety-minute movie with a plot focused on the 'coming of age story of a son destined to lead a nation'.[78] It is set in modern Los Angeles and features a cast almost entirely composed of actors of colour – that is, all the major roles except for that of Falstaff, played by Scottish actor Angus Macfadyen. The protracted dissemination of this film in itself suggests a marketing challenge inherent in so unabashedly challenging public assumptions about race, history and Shakespeare.

A white Falstaff in a film as obviously conscious of colour as *H4* immediately and quite intentionally raises the question of *why*. 'There is little explanation', James C. Bulman observes, 'of why a fat but articulate derelict like him would hang out at a black inner-city bar, nor why the Prince would find him so attractive'.[79] Chicago critic Marilyn Ferdinand posits an answer that she herself finds unsatisfactory: that Macfadyen's white Falstaff 'can be seen as American consumerist culture', and, moreover, 'a mindlessly malevolent force that keeps black men down with the hefty weight of centuries of white oppression'.[80] Although this Falstaff is a consumer, 'American' he is not, and 'mindlessly malevolent' is also not a fully accurate characterization.

Macfadyen's résumé contains some hints as to why he might have been chosen for this role. A prolific, recognizable film actor, he is best known for his breakout performance in Mel Gibson's 1995 blockbuster period epic, *Braveheart*, in which he plays heir to the Scottish throne Robert the Bruce. The story of Robert's wavering loyalties between his own countrymen and the colonizing English resonates with the various imperialist contexts of Shakespeare's history plays. Macfadyen also appeared in Tim Robbin's *The Cradle Will Rock* (1999) as a young Orson Welles, to whose lead part in *Chimes at Midnight* Macfadyen's Falstaff, like that of Beale, pays due homage.[81] As both Robert the Bruce and Welles, moreover, Macfadyen inhabited the roles of larger-than-life white men: a presence that the actor brings to the screen as Falstaff. Turning the tables on the all-too-frequent casting practice in which a single actor of colour unintentionally becomes a magnet for racializing stereotypes, *H4* deliberately places on the shoulders of Macfadyen's Falstaff the burden of representing self-consciously British, Shakespearean whiteness.

Macfadyen's whiteness is not the only thing that makes him incongruous in *H4*'s inner city world. He is also dressed in a medley of styles that include middle-aged Beatnik, rap star wannabe, Black Panther and Herbert Beerbohm Tree's late Victorian version of the fat knight. Wearing all black, he sports a matching beret and dark shield sunglasses, but also has a penchant for flashy metallic jewellery, such as a gold chain around his neck and a large golden ring on each hand. He carries a walking stick capped with an ornate silver wolf's head and frequently downs swigs from a silver hipflask (he is also constantly eating, to great comic effect). With this outfit as well as with his British accent distinguishing him from his much more casually dressed African American tavern buddies, Macfadyen embraces Falstaff's status as a fallen chivalric aristocrat.

In the sense of size, grandiosity and sheer chutzpah, therefore, Macfadyen's Falstaff differs markedly from Beale's gnome-like underdog in *The Hollow Crown*. *H4* also stages Falstaff as significantly less elderly, exhibiting just a few white hairs among his unkempt dark-brown locks and beard (Beale is only two years older than Macfadyen). However, these two Falstaffs are also quite similar in that both are disabled by their weight. In fact, Macfadyen's performed disability is even more pronounced than Beale's. He walks only with great difficulty, with the aid of that wolf-headed cane, and in many cases, he needs the assistance of one or more members of his entourage in order to rise from a supine or seated position. As in Welles's portrayal of an even more enormous Falstaff in *Chimes at Midnight*, some comedy is mined from these mobility issues, as when he tumbles off the bar along with Peto and Bardolph in their attempts to help him descend after the 'play extemporé' scene of Act 2. However, at other moments – for instance, when Bardolph brings him a folding chair from which to survey his ragged recruits and he lowers himself into that chair with a grunt of pain – it is clear that this fatness is not always a laughing matter. Like that of Beale's, the disabling fatness of Macfadyen's Falstaff signals the character's moral as well as physical ill health. In addition to marking him as an unsuitable companion for the fit young prince, this Falstaff's obesity signals the decrepitude of the old world for which he stands.

Yet at the same time, much more than Beale's or even Welles's versions of the character, Macfadyen's is an exceedingly funny Falstaff – and grows even more so with his increasing distance from an increasingly serious, goal-oriented prince. Throughout its narrative *H4* maintains the traditional comic role of Falstaff as both a critic and a perpetrator of his culture's faults. While the culture he critiques is, in the immediate sense, an American city beset by gang warfare, this Falstaff's status as an icon of Englishness and a metonym for Shakespeare also broadens the purview of that critique to include the role of Shakespeare in American and, especially, African American culture. In a *Bildungsroman* of a young Black prince who rises out of gangland Los Angeles to lead a nation, a white British Falstaff represents the dual role of Shakespeare in Black American culture as a tool that can be used both to perpetuate and to resist oppression.

Falstaff is thus a weight that Amad Jackson's Prince Hal must shed in order to come into his own, but for very different reasons than in the typical production of *Henry IV*. Although much of Hal and Falstaff's dialogue is cut in their early scenes together, physical interactions reveal the intimacy of their initial relationship. Hal first awakens the old knight from his slumbers on a couch in the Boar's Head by plopping himself down on his belly. This image of Hal sitting on Falstaff is reprised to even more comic effect at the end of Act 2, when the Chief Justice,[82] in place of the sheriff, arrives to interrupt the tavern crew's revelries. In one of several modernizations characteristic of Thompson's script, Hal's command to Falstaff to 'hide thee behind the arras' becomes 'hide thee behind my ass' (*1H4* 2.4.492). This unlikely feat is accomplished by having Falstaff sit in a chair under a black cloak while Hal sits in his lap.

Hal and Falstaff then proceed to play a version of what is known in improvisational theatre as the 'helping hands' routine, in which two actors 'speak and act as one complete person' as the hands of one actor carry out the activities dictated by the other actor's speech.[83] Here, as in most cases, the ruse is patently obvious – as the Chief Justice's initial deadpan response makes clear. The physical comedy climaxes when Falstaff, as Hal, flips her a double bird and then reaches down to scratch the prince's crotch. Apparently, this is the last straw for the Chief Justice, as the next thing we see is the prince being escorted to jail. Alongside its obvious comedy, the scene invokes an array of power relations. By requiring Hal, as the speaking 'head', to follow the dictates of 'his' hands behaviour, the helping hands device both parodies and subverts the standard body politic metaphor. The result, in this case, is not poorly applied lipstick or a chocolate-smeared face, but the imprisonment of a young Black man – royal identity notwithstanding – by a white officer. The scene thus suggests that Falstaff's power over the prince is problematic with respect to both early modern constructions of sovereignty and contemporary racial politics.

Gender additionally complicates matters. As with several male roles in this production, the Chief Justice is played by a woman: Queens-born West Indian-Polish actress Victoria Platt.[84] In contrast to Macfadyen's all-black costume, Platt wears white robes and a golden stole that to my eye recalls the style of Black Baptist Church Mothers. According to Lennix, the outfit is intended to invoke the aesthetic of the Nation of Islam, especially the MGT (Muslim Girls Training) programme.[85] Facing off in black and white, the two actors' costumes starkly contrast the two opposing figures between whom Prince Hal must choose in the wake of his father's death: the (Lord) Chief Justice representing both secular and sacred law and order, and Falstaff standing for anarchic and irreligious criminality and chaos.[86] Platt's Nation-of-Islam-inspired garb also disrupts the *Henry IV* plays' militant, anti-Islamic Christian perspective, as typified by the elder Henry's unrealized goal of sending a campaign to the 'Holy Land' (*1H4* 1.1.48 ; *2H4* 3.1.108).

In these plays, for Patricia Parker, Falstaff's chaos is feminine, while the authority of the Lord Chief Justice as 'both the father and the Law' is masculine and patriarchal.[87] By representing the law as a maternal religious and governmental figure, *H4* undermines this binary. Race is also an important aspect of *H4*'s revision, as Hal's eventual reconciliation with Platt's female Chief Justice 'lay[s] to rest the prejudice that strong black women are a threat to black masculinity'.[88] Although in their first scene together the Chief Justice authorizes the prince's imprisonment, their final union confirms the new king's rise to power while Falstaff's ostensibly innocent comic crotch-scratching is revealed to have been the more salient threat to Hal's kingship. By banishing his figure of white misrule and endorsing the authority and agency of a woman of colour, Hal proves his mettle as the leader of a modern nation.

In fact, humour is a key element of the covert villainy of Macfadyen's Falstaff. Through comedy he exercises what Stephen Greenblatt has argued is one of Prince Hal's chief verbal powers in Shakespeare's *Henry IV*: the proto-anthropological, colonialist task of 'recording' – that is, appropriating and preserving the language of another culture as a means of controlling it. In the plays this power is 'seen perhaps most clearly in Hal's own gloss of tavern slang', especially his self-proclaimed ability to 'drink with any tinker in his own language', a moment not included in *H4* (*1H4*

2.5.18–19). It continues into his rhetorical manipulations as the king in *Henry V*.[89]

In *H4*, where Falstaff rather than the prince is the chief interloper in the tavern world, the power of 'recording' is appropriated by the fat knight. Although the quantity of Falstaff's discourse is considerably trimmed in Thompson's script, what remains copious is his ability, like the textual Hal, to mimic the speech habits of the mixed American cultures into which he has been incongruously dropped. This happens most blatantly in his 'play extemporé' performance as Henry IV, where Falstaff falls from his typical 'posh transatlantic accent' to 'channel Vito Corleone'.[90] Here, instead of speaking in 'King Cambyses' vein' (2.4.381), Macfadyen overlays Falstaff's parody of theatrical kingly speech with a spoof on an iconic image of Italian-American paternal authority.

Even more insidious are the moments when Falstaff uses impersonation to mockingly appropriate Black culture. In keeping with the textual Falstaff's status as a subverter of Christian mores, he at times imitates the vocal inflections of a Black Baptist preacher. 'By the Lord' Falstaff shouts when the jig is up regarding his humiliation in Hal's robbery hoax, raising his arms to the heavens, 'I knew [you] as well as he that made [you]!' (*1H4* 2.4.261–2). Later he appropriates the idiom of the blues in a bedroom scene with 'Marion' Quickly that adapts Falstaff's melancholy conversation with Doll Tearsheet in *2 Henry IV*. As the two lie together on Marion's bed, Falstaff sings his lines to the rhythm of hip-thrusts punctuated by riffs on a harmonica: 'it grows late [mm mm mm]; we'll [go] to bed [mm mm mm]. [Will you] forget me [mm mm mm] when [you] are gone' (*2H4* 2.4.274–5). The effect is comedic rather than maudlin, and Marion dissolves into giggles.

A shift to the malign takes place in the subsequent scene when Falstaff meets his newly drafted army, all people of colour of various ages and genders. He appears before the soldiers slightly slurring, and, as discussed earlier, unable to stand on his own feet due to pain, intoxication or both. The stark presentation of his debilitation grimly frames his subsequent description of his troops. The source text's soliloquy is here privately addressed to a uniformed Peto. Retained phrases from the play that stand out in this modern American context include Falstaff's description of his soldiers as 'slaves as ragged as Lazarus', at which he laughs uproariously – a sentiment to which Peto grins in nervous agreement – and, even more pointedly, his acknowledgement that he has 'had the most of them out of prison' (4.2.25, 41). The latter line calls attention to a crucial contributor to racial injustice in the United States, the vastly disproportionate incarceration of Black men and women. As Falstaff's second in command, Peto, played by young Black actor Nick Ryan, is implicated in this inequity, thereby expanding the fat knight's destructive sphere of influence.

When the prince shows up, his loyalties now signalled by a big blue 'IV' emblazoned on his T-shirt, the contrast between his lean, mean readiness for battle and the dissipation and exaggerated comedy of 'blown Jack' is clear (4.2.49). As Falstaff delivers the line 'good enough to toss, food for powder, food for powder. They'll fill a pit as well as better. . . . [M]ortal men, mortal men', he pretends to fire into the crowd with an automatic weapon: 'POW! POW! POW! PWAH! POW!' (64–7). He thus adds to his list of ventriloquized Americanisms a penchant for gun violence – a choice that stands out further since the actual weapons used in the combat to come are baseball bats, swords and maces.

While Falstaff mocks, Hal remains dead serious about the upcoming battle and rebuffs Falstaff's attempts to engage him in playful roughhousing. So Falstaff too gets serious. Sweating and red in the face, he grabs the prince by his shirtfront. When Hal finally shakes him off and makes his exit, Falstaff delivers to Peto and the other soldiers his famous speech about honour. The soliloquy is transformed into a grandiose performance in which Falstaff works off his frustration with the prince at his on-screen audience's expense. To his soldiers' scattered laughter, he shouts, 'Well?!!!' He gestures for them to keep laughing, and as their laughter escalates, he taunts, 'No matter; honour pricks me on' (*1H4* 5.1.129–30). To underscore the phallic humour of 'prick', he holds his wolf-head cane – which is later revealed to contain a rapier – at his crotch and waggles it up and down. 'Honour pricks me on', he repeats to his now guffawing troops.

That the typical audience of live stage productions is replaced in *H4* with a diegetic audience of the very men and women whose lives are being treated so dismissively in Falstaff's speech yields an alienation effect greater than the discomfort the scene may produce in the theatre. The cinematic audience is clearly not meant to find the laughter at these soldiers' expense to be funny – or, if we do, we are meant to second-guess ourselves. Falstaff's role as both comedian and cultural critic in this scene is thus complex and multifaceted. Despite its crudeness as an instrument of physical comedy, the cane-as-phallus is subtle in its symbolic implications. All at once it is a metonym for Macfadyen's British eccentricity, a parody of the weapons wielded by impoverished urban American men and (quite literally) Falstaff's prosthetic 'staff' – a prop that signals both lameness and impotence. Falstaff thereby mounts a grimly comic critique of himself, Shakespeare and America at one and the same time.

While in the original 2012 cut of the film the scene abruptly shifts after the repeated line 'Honor pricks me on' to the first of the Shrewsbury battle scenes,[91] in the more grimly framed 2015 revision the soliloquy continues in its entirety – thereby further emphasizing the menacing nature of Macfadyen's Falstaff. With the lines 'Can honour set to a leg? No. Or an arm? No', Falstaff uses his cane to prod members of his audience in the relevant body parts (5.1.131–2). As if finally recognizing the serious stakes of their commanding officer's speech, the soldiers go grimly silent and remain that way when, even more threateningly, Falstaff draws the rapier out of his cane and waves it in their faces. Their laughter at the punchline, 'Honor is a mere scutcheon', suggests that they have become knowingly complicit in their own annihilation (5.1.140).

The troubled juncture of discourses that Macfadyen's Falstaff represents climaxes in the banishment scene. The coronation ceremony of Amad Jackson's Henry V takes place in a domed public hall that structurally recalls the US Capitol – actually an interior space of Arizona's Fairfax High School.[92] Through high double doors, a view of the Lincoln Memorial can briefly be glimpsed behind the processing royal family. It is a ceremony of presidential proportions. From a balustraded balcony above the procession, among other, mostly brown-skinned onlookers – including the members of his own crew – Falstaff waves a large American flag (Figure 5). His address to the king is sung to the tune of America's patriotic hymn 'My Country 'Tis of Thee' – originally the tune of Britain's 'God Save the King'. 'God save [you] my sweet boy!', Falstaff joyously belts. 'My King, my [royal] Jove, I speak to [you], my heart! [God save my Hal!]' (*2H4* 5.5.42, 45). This 'brilliant irony', Bulman asserts, 'draws attention to the central paradox of using a play about feudal struggles in medieval England to comment on black political culture in contemporary America'.[93]

FIGURE 5 *Falstaff and company at the coronation. H4, directed by Paul Quinn. © Triumvirate Pictures 2015. All rights reserved. Screen grab.*

It also calls attention to Falstaff's status as the production's central visual and vocal reminder of white Shakespearean Britishness. The song highlights Shakespeare's role in not only Britain's persistent cultural colonization of America but also, through America's long-standing appropriation of Shakespeare, white America's cultural colonization of Black America. Additionally, it sets the stage for Hal's rise not as the king of England, or even the king of Black America, but for a potentially more diverse and auspicious view of a novel American nation.

As Falstaff and his crew are carried off to 'County', Macfadyen gestures grandly towards unseen crowds below as he reassures his cronies, 'I shall be sent for in private. . . . He must *seem* thus to the world!' (5.5.74–5). But who makes up this world for whom the new king supposedly must 'seem'? In his final, film-ending speech, lines addressed to the king's brothers and a few other members of his court in *2 Henry IV* become this new leader's public oration to an unspecified audience. The context, however, strongly suggests that Jackson's Henry V speaks to the America of 2008 and 2012 that elected, and then reelected, a Black man as president. The closing applause thus signals a celebratory allusion to Barack Obama.[94]

With this ending in mind, Hal's rejection of Macfadyen's Falstaff is not precisely a rejection of whiteness. Nor is it a total rejection of America's Shakespearean heritage. Rather, as in Shakespeare's *Henry IV, Part 2*, it is a strategic appropriation of what Falstaff additionally represents: the potency of theatre and, especially, comedy. *H4* continues to celebrate both Falstaff and Shakespeare even as it recognizes the imperfections of such cultural icons, who carry along with their linguistic prowess the weighty baggage of history. The film's return to a comic Falstaff it promoted as 'the best loved and certainly most profane of Shakespeare's characters' is a savvy move that embraces both the power and the danger of Shakespearean adaptation.[95] MacFayden's Falstaff underscores the fundamental paradox of Shakespeare's presence in a diverse society. Although historically deployed to institutionalize white male Anglocentric privilege, Shakespeare's plays – even, and perhaps especially, his history plays – provide a tool for dismantling the same.

Coda: Falstaff south of the Equator

Such a paradox is tellingly illustrated by Falstaff's cinematic representation elsewhere in the Americas beyond the Anglophone sphere. Most importantly, Eduardo Coutinho's *Faustão* (1971) transposes the story of Hal and Falstaff to the northeast backlands of early twentieth-century Brazil.[96] This Falstaff figure (Eliezar Gomes) is the leader of a band of *cangaceiros*, or 'social bandits' – distinguished from other bandits due to their primary function as a mode of 'social protest' on behalf of the poor and dispossessed.[97] The Hal figure, Henrique (Jorge Gomes), is the son of the head of one of two rival Brazilian families who is rescued, ransomed and then adopted by the outlaw band.

Although the sole scholarly examination of *Faustão* in English downplays both its Shakespearean connection and the significance of racial difference in the film,[98] in my view this production represents a crucial link in understanding the racialized transatlantic reconceptualization of the Falstaff figure. It thus requires consideration even in a study of Anglophone history adaptations. Among the many shades of skin colour represented by the Brazilian actors who populate the film, Eliezar Gomes's Faustão stands out for his Blackness, which replaces fatness as the primary physical marker of his bodily difference; the film is sometimes titled

Faustão: O Cangaceiro Negro (*Big Faust: The Black Cangaceiro*).[99] After his father's death, Henrique (who is light-skinned) becomes the enforcer of political order and contributes directly to the downfall of his former mentor and companion. In the end Faustão wins a brief duel with Henrique but then dies heroically in a hail of bullets from the law. Although, as Stam points out, 'Robin Hood-like opposition to the rich' rather than 'black liberation' is Faustão's prime motivation,[100] race nonetheless signals both Faustão's resistance to local political authorities and what I would suggest is the film's deliberate erasure of Falstaff's original status as an icon of both (white) Englishness and Shakespeare. *Faustão*'s strategy of simultaneously invoking and obscuring a Shakespearean heritage through a Black character based in part on Falstaff suggests a further strategy of resistance to Shakespeare's cultural authority.

On the flip side of *Faustão*'s reappropriation of Falstaff as a tragically masculine Black hero, *As Alegres Comadres* – a 2003 Brazilian adaptation of *The Merry Wives of Windsor* directed by Leila Hipólito – comedically highlights pejorative constructions of race as well as femininity in its depiction of Fausto/Falstaff's disguise as an 'aunt of Brentford' (4.2.163–4). As Mark Thornton Burnett notes, this Falstaff is 'made up to resemble a "black mother", a traditional figure from Brazilian folklore, and passed off by Mrs. Lima/Mistress Page as "my servant's aunt from Africa"'. Through various cinematic means, the film makes the racialization of this character paramount. Falstaff/Fausto in blackface becomes 'a shaming ritual that exposes underlying racial ideologies and functions to endorse a construction of the social order'.[101] As this Falstaff briefly embodies a parodic representation of that so-often conspicuously absent figure in Shakespeare, an embodied Black woman, MacDonald's insistence on the centrality of these women in Shakespeare as 'necessary props' for whiteness becomes especially, troublingly visible.[102]

Both Brazilian examples spotlight the tense intersections among race, gender and nation inherent in Shakespeare's Falstaff, suggesting that the further one proceeds from the character's origins, the further such issues tend to rise to the surface. Across the globe, this rhetorically flamboyant, always already cross-gendered, increasingly racially diverse, prosthetic-yet-all-too-fleshly figure continues to be a powerful locus of theatrical agency: one means of shaping the imagined communities of our increasingly interconnected planet.

4

Straight outta Shakespeare

H4, My Own Private Idaho and the universality conundrum

The broad appeal of a character like Falstaff raises a central concern of Shakespearean adaptation in relation to race that I raised in the introduction to this book, and which I now address head-on. I refer to the commonplace notion of the plays' universality: the idea that they speak to a fundamentally human experience that transcends boundaries of both space and time. In a well-known spin on this idea, Harold Bloom has infamously characterized Falstaff as a chief example of Shakespeare's 'invention of the human'.[1] Such assertions, as Vanessa Corredera summarizes, are implicitly racializing in that they 'gloss over Shakespeare as an alienating entity – a shibboleth for approved "high" culture often imagined as white'.[2] Yet while Macfadyen's particularly white Falstaff in *H4*'s otherwise all-Black Henriad would seem to flout such a perspective, actor and producer Harry Lennix has on numerous occasions stated that the film itself is evidence that Shakespeare 'is universal'.[3]

Such apparent inconsistency goes with the territory. As Ayanna Thompson points out, definitions of Shakespeare's universality are themselves 'far from universal', revealing the concept's fundamental instability.[4] The paradox befits modern science's understanding of the capital-U Universe as the unimaginable entirety of space, time, matter and energy that is constantly expanding at an uncertain rate.⁵ So, too, does the Latin etymology of the term – from *uni*, or 'one', and *versus*, the past participle of the verb 'to turn', as in to change direction. In this original sense, 'universal' describes a reorientation of many things into a single collective whole.⁶ Such plays on time and space, multiplicity and oneness are integral to the conceptualizations of Shakespeare's universality that underlie both *H4* and an earlier adaptation of the *Henry IV* plays, Gus Van Sant's *My Own Private Idaho*. Both adaptations transpose these 'English' history plays to contemporary, distinctly American settings that incorporate human experiences not frequently engaged in traditional Shakespearean performance. In the process, both productions test the limits of the notion of Shakespeare's universality with respect to constructions of space, place and time and, especially, race.

Released in major cinemas two years following Kenneth Branagh's trend-establishing 1989 adaptation of *Henry V* but conceptualized much earlier, Van Sant's independent arthouse film, usually regarded as an adaptational anomaly, actually anticipates by over two decades concerns with race in the screen history play adaptation as more overtly taken up by *H4*. *My Own Private Idaho*'s most obvious means of testing Shakespeare's universality is its appropriation of portions of the Henriad to evoke the experience of young male sex workers in contemporary Portland, Oregon. However, while gesturing towards the universal, the film also calls attention to the particularity of this experience as a white experience.

This facet of *My Own Private Idaho* becomes especially legible in light of *H4*, which testifies to the integral role of race in the American Shakespearean history adaptation. My reading of Van Sant's film thus departs significantly from prior criticism, which for the most part has not taken account of this crucial arena. *H4*'s applicability to *My Own Private Idaho* is not solely a matter of their shared status as American appropriations of *Henry IV*, moreover, but is also a function of what both productions insist are the radically different perspectives through which Shakespeare's histories can and should be seen. With this key point in mind, and because the classroom is such a critical arena of reception for *H4*, over the course of this chapter's first half I quote from the work of four essays by students in the introductory Shakespeare classes I taught in the fall semesters of 2020 and 2021.⁷ In offering their individual perspectives on this landmark film, these students in their own ways also engage the conundrum of Shakespeare's purported universality as it collides with intersecting constructions of race, gender, class and nation in the histories and spaces of America.

'Rise up' Shrewsbury

H4's evolving perspective on its two core aims – to 'explore various aspects of African American politics in the 20th and 21st century' and to 'contribute a unique and original statement on Shakespearean performance' – can be readily appreciated by considering differences between the film's two versions.[8] The original cut was shown to select scholarly and film festival audiences, from its debut at the Shakespeare Association of America's 2012 annual meeting in Boston to its final screening at the Indie Memphis Film Festival in November of 2013. A revised version, copyrighted in 2015, was finally released on DVD and streaming video on Amazon and other online platforms in March 2020.

Both versions of *H4* as well as the differences between them reveal tensions inherent in what Lennix describes in one interview as 'the common opinion that Shakespeare is universal and timeless', a notion he believes to be 'true'. Yet Lennix also repeatedly drives home the somewhat contradictory point that prior to *H4* there had 'never been . . . a black Shakespearean film'[9] – that is, a film 'from the perspective of black people, acted primarily by black people, and . . . from the black point of view'. *H4* thus simultaneously testifies to claims of the Bard's universality and tests those claims' validity: 'If Shakespeare must be studied by every student in the English-speaking world, and beyond, because of its universal relevant themes and characters, then if it is truly universal, why do I so rarely see anyone black doing it? So with *H4* I'm saying that it is universal.'[10]

Lennix attributes his specific choice of the *Henry IV* plays for this venture to their timeless themes of troubled father–son relations and the problem of legitimate political succession. 'So I thought', Lennix recalls, 'where does that apply in black life?' The answer proved to be a moving target. Initial pre-production brainstorming focused on 'spiritual, political type leaders' like Martin Luther King, Jr, Adam Clayton Powell, Jr, and Jesse Jackson, Jr. By the end of 2008, however, another key figure had emerged on the American political scene: 'a very powerful black man in office'.[11] As I discuss in Chapter 3, that man was Barack Obama, whose concurrent presidency and recent reelection is a crucial subtext of the film's original 2012 cut as well as its 2015 revision. Yet as indicated by the lingering props of monarchy in the film, a one-to-one identification of Amad Jackson's Hal with the forty-fourth US president is also not the point. Even the Lincoln Memorial backdrop briefly seen during Henry V's coronation procession does not solely suggest a presidential context. It is also a momentary reminder of the connection between *H4*'s protagonist and that other famous 'King', who delivered his 'I have a dream' speech from that very location.

The result is a narrative as potentially confusing as a Shakespearean genealogy. Even given what Lennix has described as the film's 'parallel universe' setting in which there is, for instance, a 'king' of Los Angeles, the film never fully explains how its initial gangland plot – in which 'Harold Henry' murders his predecessor 'Kwamé Richards' in a back alley knife fight – translates into what is eventually implied to be a much broader body politic than Los Angeles alone.[12] For my student Jamir Wilson, however, such a translation is beside the point of what he sees as the film's strategy of knocking the Bard down from his cultural high horse. 'Because it is set in Compton and has many references to neighboring hoods, it's safe to make the inference that *H4* is nothing but two gangs fighting a turf war', Wilson writes. 'Because *H4* is about two gangs fighting a turf war, and the script from *Henry IV* fits Quinn's film, then everything that White people say about gang culture should also say the same about Shakespeare.' For Wilson, Amad Jackson's King Henry V is not a figure of the political establishment represented by Barack Obama but rather a figure of a series of culturally marginalized individuals that includes rappers, poets, former gang members and activists:

> We see a Black king in Washington D.C. talking to America. . . . He is saying 'look at how the Black community heals as a unit'. He is making people listen and that is representative of what this play means in a critical way. He is Nipsey Hussle, the Killer Mikes, Noname, Common, G Herbo. He is all the Bloods and Crips who are now coming together to protect the youth and make sure the streets are safer.[13]

From Wilson's perspective, the king's final speech is less about establishing consensus across racial lines than about unifying the

Black community against internal violence, while also resisting external oppression – including the cultural capital of Shakespeare.

Additional elements of the adaptation further complicate *H4*'s political narrative. In a 2011 interview, Thompson described how 'Welsh, Scottish, and English factions' in the plays translate into 'tensions between recent Black immigrants from the islands and Africa and African-Americans who have been in the U.S. for a long time'.[14] Thus the Scottish warrior Douglas is transformed into a Jamaican, while King Richard's 'Irish expedition' from which he returned to be deposed becomes his 'Cuban expedition' (*1H4* 1.3.149). Costumes in the film represent these factional differences, from the Douglas's cape and hat sporting the green, black and gold colours of the Jamaican flag to the casual American street attire modelled on rappers and gangsters as worn by Prince Harry and his crew. As mentioned previously, the aesthetic of many of the film's costumes was derived from the traditional garb of the Nation of Islam, which to Lennix 'symbolizes rectitude, uniformity and discipline'.[15] While all these elements invoke aspects of Black American politics, there is no precise one-to-one correspondence with the story of Hal as Barack Obama, M. L. K. Jr., Nipsey Hussle, or all three.[16]

Part of the explanation for these multiple coexisting narratives is, of course, *H4*'s non-realist approach to adaptation – an approach epitomized by its use of space and medium. Roughly half the film's action (all the prose parts) take place on location in Los Angeles and the other half (the blank verse parts) in an ambiguous space on the stage of an old theatre. For Lennix these spaces represent two different 'worlds' created by Shakespeare's variable use of language.[17] According to the film's creators, 'the iambic pentameter was shot in a theatre to suggest a heightened reality – abstracted, lyrical, and symbolic, while the prose was shot on location – more realistic, literal, and visceral'.[18] Co-executive producer Giovanni Zelko calls the result a 'fusion hybrid film: part play, part movie', which he sees as *H4*'s chief artistic innovation. Like shooting a Black Shakespeare film, this combination of media and aesthetics is something that had 'never been done before'.[19]

While the word 'universal' is not used in these commentaries, the notion potentially underlies their description of the theatrical space as 'a heightened reality – abstracted, lyrical, and symbolic'. The theatre is the space where, accordingly, apparently universally human rituals take place. Father and son carry out the age-old rite of succession; two arch-rivals meet for a trial of strength-in-arms in which only one will emerge alive. Perhaps the chief 'universal' idea the theatre setting evokes is the plays' concern with the nature of kingship as a theatrical construct, which is readily translatable to the image- and spin-obsessed politics of the twenty-first century. Both Lennix and Zelko emphasize *H4*'s interest in metatheatricality, especially the collapse of 'the distinction between statecraft and stagecraft' in both Shakespeare's time and our own.[20]

On the other hand, 'realistic, literal, and visceral' read like code words for the particularities of racialized experience invoked in Los Angeles's urban world. Such specific local and racial differences emerge in emendations to Shakespeare's dialogue: that Harry is the 'Prince of Watts' rather than the 'Prince of Wales', or that 'four white men' are robbed rather than the 'king's exchequer' in the Gad's Hill robbery scene – which takes place not on Gad's Hill but 'on a tour of Kings County' (*1H4* 2.2.53). The disparate venues of street versus theatre offer two seemingly alternative perspectives on Shakespearean universality. While the on-location scenes highlight the plays' ability to accommodate a vastly different set of experiences than Shakespeare could ever have imagined, the theatre emphasizes universal themes seemingly blind to particularities of setting.

Yet as simultaneously underscored by the film's undisputed consciousness of the Black bodies populating both venues, this binary proves specious – not unlike the supposed class binary of blank verse versus prose on the Shakespearean stage, in which the former is conventionally associated with the upper social ranks and the latter with the lower. The association between form and venue in *H4* is far from happenstance; the poetic constructedness of blank verse is part of what grants the theatre scenes in *H4* their air of 'heightened reality'. As I note in my introduction, however, *H4*'s adaptation of Henry IV's death scene, which takes place on the 'universalizing' stage of kingship, must make a key substitution in Shakespeare's text, replacing Shakespeare's 'English kings' with the phrase 'great Black kings' (4.3.168). Although preserving the metre of the original blank verse and thus the veneer of a universalizing aesthetic, the change in content nonetheless calls direct attention to a four-century gulf of racializing history. Similarly, one of the most starkly contemporary and racially conscious moments in the film, Prince Hal's imprisonment after the Chief Justice's discovery of the robbery plot, takes place in a backstage area of the theatre reconfigured as a jail.[21] Contemporary racial politics prohibit a fully universalizing view of this scene as the age-old conflict between patriarchal authority and a rebellious son. The same moment that shows Hal justly punished for his criminal behaviour exposes the particularity of America's racist judicial system as the concealed inner workings of the state's 'universal' theatrical power.

Even the sword fight between Hal and Hotspur reveals what my student KiaJah Rhodes spotlights as a crucial twenty-first-century intersection between race and class. Rhodes identifies *H4*'s Los Angeles setting with 'racist policies like redlining, a government initiative to exclude marginalized communities from advancement services and opportunities that were allotted to white, affluent communities', thus causing 'urban low-income neighborhoods' to be 'riddled with crime and a lack of resources'. She goes on to analyse the scene in question:

> Quinn uses Prince Hal's murder of Hotspur in *Henry IV, Part 1* Act 5, Scene 4 to communicate that the consequence of political disenfranchisement is violence. Hal is hesitant to wound Hotspur until he sees his own reflection in the sword and realizes that if he does not kill Hotspur then he will be killed. After Hotspur is fatally wounded he speaks to Hal,
>
>> Oh, Harry, thou hast robbed me of my youth.
>> I better brook the loss of bitter life
>> Than those proud titles thou hast won of me.
>> They wound my thoughts worse than the sword my flesh.
>> But thought's the slave of life, and life, time's fool,
>> And time, that takes survey of all the world,
>> Must have a stop. (5.4.79–85)
>
> Quinn presents this scene (01:01:15–01:02:32) with Hotspur lying on the wood floor of the theatre. The spiraling of the overhead camera positioned above Hotspur is speaking to the cycle of life and time. Hotspur says that the cycle must come to a stop and the camera spirals into focus overhead of Hotspur's body, recognizing him as an endpoint in this cycle. Violence, and in Hotspur's case death, is a predetermined endpoint for Black people in the cycle of institutionalized racism.[22]

For Rhodes, this scene reveals not the universality of Shakespeare but the cyclicality of structural racism's inevitably violent outcomes. These meanings coexist with the creators' intent of emphasizing the innate theatricality of the transition of power between the two 'Harries', with Hotspur 'literally . . . dying on the boards'.[23]

Such a cycle of violence is prefigured in an opening scene that only exists in the film's 2012 cut. In that earlier version of *H4*, a prologue sequence dramatizes the deposition and murder of Kwamé Richards, a swaggering dandy in a cape and derby, by the lean and mean young gangster Harold Henry and his crew. The opening portion of the scene takes place in the 'real world' but also provides a transition into the theatrical realm. Dying against a chain link fence from a crowbar's blow to the head, in a final show of resistance, Richards headbutts his usurper, catching him in the eye with a point of his crown. Half-blinded and bleeding, Harold stumbles through the back entrance into a nearby building that turns out to be the abandoned theatre – the same space in which subsequent scenes of statecraft-as-stagecraft will take place. There he appoints himself both with an eyepatch and the literal costume of monarchy: a new crown, a jewelled sash and a collection of medieval-style swords that he finds among the backstage props. The gleeful young king then sits down at his desk centre stage.

This is the same position in which he wakes up, according to the caption, 'twenty years later', having transformed into the middle-aged Lennix. Now in modern business/monarchical attire, this older King Henry IV receives a call from the smartphone buzzing under his crown that his 'son is at it. Again'. When he leaves the dark theatre for the sunlit alley outside, the king's expensive suit, dress shirt and sash suddenly morph back into camouflage pants and a T-shirt. The two swords he had grabbed on his way out turn into a crowbar and a baseball bat. The king is clearly aware of this transformation. He looks down at himself, bemused, before setting off in his limo to a Crenshaw bar where the prince is reportedly wreaking havoc.[24]

By highlighting the discrepancies between the 'literal', 'visceral' street scenes and the more 'lyrical', 'symbolic' theatre scenes, this prologue potentially undermines the ontological reality of the latter. According to one confused 2013 film festival reviewer, 'half the time it feels like we're meant to understand that the characters are play-acting, not going through the literal reality of their story'.[25]

Perhaps with such criticisms in mind, a crucial revision made in the 2015 DVD/streaming video version of *H4* was to cut the opening prologue sequence, thus removing the implication that the theatre scenes are less real than the on-location scenes.

However, while clarifying to some degree the production's use of space, the revision wreaks havoc with its use of time. *H4*'s initial script takes a comparatively straightforward approach to chronology. Beginning with key events from Shakespeare's *Richard II*, it proceeds in order through selected portions of *Henry IV, Parts 1 and 2*, packaging them as 'the coming of age story of a son destined to lead a nation'.[26] The 2015 version replaces the story of Richard's deposition – which is transposed into a series of brief flashbacks later in the narrative – with a new preliminary sequence. A series of newspaper front pages dated during the first week of October 2015 is intercut with the opening credits as well as a series of video and audio clips of civil unrest. Boots stomp on the pavement, a bomb explodes in a city square, police in riot gear fire tear gas at crowds, protesters march, sirens blare and helicopter blades whir threateningly in the sky. Instead of providing backstory with respect to the past, the revised opening contextualizes the film's events with respect to a present that is, disorientingly, simultaneously diegetic and extradiegetic.

The (fictional) paper is titled *The International Gazette*; the masthead further identifies it as 'Shakespeare's English daily, established 1922', owned by the 'Global View News Group' and 'published in Watts'. Each headline describes a key event from the film's narrative with the byline 'John Masro reporting from Crenshaw'. Directly below, each cover story transcribes the relevant act, scene and lines from Shakespeare's play in the typographic style of old playscripts, while a corresponding image from later in the film, initially in colour, morphs into a black-and-white newspaper photograph with an explanatory caption. For example, the first cover page shown, dated 1 October 2015, is headlined 'King Henry IV Postpones His Holy Land Expedition' with the subtitle 'Rebels Attack the King'. The story features lines from the opening scene of *1 Henry IV*. A photograph from the original prologue, showing Lennix as the newly aged King leaning forward at his desk, has a caption reading, 'King Henry calls for chief cabinet members to prepare for war'. Each complete cover page not only provides a snapshot linking a specific moment in Shakespeare's text to a specific moment in the film; it also introduces both global and local geographies as it connects a diffuse Shakespearean past with an immediate American present.

That present, moreover, invokes a specific historical context that postdates *H4*'s original 2012 release. Some of the intercut stock footage references the Black Lives Matter movement, which 'was not in the Zeitgeist' during the film's initial shooting in December of 2010'.[27] Even more specifically, it references 'Rise Up October': a three-day series of mass protests that took place in October 2015, the same period referenced by the newspaper cover pages. Protesters hold aloft a poster featuring an enlarged black-and-white photo of Natasha McKenna, an African American woman who died in police custody earlier that year. Other protest signs read, 'Rise up. Stop Police Terror' and 'Which side are you on?'. While some footage directly invokes the year 2015 and particular places like New York City, however, other clips are difficult to localize in terms of both date and geography. The 'universality' of this type of violence and civil unrest is clearly also part of the point.

The same mix of video clips recurs midway through the revised film, right before the Battle of Shrewsbury – reconceived as the 'Battle of Compton'. Accompanying these visual excerpts of twentieth- and twenty-first-century race-based violence, on the soundtrack a newscaster narrates as follows: 'Breaking news. Today another round of fights between the insurgent Hotspur's militant force and King Henry's national guard broke out. Large plumes of smoke were seen in the downtown Los Angeles area. There is no word so far on military or civilian casualties at this time.' As Lennix notes in his audio commentary on the 2015 film, Black Lives Matter began during Obama's presidency. 'Black leadership' doesn't preclude the necessity of civil unrest.[28]

By linking the climactic action of Shakespeare's Battle of Shrewsbury to this series of displaced moments from US history, moreover, *H4* potentially provides a larger commentary on Shakespeare, racism and violence. These video clips are both diegetic representations of the events of *H4*'s narrative and extradiegetic context for the film as a whole. As such, they represent two alternative versions of Shakespeare's relationship to violence through time. According to one possible reading, they demonstrate the timelessness of the type of violence depicted in Shakespeare's plays – the presumed result of human nature or, as Jan Kott asserts, of Shakespeare's paradoxical status as 'our contemporary'.[29] On the other hand, they represent the particular result of a series of human choices that have cumulatively given rise to the forces of institutional racism – choices that include a four-century history of performing Shakespeare's Henriad. In other words, Shakespeare is both an expression of the universal human condition and a particular cog in a cycle of violence that so desperately needs 'a stop'.

The latter possibility gains further impetus through another aspect of *H4*'s 2015 revision. In the 2012 film, bridge shots from a moving vehicle highlight, documentary-style, various particularities of the LA Black experience. Neighbourhood landmarks are prominently featured, including Skid Row's Union Mission, the 'Great Wall of Crenshaw' (a streetside mural featuring iconic historical African Americans), the bizarre metal spires of Watts Towers and the curiously transplanted Watts Obelisk – ancient Egyptian symbols and all – on S. Wilmington Avenue.[30] In between, the handheld camera offers glimpses of daily life: kids shooting hoops, a city bus passing by and a man walking down an urban street. In order to frame its narrative with archival riot footage, the 2015 version of *H4* largely eliminates such details, thereby communicating the universality of the violence plaguing the Black community across both space and time.

A disjunct persists, however, between the temporally and geographically unlocalizable aspects of the stock footage, on the one hand, and 'to-the-minute' reporting of the interpolated newscaster's voiceover, on the other. Along with persistent tension between the 'universal' setting of the theatre and the 'particular' spaces of various LA locations, this disjunct adds to the revised *H4*'s unsettled presentation of both space and time. The film's link to Shakespeare further exacerbates this geographic and temporal instability – as exemplified by those newspaper front-page shots which present text directly culled from the plays as on-site, up-to-date reporting from Crenshaw in October 2015. At the very moment of offering Shakespeare's timelessness in this hyperbolic form, the play text's presentation in old-fashioned typeface immediately calls that purported location and date into question.

In the end, the revised *H4*'s desire to foreground the timeliness as well as timelessness of its story results in a multimedia framing which, through excess, almost undoes its intent. A reprise of the newspaper device immediately follows King Henry IV's death. This time the headlines read, 'Prince Hal named King in H4 succession: The King Dies Peacefully in the Arms of his Two Sons'. There is no irony whatsoever here; the headline describes precisely what we have just seen, as does a photo of the king's final resting pose in his royal bed along with an excerpt from the very dialogue we have just witnessed from Act 4, Scene 3 of *2 Henry IV*. A close shot of this newspaper image accompanied by traffic noises on the soundtrack pulls back to reveal the paper's location in a news box on a street corner, as a hand reaches inside to extract a copy of *The International Gazette*. Not insignificantly, there is an apparent typo in the paper's date, which reads 'December 31, 2061' instead of '2016'. The forward jump of nearly half a century instead of a single year, which suggests a more future-oriented transposition than the show's creators likely intended, underscores an already palpable strain in the film's time-straddling chronology.

Alongside TV news and newspapers, well on their way to being outdated media even in 2015, other efforts are made in the film to showcase modern communication devices. A rebel messenger takes notes in one scene on a tablet PC, and Hotspur's Act 2, Scene 3 reading of the refusal letter from a would-be conspirator takes place via text messages on a smartphone – albeit an already outdated Blackberry. This technology is emphasized in the film's second cut by inserting close-ups of the handheld device, rendering both the texts and the smartphone more visible. Along with the likelihood that many viewings of the 2015 version of *H4* will themselves take place, via various streaming video services, on some version of a computer screen, this pastiche of media modes highlights *H4*'s race to catch up with an ever-receding present. In its exertions to establish Shakespeare's timelessness and timeliness alike, *H4* reveals self-reflexive anxieties about its own particular, self-inscribed temporality.

'That [our] great body of [the] state may go'

Further complicating *H4*'s evolving portrayal of history with respect to the ever-moving target of the present is the timeline of the film's distribution. *H4* was initially well received at both the Shakespeare Association of America conference in Boston and the International Shakespeare Conference in Stratford-upon-Avon, coinciding with London's Summer Olympics of 2012. It reached a somewhat broader audience through its October and November 2013 film festival screenings in Chicago and Memphis. However, although the 2015 revision of *H4* eventually made it to Amazon in March of 2020, a planned distribution deal between Lennix's production company, Exponent Media Group and Nehst Media's Digiplex chain never bore fruit; as of this writing, the film has not been released in the commercial cinema.[31]

Yet the story of *H4* is far from over. The 'digital revolution' in film culture,[32] which has only accelerated in the wake of the Covid-19 pandemic, is reshaping the landscape of viewing practices just as *H4* has become widely available via streaming video – and also as the ongoing issues to which the film directly speaks have risen to the surface of cultural awareness. There are thus many possibilities, especially for academics, in promoting *H4*'s continued dissemination. Ayanna Thompson emphasized in her 2011 interview with *The Arizona Republic* that the film's primary audience was from its origins 'expected to be in secondary schools and universities' – 'a great way to initiate conversation in the classroom'.[33] As indicated by the two essays quoted earlier, through my own use of *H4* in this setting I have seen its contemporary relevance inspire students as they grapple with American politics.

When I taught *H4* for the first time in the fall of 2020, my class's viewing of the film happened to coincide with the tumult surrounding that year's presidential election – decided in so many places by razor-thin margins where the Black vote was often a critical factor. Never had the internal political divisions represented in Shakespeare's *Henry IV* plays seemed so immediate and pressing. That semester one of my students, Devin Gaffney, wrote her final essay on what she saw as parallels between the conclusion of *H4* and the election of Kamala Harris as the first Black as well as the first female American vice president (VP). Gaffney's focus was the Chief Justice as played by biracial actress Victoria Platt, whose circumscribed yet symbolically momentous power she compared to that of the newly elected VP. 'On her own, Kamala Harris wasn't able to win the Democratic Presidential nomination, but running behind Joe Biden, she was able to become the next Vice President of the United States', Gaffney observed. Similarly, in the first half of *H4*, Prince Hal is dismissive of Platt's Chief Justice. However, 'The relationship between Hal and Chief Justice pivots from *Part One* to *Part Two*. Once Hal is given the title of King, he seems to gain a different level of respect for the female Chief Justice. He chooses to entrust her to "bear the balance of the sword (*2 Henry IV* VI.ii.102)"'.[34] Indeed, the scene of the new Henry V bowing to Platt's Chief Justice is, for Harry Lennix, the film's 'most significant moment'[35] (Figure 6). Gaffney's link between Kamala Harris and *H4*'s brown female Chief Justice aptly underscores not only both how far America has come and how far we still have to go in terms of placing women of colour in positions of national power but also how crucial representation is. My two biracial daughters, then five years old, stayed up the night of 7 November 2020 to watch the first televised speech of a vice president who looked like them. *H4* is a film I plan to show them one day in part for similar reasons.

Both the limitations and possibilities of an empowered Black future in *H4* are encapsulated in slight but significant alterations of two key lines in Hal's last speech, as he addresses an unspecified audience that includes the film's viewership on the other side of the camera's lens. The lines

FIGURE 6 *Henry V kneels to the Chief Justice.* H4, *directed by Paul Quinn.* © *Triumvirate Pictures 2015. All rights reserved. Screen grab.*

Now call we our high court of *parliament*
And let us choose such limbs of noble counsel,
That *the* great body of *our* state may go
In equal rank with the best-governed nation

(5.2.133–6, ITALICS MINE)

become

Now call we our high court of *advisors*
And let us choose such limbs of noble counsel,
That *our* great body of *the* state may go
In equal rank with the best-governed nation.

More significant even than the change from 'parliament' to 'advisors' is the pronoun/article switch, which encapsulates the tension between two distinct models of the body politic. In Shakespeare's *2 Henry IV*, Hal deploys the royal 'we' – here, the royal 'our' – to describe his ownership of the state, while the definite article modifies, and thereby further aggrandizes, 'the great body', of which he is head. The transposition of 'our' and 'the' in Amad Jackson's version of the speech renders 'our', instead, an inclusive pronoun that numbers Hal among the people of the state he now leads.

One of my fall 2020 students, Kyle DiPofi, identified an additional significance in the king's use of pronouns. A 'shift in the connotation of the word "our"' from the royal, singular 'our' of 'our high court of advisors' to the inclusive, plural 'our' of 'our great body of the state', DiPofi noted, 'marks the separation between the values of Shakespeare's England and *H4*'s America, and helps to further the idea of the American nation as a place that has a role for everyone in equal measure'.[36] In numbering the king as merely one of many members of the body politic, this use of 'our' adumbrates a distinction between republican and monarchical understandings of nation. Whether by design or by a slip of the tongue, this moment of the text in flux encapsulates on a micro scale what Thompson has described as the productive 'instability' of Shakespeare in contemporary America.[37] Instead of postulating any static universal or timeless values, *H4* reveals both space and time in Shakespeare's histories to be dynamic and therefore mutable – ripe, in other words, for 'an infinite variety of appropriations'.[38]

'The Coming of the White Man'

H4's approach to the history adaptation not only unsettles its own historical moment's relationship to Shakespeare but also provides a lens through which to better apprehend how the histories have been adapted in the recent past. That lens is especially applicable to Gus Van Sant's *My Own Private Idaho* (1991), which like *H4* is a distinctly American *Henry IV* conflation concerned with Shakespeare's purported universality. This early contribution to the 1990s Shakespearean cinematic resurgence additionally shares with *H4* an interest in race, but from an alternative perspective. By transposing Shakespeare to an American setting, *My Own Private Idaho* reveals both Shakespeare's and America's intersecting enmeshment in constructions of whiteness.

Unlike Lennix, Van Sant has not (to my knowledge) publicly expressed a desire to demonstrate Shakespeare's universality by adapting his plays to a human experience outside the range of dominant, normative cultural values.[39] However, that seems to be precisely what his film does. As mentioned previously, *My Own Private Idaho* reimagines Shakespeare's Eastcheap inhabitants as homeless young male sex workers in contemporary urban Oregon. As the film's Falstaff stand-in, itinerant gay drug dealer and dubious father figure Bob Pigeon (William Richert) presides over this decidedly fallen crew. The world of Henry IV's Westminster court undergoes a corresponding metamorphosis. Prince Hal is reconceived as Scott Favor (Keanu Reeves), the only son and heir of the wealthy but moribund, wheelchair-bound Mayor of Portland, Jack Favor (Tom Troupe). Scott's 'reformation' as the inheritor of his father's wealth and social position plays out as the exchange of the down-and-out life of a seemingly homosexual street hustler for that of an upper-class existence and normative heterosexual marriage by the end of the film (1.2.205). In a line interpolated into an adapted version of Hal and Falstaff's opening conversation about the 'time of day' in Act 1, Scene 2 of *1 Henry IV*, Scott at one point himself articulates an expression of the Bard's universality by stating, 'We are timeless' (1.2.1).

Complicating this picture, however, is the film's far from straightforward adaptation of *Henry IV*. It combines the Hal/Falstaff narrative with the story of Mike Waters (River Phoenix), Scott Favor's gay, homeless, narcoleptic best friend and fellow street hustler, whom Scott accompanies on what turns into an intercontinental search for Mike's mother. Scholars have made various attempts to locate Shakespeare's *1* and *2 Henry IV* in portions of *My Own Private Idaho* that don't directly arise from these two plays. Mike, for instance, has been read as taking on aspects of characters including Ned Poins, Hotspur, Doll Tearsheet and even Falstaff himself.[40] Nonetheless, following Van Sant's own description of the film as a collage of 'three different screenplays' – one about Mike and Scott, one about a narcoleptic street hustler, and one a 'modernized version of *Henry IV*', with 'segments of each ... mixed and cut together'[41] – criticism of the film as a Shakespeare adaptation has, for the most part, separately considered its 'Shakespearean' and 'non-Shakespearean' elements as components of a larger postmodern bricolage narrative.

Via both its Shakespearean and postmodern heritage, *My Own Private Idaho*, like *H4*, convolutes any straightforward understanding of time or space. Numerous historical moments, Shakespeare's among them, intersect in the film's nonlinear time scheme. Despite being released in 1991, the street culture *My Own Private Idaho* represents is primarily that of the 1970s and 1980s, later 'quashed by urban renewal and AIDS'.[42] Geography is also up for grabs. A series of vividly coloured title cards identifying each of the film's settings does little to alleviate the anxieties of dislocation when Mike falls asleep only to wake up somewhere else altogether with no idea how he got there. Moreover, for all this apparent movement, narrative progress is never achieved. The film begins and ends in the same place on the same stretch of road in rural Idaho, a road that Mike speculates 'probably goes all around the world'.[43]

Regarding its status as a Henriad adaptation, *My Own Private Idaho* has most often been read as mediated through yet another work, Orson Welles's *Chimes at Midnight* (1965). Portions of its representation of the Boar's Head Tavern scenes from Acts 1 and 2 of *Henry IV, Part 1* as well as the Gads Hill's robbery and its aftermath are nearly a 'frame for frame imitation' of the same scenes from Welles's movie. But whereas Welles constructs his tavern world out of conscious nostalgia for a bygone 'merrie England', Van Sant, according to Kathy Howlett, 'intentionally and obviously degrades Welles' vision of a utopian tavern world'.[44] That degradation is, moreover, an Americanization: a transposition of both Shakespeare's and Welles's stories about England and English values into what Andrew Barnaby describes as 'a dark fable of the American dream'.[45] Viewing the film through the additional lens of Lennix, Quinn and Thompson's *H4* allows the racial component of *My Own Private Idaho*'s critique of the American dream to come more clearly into view.

As a Shakespeare adaptation of the early 1990s, *My Own Private Idaho* occupies a peculiar position within that decade's cinematic Shakespearean renaissance. Writing in 1997, scholar Curtis Breight situates Van Sant's film with reference to both the conservative politics and 'straight narratives' of Branagh's *Henry V* (1989) and the concomitant 'declaration of cultural wars' by right-wing politicians in the United States. He argues that by 'privileging the lower class world to reveal its inhabitants as social victims of institutional power', *My Own Private Idaho* exposes contemporary America as the product of imperial history traceable back through 'the early modern dawn of European imperialism, the Renaissance', whose vision of global conquest 'was ideologically based on the Roman Empire'.[46]

According to Breight's argument, with which I am largely in agreement and with which my subsequent analysis is frequently in dialogue, the film accomplishes this critique largely indirectly, through 'gradual accretion' of 'images, allusions, jokes, and songs' through the entirety of its narrative. For instance, the soundtrack includes 'multiple repeats of "America the Beautiful" at key moments in the film, played slowly and fragmentarily', as well as quintessentially American cowboy tunes such as Tex Owen's 'Cattle Call' and 'Home on the Range'. Shakespeare's role in the story, far from limited to the Hal/Falstaff bits, also appears in images of Tudor and/or Elizabethan culture – including references to Shakespeare's plays themselves – sprinkled throughout the film. Mike's brother/father lives in 'Globe, Idaho' and at one point Scott drinks from a bottle of Falstaff Beer. The British Empire is referenced through disparate elements such as a 'wall clock . . . featuring an "RC" or Royal Crown (Cola) advertisement' and a 'British flag' T-shirt worn by a street kid named Digger, whose name recalls for Breight the seventeenth-century English agrarian socialist movement whose members went by the same moniker. Finally, the journey to find Mike's mother takes the protagonists all the way to the 'cradle of Western imperialism', the city of Rome, where Scott meets an Italian woman whom he later marries.⁴⁷

Conspicuously missing from Breight's account, however, is the status of race in *My Own Private Idaho*, especially with respect to its cast. While the major roles are all played by white or apparently white actors, an 'Indian Cop' (Oliver Kirk) appears in two key scenes, and the rest of the film includes scattered non-speaking characters of colour everywhere *except* among the Portland street hustlers who stand in for Shakespeare's tavern crew. Also significant is the fact that one of the film's two main protagonists, Keanu Reeves's Scott Favor/'Prince Hal', presents as white but also can compellingly be read as a racially 'other' character. Particularly with twenty-first-century hindsight, such casting choices are legible as part of *My Own Private Idaho*'s discourse of both American and Shakespearean culture, where they are integral aspects of its representation of class, sexuality and nation.

One frequently cited image early in the film highlights Van Sant's own seriocomic interest in the intersections among race and these various categories. In this scene Mike awakens from a narcoleptic episode in the arms of Scott. They are at the foot of a monument an April 1989 screenplay draft describes as 'a statue . . . of two Indians pointing out across the horizon', which is realized in the film as a sculpture of a single Native American astride a heavily antlered elk.⁴⁸ On the statue's pedestal is the conspicuous legend, 'The Coming of the White Man' (Figure 7). This extended shot, which lasts a full thirty seconds, has numerous intertwined implications. Foremost for the film's director is a sexual pun that is also a specific, localized reference to Portland's queer culture. Although born in Louisville, Kentucky, Van Sant grew up in Portland and considers the city his hometown. As the director told *Rolling Stone* magazine in 1991, the statue he intended to use in the shot is the one described in the screenplay, a bronze statue in Portland's Washington Park 'that used to be a gay pickup scene. "It's of two Indians, one pointing off into the distance, and it's called *Coming of the White Man*. I always thought it was ironic"'. Because the original statue was 'surrounded by too much greenery', to make the shot work Van Sant instead had a crew member wearing 'Indian garb' and body paint sit astride Portland's downtown Elk Fountain statue, which has no rider, and altered the original engraving.⁴⁹

While Van Sant did not specify what he believes is 'ironic' about the original statue, as recreated in *My Own Private Idaho* its

FIGURE 7 *'The Coming of the White Man'*. My Own Private Idaho, directed by Gus Van Sant. © New Line Cinema 1991. All rights reserved. Screen grab.

irony functions on multiple levels. As a broad punning reference to the male sexual experience, it is also a sly in-joke regarding Portland's location-specific gay subculture. As a monument to dispossessed Native Americans, the statue's legend backhandedly commemorates those who dispossessed them. Paralleling the status of Shakespeare's Henriad in the film, it is not only a piece of Americana but simultaneously an appropriation of Renaissance European art – that is, Michelangelo's *Pietà*, a statue of Mary cradling Christ's crucified body which Scott and Mike's posture at the statue's base mimics.[50] The pun on 'coming' ultimately links Christ's future messianic return, the genocidal arrival of Europeans in the Western Hemisphere and the orgasms of both a single fictional sex worker and a whole community of real-life gay men. In the process, moreover, the shot demonstrates a clear if tongue-in-cheek awareness of whiteness as a racial identity.

Going down on history

Whiteness also informs another moment in *My Own Private Idaho*, in which multiple embedded historical and cultural references intersect to create unexpected meanings. In a memorable expository scene, cover models on gay skinmags on display in an adult bookstore come to life and speak. The magazine titles are things like *Torso*, *Honcho*, *Mandate*, *Joyboy* and *Butch*. Several of the models are also characters in the film; their conversation about their motives for selling their bodies takes on multiple levels of significance.

From his position on the cover of *Male Call*, the Prince Hal figure Scott begins by insisting that for him having sex with men is exclusively about money: 'It's when you start doing things for free that you start to grow wings. . . . You grow wings and become a fairy.' When his friend Mike, summoned to speak from his own magazine cover, calls him out on his hypocrisy – in fact, as a wealthy heir to his family fortune, Scott doesn't really need to earn money at all – the other cover boys join in, taunting, catcalling and whistling. One model, later revealed to be the minor character identified in the credits as Digger, asks disparagingly, 'So what are you doing on the cover of that magazine, slumming?' Unabashed, Scott looks squarely at the audience as the camera zooms in. He replies, 'Actually Mikey's right. I am going to inherit money. A lot of money'.

The thematic focus in this scene on class and sexuality all but elides the salient fact that every one of the models is white. That is, everyone except for Scott himself as embodied by the actor Keanu Reeves, to whose non-white ethnicity I allude previously. Although he often plays white characters, Reeves inhabits a racially ambiguous representative space due to his transnational, multiethnic status. As Julian Cha summarizes, 'His father is of Chinese and Hawaiian descent, and his mother is Caucasian; he carries citizenship in the U.S., Canada, and England'. Reeves's ability nonetheless to '"pass" as white' and to 'dodge having his body marked by "otherness" and its subsequent stereotypes' is, for R. L. Rutsky, an 'example in Hollywood's long history of effacing the ethnicity of its stars while retaining some measure of their "exoticism"'. But it also endows him with a 'lack of fixity that is often figured in [his] films' emphasis on movement'.[51]

Although *My Own Private Idaho* emphasizes Scott's geographic movement as well as his fluidity across barriers of sexuality and social status, a variety of the film's creative choices seemingly obscure his equally ambiguous race. Scott's father, Jack Favor, is played by an unambiguously white actor (although the ethnicity of Scott's mother, who appears only in a brief veiled shot, remains unclear). Scott's whiteness would therefore seem to mark his privileged status as Portland's 'heir apparent'. Finally, Scott is presented as a Shakespearean figure at a time when cinematic Shakespeare was almost exclusively the province of white performers. Yet in the skinmag scene in which Scott openly admits to misrepresenting his privileged identity in the role of street hustler, his magazine, which features a Western theme, depicts him 'passing' in yet another way – by playing the archetypically white, American role of the cowboy. The cover displays a bare-torsoed, erect-postured Keanu Reeves, hand on abdomen, jeans suggestively unzipped below and a black Stetson prominently perched on his head; the headlines read, 'Ready to Ride', 'Homo on the Range' and 'Cowboys and Indians All Tied Up'. Reeves's performance of whiteness becomes obliquely visible alongside his character's various other performative identities.

Scott's Shakespearean role-playing, moreover, intersects with his other theatrical poses – to which another magazine, the fall issue of *Torso*, calls direct attention. This cover features two shirtless models with a red theatre curtain and movie spotlight in the background. One of the models is Digger, sporting girlishly wavy long blond hair and gazing seductively outward at the viewer. He wears a distinctly crown-like green-and-black hat and holds both a sword and a glittering chalice. His companion, a taller young man with a more contemporary, butch blond haircut, possessively grips Digger's shoulders and stares down at him from behind. The cover lines on this magazine are all spoofs on Shakespeare play titles that might potentially describe its cover scene: in the largest typeface, 'King Leer', followed by 'Two Gentlemen of Pomona', 'Pleasure for Pleasure' and 'Julio and Ron Dewet'. Also adding to the entire scene's Shakespearean quality is the soundtrack: a jaunty Renaissance-style melody plays throughout, music that is reprised during the later scenes directly taken from *1* and *2 Henry IV*.

The status of Shakespeare with respect to the cover models'/street hustlers' various intersectional identities is itself heterogeneous. On the one hand, the transformation of Shakespearean titles into gay skinmag soundbites takes a dig at the Bard's contemporary highbrow cultural status, appropriating the plays as an especially uncouth, non-normative form of lowbrow culture. In the process, as Breight points out, Shakespeare becomes an object of *My Own Private Idaho*'s anti-capitalist, anti-imperialist critique. Alongside

Scott and Digger, Mike appears mid-pole dance on a magazine called *G-String* along with the taglines 'Pillars of the Roman Empire' and 'Go Down On History'. The proximity among the Shakespearean, American and Roman magazine themes is 'used to help establish imperial and sexual connections across two millennia'. Situating these models, like the street hustlers they represent, as the victims of a capitalist system that requires them to sell their bodies to survive, the scene demonstrates how this system has harnessed their images in order to perpetuate an imperialist agenda. It is notable that of the three identifiable cover boys – Scott, Mike and Digger – the latter two are presented in ways that portray their victimhood. Mike's shirtless pose against the pole 'evok[es] the crucifixion', while Digger, despite the paraphernalia of monarchy, is portrayed as the feminized object of his fellow cover model's sexual aggression.[52] Only Scott, who in 'real life' is a member of the entitled upper classes, adopts an uncompromised pose of power. His black hat, via common cinematic shorthand, further suggests villainy.

In stressing these youths' status as victims of imperialist/capitalist culture in the magazine scene, Breight's argument reveals a tension both within its own logic and within *My Own Private Idaho*'s appropriation of Shakespeare. While Breight elsewhere insists that the film deploys Shakespeare's criticisms of Renaissance England's unequal society against modern American structures of power,[53] his analysis of the magazine cover scene positions Shakespeare from quite a different vantage. Here, the Bard functions as an agent of Renaissance imperialism's forward propagation into contemporary American capitalist culture and thus as an object of the film's critique rather than its mouthpiece.

For like *H4*, *My Own Private Idaho* reveals Shakespeare as a simultaneous agent and critic of the imperialist impulse – with constructions of whiteness at the heart of this contradiction. The hustlers' status at the intersection between white privilege and more obvious forms of victimization emerges most starkly in the scene immediately following the extended 'Coming of the White Man' shot, during which Digger (Michael Parker, wearing his Union Jack T-shirt) and another street hustler played by Scott Patrick Green provide what appear to be improvised narrations about their traumatic first 'dates' as sex workers. Filmed documentary-style in a Portland restaurant, each intercut anecdote concludes with the young man in question being raped by his client. Green describes his client-turned-assailant as a 'big Black guy' with a lot of drugs as well as money. After explaining how the man forced him to perform fellatio under the threat of violence, he repeats, 'This Black guy – he had a big old fucking cock and shit', miming the man's penis size with his index fingers spaced an improbable distance apart.

While the racist stereotypes invoked in Green's story appear to be a function of unscripted speech, their inclusion in the film is a choice on the part of the film's creators that must be considered alongside other choices. One such choice is the original inclusion and subsequent elimination of an episode in the April 1989 screenplay draft that depicts 'three Black Boys' in Las Vegas attempting an armed robbery on the sleeping Mike. The assault on Mike includes both physical violence – the Black Boys cut Mike's hands with a knife when he refuses to surrender his duffle bag – and verbal violence when they call him both 'white boy' and 'faggot'.[54] The elimination of this scene in the film's final cut suggests a discomfort with the stereotyping attribution of violence to a non-white racial group. Yet the troubling stereotype of Black male brutality is preserved in the second street kid's narration. There, casual racism along with the experience of sexual violence are presented as inextricable components of life on the streets.

The street hustlers' role in these documentary-style scenes also has a direct Shakespearean parallel. As they break the fourth wall to address the film's audience, both Digger and Green's unnamed character function as modern versions of Falstaff's Boy. The Boy, as we have seen, likewise describes dealing with older men who want forcibly to 'serve [anally penetrate]' him – older men whose bodies he disparages with racializing language (*H5* 3.2.29). What Breight argues is Van Sant's revision of Shakespeare's idea of the nation to comprise 'young people intensely passionate and intensely victimized'[55] remains a nation where whiteness is defined in opposition to an alien, criminalized Blackness.

Subsequent scenes that incorporate dialogue directly from *1* and *2 Henry IV* are framed by these moments that place both Shakespeare's coercive cultural capital and racializing constructions on display. *My Own Private Idaho*'s tavern world is therefore set up to be assessed for its own contradictions – and such contradictions prove numerous. Although the text used in these scenes exposes the 'menacing forms of power and terror exercised by Prince Hal and Falstaff in *1 Henry IV*', Van Sant's version of Eastcheap also incorporates the 'warm atmosphere of Welles's festive tavern world'.[56] While not exactly 'merrie old England', that world remains conspicuously white as well as mostly male. The only exceptions are Jane Lightwork (Sally Curtice, a stand-in for the Hostess whose name, transposed from Jane Nightwork, is borrowed from a line from 2 Henry IV) and a single female sex worker named Denise (Jessica Makinson) – who at one point exchanges a kiss with Scott to highlight the latter's not strictly 'homo' sexuality, thereby counteracting Mike as an alternative, heteronormative Doll.

These rare female bodies excepted, the social composition of the 'tavern crew' is therefore as self-consciously Shakespearean as the scene's borrowed dialogue. Moreover, along with reflecting the all-white, all-male acting companies on the Shakespearean stage, these performers invoke the simultaneously fetishized and marginalized bodies of Renaissance boy actors. As David Roman points out, the hustlers themselves, their skinmag avatars and the boyish adult celebrity actors who play both Mike and Scott in the film reinvent the boy player's commodified sexuality in contemporary terms.[57] At the very moment that My Own Private Idaho seems to be constructing a Welles-like nostalgic moment, it thus maintains an ironic, critical distance that at times becomes self-implicating. While the film uses subversive elements in Shakespeare's dialogue to comment on contemporary social injustice, it simultaneously highlights the contradictions embedded in both Shakespeare's social commentary and its own.

Such contradictions infuse the film's deployment in these 'tavern' scenes of the trope of universality briefly cited earlier. When Scott awakens Bob Pigeon from his slumbers, the pair commences with an updated version of Hal and Falstaff's initial conversation in 1 Henry IV:

BOB   How are you? What time is it?
SCOTT   What do you care? Why, you wouldn't even look at a clock unless hours were lines of coke, dials looked like the signs of gay bars, or time itself was a fair hustler in black leather. Isn't that right, Bob? There's no reason to know the time. We are timeless.

While the most obvious alterations of the text transform the sack-guzzling, woman-wanting Falstaff into the cocaine-sniffing, man-desiring Bob, the exchange also spotlights the notion of Shakespeare's timelessness without clearly endorsing it. Having the quintessentially role-playing Scott claim to embody Shakespearean universality suggests that the idea may not withstand scrutiny. Hence Breight's claim that *My Own Private Idaho* 'interprets the *Henriad* as a timeless story about dispossessed people'[58] must be qualified. In the very act of deploying the trope of timelessness, the film calls it squarely into question. Moreover, that questioning involves a self-consciously white Shakespearean aesthetic that always threatens to be undercut by the ambiguous race of Scott Favor/Keanu Reeves himself.

Scott's potentially performative whiteness is supplemented by the presence of *My Own Private Idaho*'s most obvious racially othered character, the Indian Cop. We first encounter this figure when Mike and Scott flee Portland on a stolen motorcycle to visit Mike's brother in Idaho. After the motorcycle breaks down, the boys are forced to spend the night camping out by the roadside. While their subsequent intimate fireside discussion in which Mike obliquely admits his homoerotic love for his friend has been a frequent topic of scholarly analysis, less attention has been paid to how the entire sequence treats Native American otherness. In the script, the following directions set the scene: 'At night, Scott and Mike sit next to a fire they have made on the side of the road. We can hear Indians in the distance dancing and chanting a song. . . . The music is getting louder. It sounds like a war chant.'[59] Dimly audible as the backdrop of the friends' conversation, the chant highlights an important tension between the dispossessed American natives and the dispossessed white boys of Portland, who enter the natives' space as colonizers.

The next scene realizes in comedic terms the actual confrontation between 'Indian' and white man. The following morning, as Scott still unsuccessfully attempts to start the motorcycle, a Native American state trooper drives up behind him and Mike. Their distinct responses to this authority figure underscore the two characters' vastly different senses of their own privilege. Meanwhile the cop's response to Scott and Mike subtly demonstrates the cultural chasm between himself and both young men. The moment Mike sees the approaching police vehicle, he takes off through the open field. When a narcoleptic spell hits and he collapses face down 'in a cloud of dust', the screenplay notes, 'The policeman, a full blooded

American Indian, seems amused at his power'.[60] Meanwhile Scott holds a cordial conversation in which he asks for the Indian Cop's assistance with the faltering motorcycle.

Although the cop is nothing but helpful as he assists Scott in starting the bike before driving away, the scene clearly marks him as a figure of otherness. Even in the absence of stage directions, his long black ponytail and slightly accented deadpan drawl identify him as an outsider. As the physical embodiment of the war chants, he exemplifies an alien/alienated aspect of the Idaho world related to, but distinct from, signs of the white man's presence in the Great American Desert, such as the empty houses within Mike's various dreamscapes and the repeating figure of the road itself.

The Indian Cop is also yet another figure of dispossession – the 'Coming of the White Man' statue rendered flesh and transported into the film's present. Stripped of his heritage, he is reduced to wielding the modicum of power bestowed upon him in white America's empire: to inspire fear in white motorists or, as in a later scene, to give them tickets for speeding. The script implies that his knowledge of his own otherness is the true source of his amusement – more particularly, his awareness of the simultaneous ironies that he has power over his oppressors and that this power really isn't power at all. Although the Indian Cop scene is not directly Shakespearean, moreover, its significance is heavily inflected by Scott and Mike's status as Shakespearean figures. That is, they are figures of what has become, through history, Shakespeare's status as the ultimate 'White Man' – whose 'coming' is simultaneously a bawdy joke and a menacing truth in a not entirely post-colonial world.

The coming of the Black man?

While Kirk's 'Indian Cop' is the sole obviously non-white speaking role in *My Own Private Idaho,* he is not the only visible character of colour in the film. Scattered BIPOC actors noticeably populate all the Portland scenes except for the tavern crew scenes from *Henry IV.* Moments including diversely cast extras include a scene modified from *Richard II*, where Jack Favor asks his police chief and aides – one of whom is Black – to locate his missing wayward son, and Falstaff's banishment scene, which takes place at a posh Portland restaurant where several faces of colour appear among the mostly white onlookers. Similarly, a Black woman and man are silent but visually prominent attendees at Mayor Favor's funeral. Despite the minor nature of each of these roles, collectively they are not inconsequential. As I have suggested previously, these casting choices frame the exclusive whiteness of the crew of Portland street hustlers as an anachronistic anomaly – not unlike Jane Lightwork's Elizabethan collar or Bob Pigeon's prominent codpiece.

This distinction ends, however, in the film's penultimate scene, which tellingly involves another key figure of racial otherness: a Black accordion player who subversively officiates at Bob Pigeon's funeral. Like Hal in Shakespeare's *Henry IV*, at the end of *My Own Private Idaho* Scott loses both his biological father and his chief father figure – the man whom, even in the banishment scene, he claims to love more than the man who sired him. Jack Favor dies off screen; Bob Pigeon's death from a heart attack occurs on screen immediately following – and presumably as a result of – Scott's public rejection of his friendship. The staging of these men's funerals at the same time and in the same cemetery both brings the story of paternal loss to a dramatic, tragicomic denouement and emphasizes the connection as well as the opposition between Scott's two dads.

Tellingly, in Van Sant's version of *Henry IV* the 'king' rather than the Falstaff figure is physically disabled. Jack Favor's wheelchair marks not only his moribund status but also the demotion and hollowness of the power and privilege he represents. The fact that he shares a first name as well as initials with the original Jack Falstaff signifies that Mayor Favor, too, even more than Bob Pigeon, is a figure of fallen masculinity. Not unlike Angus Macfadyen's Falstaff two decades later, he is also, the funeral scene suggests, a figure of fallen Shakespearean whiteness.

Officially, of course, the two men's ceremonies are entirely separate affairs. The formal interment of the mayor is presided over by a collared priest and attended by several rows of mourners in sombre black attire. Flanked by his veiled mother on one side and his solemn Italian wife on the other, Favor's son and heir Scott is the focal point among them. Meanwhile, in a less fashionable corner of the cemetery, a motley gang, including Mike Waters, participates in a much rowdier celebration of the life of Bob Pigeon. Presiding over the latter is the most visible as well as the most audible Black character in Van Sant's film. An accordion-playing man in a black suit and red and white polka-dotted shirt makes his first appearance standing on Bob's plain wooden coffin. Conspicuously idiosyncratic even within the crowd of drifters, he performs at the centre of the riot that disrupts the rites over the dead mayor a few yards away.

Juxtaposed against the officiating priest's solemn intonations from the King James Bible is a song in which the accordion player leads his own congregation of the urban dispossessed. The song's only lyric is the single word 'Bob', initially sung to a drawling, melancholy tune. The music ceases, however, when Bob Pigeon's closest sidekick, the bleached-blond Budd (played by Red Hot Chile Peppers' Flea) suddenly explodes with anguish, throwing a lawn chair as he gutturally roars his dead companion's name. First as a defiant chant but in an increasingly celebratory mode, the crowd – Mike among them – continues to shout, 'Bob! Bob! Bob! Bob!' Riotous fighting among the mourners turns into orgiastic man-on-man kissing as the men finally pile in a frenzied heap upon Bob's supersized coffin. All the while, frequent cuts back to Scott and his cohort's disapproving stares emphasize the link as well as the dissonance between the 'aristocratic' and 'tavern' worlds.

At the same time, a striking opposition develops between Bob Pigeon's churlish, linguistically prolific Falstaffian living presence and the carnivalesque, anti-linguistic behaviour of his crew after he is dead, where his vacant leadership role has apparently been filled by the never-before-seen accordion player. With his Blackness, festive demeanour and one-word song, this musician functions in another sense as an anti-Falstaff, or, perhaps, as an anti-Shakespeare, rejecting all at once the oppressive ideological apparatus of both whiteness and Shakespearean verbosity. Notably, he alone in the scene remains separate from the coffin-top orgy, leading yet refusing to fully participate in the white men's final exuberant ritual of mourning for Bob.

While Van Sant's funeral scene has no analogue in Shakespeare's Henriad, it does have one in the final scene of Welles's *Chimes at Midnight*, which also focuses on the larger-than-life coffin of its permanently fallen Falstaff. At the end of Welles's masterpiece, after Mistress Quickly delivers her narration of Falstaff's death from *Henry V*, an extreme long shot centres on three of the fat knight's former crew members as they laboriously wheel his coffin up a desolate dirt path. Their journey is framed by the ramshackle tavern in the foreground and the castle's austere battlements in the distance. Meanwhile Ralph Richardson's voiceover cites lines adapted from Holinshed, praising the 'new king', Henry V, for his humanity and justice, and concluding that he 'lived and died a pattern in princehood, a lodestar in honor, and famous to the world alway'. That coffin and its arduous journey, as Barbara Hodgdon notes, take over the final scene, where 'Falstaff's body inhabits a no-man's-land between the two spaces over which the voice of "history" provides, circumscribing and replacing Quickly's report of the fat knight's death with Henry V's chronicle epitaph'. This epitaph, of course, is utter propaganda; Falstaff's body is the terrain onto which Welles 'remaps the traditional territory' of Hal/Henry V's rhetorical performances, casting 'the spectacle of rule into question'.[61]

In Van Sant's adaptation, the paired funerals – one with its biblical texts read by the priest and one with its monoverbal song led by the accordion player – roughly parallel the duelling histories – Holinshed's and Shakespeare's/Mistress Quickly's – in Welles's version of the scene. However, rather than the voice of chronicle history supplanting Quickly's narrative, the 'Bob' song drowns out Jack Favor's more formal funeral rites. Bob's large coffin, although an initial focal point, is itself soon overwhelmed by the bodies of his mourners – which are subsequently also displaced when the camera's point of view, along with that of the narcoleptic Mike, moves skyward.

The 'no man's land' with which *My Own Private Idaho* ends is a different place altogether: the same road 'with a fucked-up face' with which the film began. There Mike briefly awakens before having his final narcoleptic episode. After he is robbed by two passers-by, his shoeless, sleeping body is found by a more altruistic motorist who stops to load him into the front passenger seat of his sedan. In parallel to Falstaff's corpse at the end of *Chimes at Midnight*, Mike's invisible form is then slowly wheeled away as the object of the viewer's final receding gaze.

While Welles asks his audience to mourn 'merrie England' as a timeless mythical Shakespearean value for which Falstaff stands in synecdoche, in *My Own Private Idaho*, Shakespeare – along with Mike, Bob, Scott and other members of the tavern crew – is revealed as something other than timeless. Rather, Shakespeare embodies a set of particular, self-contradictory values involving race, sexuality, gender, class and nation. As in *H4*, what forever returns is not the universal Bard but what that road in Idaho represents: the oppressive effects of institutional power which Shakespeare, in all his multiplicity, may either uphold or resist, according to his particular uses.

5

Film Noir, *White Heat*, 'Top of the World'

Loncraine's *Richard III* in Nazi-face

The germinal seed from which this chapter springs is a question my students raised the first time I taught Richard Loncraine's 1995 blockbuster, *Richard III*, in my undergraduate Shakespeare class: What is Al Jolson's 'Sitting on Top of the World' doing in this film's conclusion? Or to be more precise, what is a song from a 1920s American 'talkie' musical drama sung by a Jewish singer famous for performing in blackface doing at the end of a movie about the downfall of a medieval Shakespearean tyrant updated as an English Hitler? The answer turns out to be a fitting topic for the next-to-last chapter in a book about adaptation, race and intersectionality in Shakespeare's histories on screen. To get there, I present an investigation that explores the stage performance history of *Richard III*, 1920s American blackface musical drama, classic gangster movies, film noir and the 1990s cinematic Shakespeare renaissance. At a moment when nontraditional casting was starting to become an accepted norm in Shakespeare on screen, Loncraine's all-white *Richard III* subversively intertwines the racializing language and performance legacies of Shakespeare's most popular history play with American cinema's foundational racist history.

Overseen by a director from the south of England, starring well-known English actor Sir Ian McKellen and based on a 1990 stage performance directed by Richard Eyre for the Royal National Theatre, Loncraine's *Richard III* would appear to be a thoroughly Anglocentric production. Yet by presenting Richard III as a fascist tyrant in a dystopian version of 1930s England while also referencing multiple stage and screen predecessors, this Shakespearean history adaptation obliquely but persistently invokes the enormous historical and cultural burden of Western racism more broadly considered. McKellen, who in 1995 was an established Shakespearean actor on the classical stage but not widely known in film, and Loncraine, who then had a great deal of previous experience shooting successful commercials but none whatsoever with Shakespeare, made for an unlikely but ultimately productive pair on this project.[1] As the first full historical transposition of one of Shakespeare's plays for the cinema, their film was, and remains, a groundbreaking experiment.[2]

The critical conversation about Loncraine's *Richard III* so far has emphasized its engagement with Richard's bodily difference through the linked lenses of queer and disability studies and also examined its metacinematic fascination with multiple forms of media – both areas that connect with the film's Nazi themes. McKellen's characterization of Richard presents contemporary signifiers of homosexuality that contribute to both his alterity and his allure. These include the setting of the second half of Richard's seductive opening soliloquy in a men's urinal, numerous occasions that suggest Richard's attraction to other male characters, his rejection of his wife's sexual advances and, perhaps most obviously, the widely known fact that McKellen himself is gay.[3] As both a 'crip' and a 'queer', McKellen's Richard, according to Robert McRuer, 'expose[s] the ways in which the marriage of compulsory heterosexuality and compulsory able-bodiedness has no future'.[4]

Yet other scholars have noticed that what stands out in McKellen's performance is a conspicuous lack of disfigurement. The usurper king's original deformity is, rather, in part 'transposed onto Richard's status as a solider and a Nazi', so that his monstrosity is not only about his misshapen body but also about his misshapen politics.[5] This Nazi motif is made visually explicit in 'the black SS uniforms of Richard and his followers, his red flag with a stylized black boar's head recalling the swastika, and the raised arm salutes'. It is also present in smaller cinematic details such as Hitler's purported 'fondness for chocolates, newsreels, and early morning meetings', as well as McKellen's own screenplay notation 'that Jim Broadbent's Buckingham features "Himmler glasses" and a "Goering smile"'.[6] Unlike the 1990 stage production, moreover, the film strives not only to consider the historical possibility of an 'English Hitler' but also to comment on its own cinematic medium. By presenting the story through a 'post-modern bricolage of photography, film, telegraphy, and other media', Loncraine's direction of *Richard III* exposes the spectacular nature of fascism and the danger posed by these media themselves.[7]

This exposure additionally presents an opportunity to interrogate the racist legacy of Anglo-American cinema – an interrogation that remains viable, I submit, whether or not the film's creators were conscious of their allusions' connection to that additional legacy. Situated in the 1990s at a moment where the question of racial representation in the screen Shakespeare adaptation had reached a pinnacle of debate, *Richard III*'s interest in contemporary media intersects productively with what is only now, in the twenty-first century, emerging in Shakespeare criticism as an understanding of the racializing work of the English histories.

In a 2020 book chapter Urvashi Chakravarty provides a compelling argument for how Shakespeare's *Richard III* articulates 'the promise of homonationalism'. The term 'homonationalism' comes from contemporary American race and gender studies; Chakravarty applies it to early modern drama to describe 'the possibility for dynastic futurity through sameness and stasis rather than change'. The tyrannical antihero's 'improperly queer', racialized as well as physically monstrous, ungenerative body and politics enable this possibility by catalysing their own replacement by Richmond's 'properly queer', 'fair and future-affirming' body and politics.[8] In other words, Richard and Richmond are two sides of the same queer coin. Richard's Black, deviant, deadly queer terrorism gives way, by the end of the play, to Richmond's white, redemptive queer homonationalism. By articulating Richard's Blackness, queerness and disability through parodic allusions to earlier Anglo-American cinema, Loncraine's adaptation makes visible the artificial logic of race as it intersects with these other categories of otherness. Through the interweaving of these discourses, the updated *Richard III* exposes whiteness, rather than Blackness, as the genuine evil.

Ugly Americans, blank(er) verse

Loncraine's artistic decisions in *Richard III* must be considered in light of both the long history of nontraditional casting on the Shakespearean stage and the more immediate changes taking place in cinematic Shakespeare in the 1990s. Especially in the United States, where (as discussed in Chapter 3) *Richard III* was from colonial times through the nineteenth century the most popular Shakespearean play on stage, the relationship between Black actors and the role of the hunchbacked Richard has been an especially important one. This aspect of the character has direct bearing on Loncraine's invocations of US racial history via America's cinematic heritage. In addition, the transatlantic cinematic climate in which the 1995 version of *Richard III* was released linked British concerns about the Americanization of Shakespeare with the growing pains of the film industry's gradual and often grudging acceptance of racially diverse actors in its ranks. Both contexts provide important frameworks for considering how, in Loncraine's *Richard III*, cinema itself mediates the linked representations of twentieth-century racist and xenophobic violence with the racializing nationalism of Shakespeare's early modern English history play.

As noted in Chapter 3, the inaugural performance of Shakespeare by the all-Black African Grove Theatre Company in Manhattan in 1821 was a production of *Richard III* with James Hewlett playing Richard. The performance inspired fervent protest on the part of white Americans who 'wished to maintain racist notions of blacks (particularly their lack of intellect)' – a conflict fictionalized in Carlyle Brown's play, *The African Company Presents Richard the Third*. In subsequent decades, the role continued to be performed by African Americans such as Ira Aldridge, Paul Molyneaux and J. A. Arneaux, either in all-Black productions or, as in the case of Aldridge, while in white-face.[9] Historian Shane White has suggested that the role initially appealed to African Americans due to the disabled Richard's correspondence with 'the trickster figure in African American culture', similar to slaves who used verbal manipulation to 'negotiat[e] their freedom with their masters'.[10]

More recently, ostensibly colourblind US productions of *Richard III* featuring Black actors in the title role have created problematic intersections between Shakespeare's depiction of a monstrous tyrant and contemporary stereotypes of Black masculinity, participating in 'a history of the representation of the black male body as something not quite human'. For instance, Lisa Anderson describes the stereotypes inadvertently engaged in a 1996 Chicago performance in which Brendan Corbalis as Richard and Richard's two murdering henchmen were the only Black actors in the cast. This Richard's seduction of a white 'Anne recall[ed] the Black Buck, the black man who is "oversexed and savage, violent and frenzied as [he] lust[s] for white flesh"'. Anderson speculates that negative reviews of the production, which never mentioned the actors' races but criticized Corbalis as '"fairly bland and ineffectual"', in part emerged from 'the reviewers' struggle to avoid noticing' these discomfiting images.[11] A 1990 New York Shakespeare Festival staging of *Richard III* with Denzel Washington in the title role as well as Black actresses playing Anne (Sharon Washington) and Margaret (Mary Alice) – likely the first Black Margaret in a multiracial production – resulted in reviews that similarly found Washington's Richard lacking in 'feral and emotional assertiveness', while Alice's Margaret was perhaps backhandedly praised for her 'fierce[ness]' and 'savage[ry]'.[12] As with reviews of Corbalis's performance, although these articles never mention race, it remains a key subtext.

In the UK, where the performance history of *Richard III* is considerably whiter, Richard Eyre's mostly white 1990 National Theatre production on which Loncraine's film is based was far from unusual. The original production included only a single BAME cast member, British-Nigerian actor Hakeem Kae-Kazim, as Tyrell.[13] However, translating this production into the medium of cinema in 1995 brought additional considerations to the table. Just six years after Kenneth Branagh's *Henry V* with its all-white, all-British cast inaugurated a renaissance in Shakespearean screen adaptations and four years after Van Sant's *My Own Private Idaho* presented its mostly white spin on the Henriad's Prince Hal-Falstaff story, the cinematic Shakespeare world had changed significantly. Starting with Denzel Washington as Don Pedro in Kenneth Branagh's 1993 production of *Much Ado about Nothing*, actors of colour began appearing in some, if certainly not all, Shakespearean film adaptations. Branagh's *Much Ado* also featured multiracial if ostensibly 'white' Canadian actor Keanu Reeves as Don John as well as several well-known white American actors in other key roles, such as Robert Sean Leonard as Claudio and Michael Keaton as Dogberry. While Branagh does not mention race directly in his published comments on the screenplay, he describes seeking 'different accents, different looks' in order to produce 'a Shakespeare film that belonged to the world'.[14] In subsequent productions, the Belfast-born director's self-advertised endeavours to 'reshape the ethnic makeup of a typical Shakespearean cast' became 'a signature of his work'.[15]

The growing pains of nontraditional casting in cinematic Shakespeare can be clearly seen in productions of this era. Another 1990s Shakespeare adaptation to cast a diverse range of actors was Baz Luhrmann's *William Shakespeare's Romeo + Juliet* (1996). Lurhmann's modern-day setting in 'Verona Beach' made a diverse cast, including African American and LatinX performers, who were all asked to speak '"in their own American accents"', a relatively logical choice even for an uninitiated audience.[16] Yet as Nicholas Radel and I have each discussed elsewhere, in this context, the whiteness of the primary couple combined with a text preoccupied with the symbolism of darkness and light led to persistent racial and gendered stereotyping.[17] In 1996, Branagh cast several actors of colour in minor roles in *Hamlet* – possibly 'seeking to avoid the charge of tokenism' raised by Washington's presence as the sole Black actor in *Much Ado,* but thereby inadvertently engaging the 'discourse of Orientalism'.[18] In two later films, *Love's Labour's Lost* (1999) and *As You Like It* (2006), Branagh avoided Don Pedro's disturbing outsider status in *Much Ado* by including 'inter-ethnic couples' in the casting of major characters. However, other problems persisted, notably in the colonial, Japanese setting of *As You Like It*, which oddly included very few Asian actors.[19]

The primary impetus behind what Branagh advertised as his 'global' casting, really a mix of '"British actors"' and '"American stars"', appears to have been a commercial one.[20] Branagh's *Hamlet* featured numerous 'international "names", particularly Americans', in order to 'cope with the dominance of Hollywood in the industry as a whole'.[21] Similar considerations went into casting decisions in Loncraine's *Richard III*. Distributors of the film 'insisted that at least two of the cast had to be "internationally famous"' – or, in other words, '"American"'.[22] This requirement led to the casting of Annette Bening as Queen Elizabeth and Robert Downey, Jr, as her brother, Lord Rivers, both actors with box-office appeal and a command of the big screen. While economically sensible, the casting of American movie stars with little or no classical Shakespearean training met resistance from viewers accustomed to hearing

Shakespeare's language spoken in a particular way. Although reviews of these productions almost never directly commented on race, the question of accent and the ability to properly enunciate Shakespearean verse was the site onto which concerns about the linked issues of the Americanization of Shakespeare and the rise of nontraditional casting were frequently projected.

The year 1995 represents a pinnacle of these debates. Alongside Loncraine's *Richard III's* appearance as the first full-length, original-language Shakespearean screen adaptation to feature an updated setting, Oliver Parker's *Othello*, starring Laurence Fishburne, arrived in cineplexes as the first major film version of that play to feature a Black actor as the title character. Because of their release the same year and the presence of non-Shakespearean American actors in both films, Parker's *Othello* and Loncraine's *Richard III* were often subject to similar criticisms, and at times direct comparisons, in the press. 'The words don't exactly trip off the American tongues of Annette Bening as Queen Elizabeth and Robert Downey Jr. as her hapless brother', wrote a reviewer for *Rolling Stone*, 'but the actors do get into the daredevil spirit of things'.[23] Writing for *Cinéaste*, Gary Crowdus largely praised Bening: 'Although Annette Bening's American accent initially sounds jarring amidst all the Britspeak, she gives a spirited and often moving performance as the victimized but combative Queen Mother.' Against Robert Downey, Jr, however, he deployed a particularly trenchant pun: 'blank verse has rarely been delivered so blankly.'[24] Laurence Fishburne's vocal style in *Othello* met comparable disparagement. A reviewer for Toronto's *Globe and Mail* damned Fishburne with half-hearted praise that once more invoked that oft-used line from *Hamlet*: 'A superb actor in the U.S. naturalistic tradition, Fishburne certainly commands the screen (no surprise there), but he has a tiny problem with the language – Elizabethan English doesn't exactly roll trippingly off his tongue.'[25] More pointedly, another reviewer for the *Ottawa Citizen* asserted that while 'Fishburne is a fine Ike Turner (*What's Love Got To Do With It*) and a great Southern cop (*Just Cause*)', the African American actor was 'no Shakespearean. The language is beyond him; the passions of the character elude him. . . . Fishburne is the first black actor to play Othello on screen, which is terrific for racial equality, but his portrayal doesn't do much for the Bard'.[26]

As usual, of course, race does make a difference. Although Bening, Downey, Jr, and Fishburne alike received criticism for their untrained American enunciations of Shakespeare, reviews of Fishburne were particularly attuned to the actor's status as a Black American man in a Shakespeare film. Using what Barbara Hodgdon identifies as 'coded terms' for 'racist ideologies' that do not wish to mark themselves as racist, the critics I just quoted delimit Fishburne's repertoire to what one calls 'naturalistic' acting, while another goes so far as to salute 'racial equality' while simultaneously implying that African American actors should stick to African American characters like the notorious wife-beater Ike Turner or a 'Southern cop'.[27]

A further element distinguishing Loncraine's casting of Downey, Jr, and Bening not only from Fishburne's role in *Othello* but also from Branagh's casting of American and Canadian actors in *Much Ado* is what Peter Holland points out is the former's productive use of nationality and accent to portray Bening's and Downey, Jr's characters as 'American arrivistes'.[28] Loncraine's use of nationality and accent is thus in one sense comparable to the use of race in colour-conscious casting. Both Queen Elizabeth, who has married into English royalty, and her tagalong brother, Lord Rivers, are stamped via their American accents as upstart interlopers in English society. Richard and others look down on them as social inferiors just as reviewers look down on Bening and Downey, Jr, as shoddy Shakespeareans.

However, although ostensibly making them verbally inferior to 'proper' English speakers around them, their accents also obliquely grant these American actors as well as their characters a form of power that Loncraine's film places under a critical lens. First, the presence of American actors in a British film 'as imported star power' indicts America for its cultural imperialism, namely 'the destructive extent to which American mass media came to dominate British culture in the years after the war'.[29] A resentful awareness of such 'harsh realities of commercial filmmaking' is one reason behind what Lisa Hopkins sees as McKellen's 'anti-American animus' that comes through in both his adaptation of *Richard III* and in his screenplay notes on the production, extending to the portrayal of Queen Elizabeth not only as a social upstart but as a likely Nazi. For as other critics have also observed, Bening's Elizabeth betrays more than a passing similarity with American socialite and probable

Nazi sympathizer Wallis Simpson, whose engagement to Edward VIII – who also likely held fascist sympathies – led to the abdication crisis of 1936.[30] In a related vein, the Americanness of Elizabeth's brother is marked by even more blatant signs of white America's imperialist, genocidal history as encapsulated by the cinematic genre of the Western: the Native American headdress worn by Rivers over breakfast, while his nephew, the young Duke of York, wears a cowboy outfit and pretends to shoot him with a toy cap gun. The scene suggests the casual passing down of this legacy to a near-heir to the English throne.

Yet the film's grimly comic parody of American imperialism coexists with what Loehlin identifies as the film's parodic take on the 'idea of Englishness', especially the 'wholesome hierarchical "English" values' of the English heritage film.[31] *Richard III* features numerous famous English landmarks, such as St Pancras Rail Station transformed into King Edward's Palace of Westminster, Brighton Pavilion as the ailing king's royal retreat and South London's abandoned Battersea Power Station as a military base where the climactic Battle of Bosworth Field takes place.[32] In addition, Bening and Downey, Jr excepted, its cast list is a veritable 'who's who' of English heritage actors: Maggie Smith, Nigel Hawthorne, John Wood, Christopher Bowen, Edward Jewesbury and, of course, the most well-known classical Shakespearean in the mix, Sir Ian himself as the Hitler-esque King Richard.

Although Bening's and Downey, Jr's position in the plot of *Richard III* puts them squarely in this tyrant's gunsights, Loncraine's film is quite shrewdly aware of their mutual implication in the desire for power, which in this film's universe translates into Nazism. Rivers's interpolated death scene, in which he is having sex with a Pan American flight attendant, underscores both his American origins and what Kathy Howlett aptly reads as his strange parallelism with Richard, linking both to the horrors of Nazi Europe as mediated through the art of cinema.[33] That one of Rivers's hands is tied to a bed frame positions the American playboy in a similar physical bind to that of the disabled king with his paralysed left arm. Near orgasm, Rivers is suddenly stabbed through the abdomen by a blade that emerges from beneath, wielded by an unseen assailant striking through the mattress to which Rivers is bound. This through-the-bed stabbing is 'more symbolic than realistic', resembling a 'perverse birth' that recalls both Richard's own self-described obstetric origins and his violent boundary-busting tendencies – literalized in the film by the opening scene in which his tank 'bursts through the walls of Prince Edward's headquarters'. The scene is a key example of what Howlett, citing Erving Goffman, calls 'vivid negativity', which bequeaths the power of legend to representations of especially traumatic, if relatively recent, historical events like the Nazi Holocaust.[34]

The moment also makes a crucial extradiegetic allusion to a famous scene in Alfred Hitchcock's 1935 thriller, *The 39 Steps*, when a woman's scream as she discovers a murder victim blends on the soundtrack with the whistle of a train emerging from a tunnel. Mimicking Hitchcock's device, the flight attendant's scream as Rivers is stabbed fades into the whistle of a train – the same one carrying the soon-to-be-crowned young Edward V back to London. That whistle, in turn, becomes the lesser calibre whistle of the young Duke of York's toy train, a visual pun derived from Buckingham's line 'and with some little train' (*R3* 2.2.120).[35] Along with his mother (Annette Bening's Queen Elizabeth) and grandmother (Maggie Smith's Duchess of York), the boy plays on the floor of a sitting room in his father's palace, accompanied on the soundtrack by his sister Elizabeth's tinkling practice at the piano.

The symbolic implications of Loncraine's use of the train and its whistle are altered from the original. In *The 39 Steps*, an immediate view of the locomotive in a tunnel takes the place of the screaming woman's mouth as the whistle supplants her scream.[36] In Loncraine's version, before we see the tunnel, the entire train appears in a wide shot of the English countryside where, in the foreground, a farmer with two plough horses tills a field. Rather than blur the boundary between woman and train, the image ironically juxtaposes and implicitly parodies both the flight attendant's terror over Rivers's murder and the idyllic view of English life – in countryside and palace alike. This parody takes place, moreover, through a self-referential framing device that in this case invokes a well-known British film.

Another subtle Hitchcock allusion occurs even earlier in Loncraine's *Richard III*, during the opening ball scene. Richard delivers the first half of his 'Now is the winter of our discontent' soliloquy as a public monologue, speaking from a stage microphone to a slightly inebriated, applauding crowd (1.1.1). Midway through the speech, right before the jump-cut to the urinal,

> the camera moves in to frame the movements of his brutal, willful jaw, showing his teeth in extreme close-up. The shot alludes, perhaps, to the famous long tracking shot in *Young and Innocent* (dir. Alfred Hitchcock, 1937), in which the camera slowly moves from the upper balcony at the back of an immense dance hall to a close-up of the drummer in the band onstage, a close-up tight enough to reveal the flaws in his blackface makeup and discover the murderer's disguise.[37]

These shots in both films link disturbing exteriors to even more disturbing interiors. The turn to the villain's mind – Richard's calculated self-exposure at the urinal, or as occurs in Hitchcock's film, the killer's panicked self-exposure on stage – is accompanied in both instances by an intimate focus on bodily detail that reveals flaws in both characters' presenting personae. In *Young and Innocent*, moreover, blackface functions as revelation as well as concealment; it is the racialized exteriorization of a white man's villainy.[38]

The simultaneously revealing and concealing power of blackface in this moment resembles the similar paradox of Richard's disability not only in Loncraine's film but also in Shakespeare's play. While often explained by modern critics as a clear externalization of Richard's internal evil, the relationship between the deformed body and deformed mind was, as Michael Torrey points out, considerably less self-evident for early modern theorists of physiognomy, who demonstrate 'ambivalence about the reliability of the science they describe', thus 'cast[ing] doubt upon its promise to decode the semiotics of bodily form'. This ambivalence fits the epistemological uncertainty actually demonstrated by Shakespeare's *Richard III*, in which characters are clearly deceived by Richard in spite of his disfigured appearance: 'Richard both conceals and reveals his moral status. . . . In crucial scenes his deceptions redefine the meaning of his deformity as he bends the semiotic power of his body to his own purposes, making it signify what he wants it to signify.'[39]

Yet in this scene the camera's gaze works against Richard's rhetorical intentions. Zooming in on McKellen's mouth as he speaks the lines 'Grim-visaged War ha[s] smoothed his wrinkled front; / And now, instead of mounting barbèd steeds / To fright the souls of fearful adversaries', the shot reveals the combined sources of this Richard's dangerous power: his corrupt rhetorical organ and his composed self-presentation as a soldier (1.2.9–11). Richard himself is the personification of 'Grim-visaged

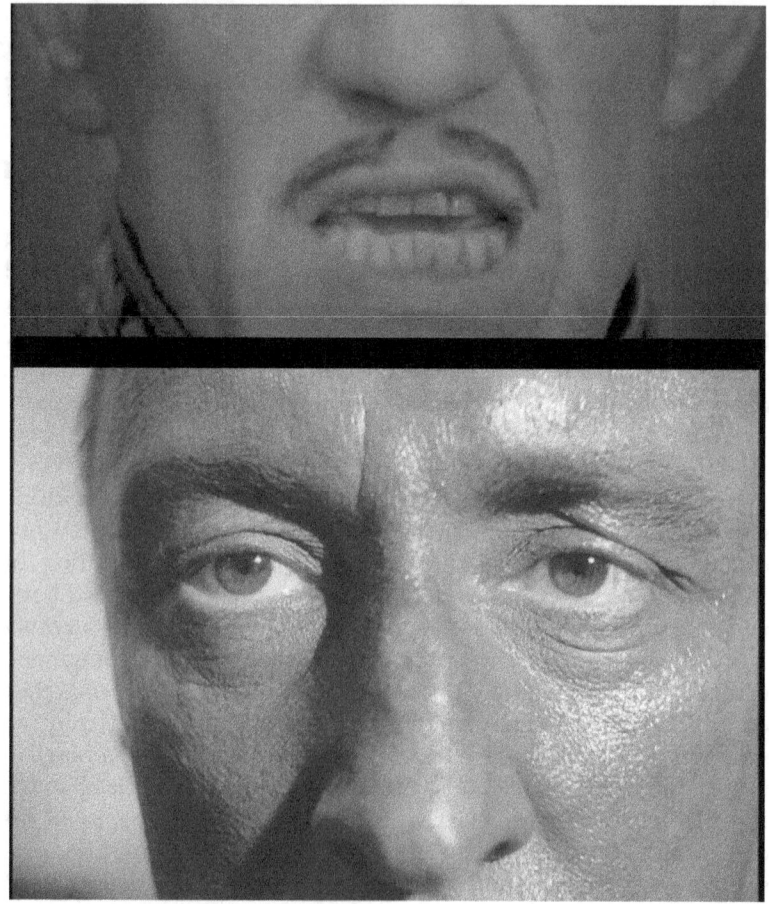

FIGURE 8 *Two villains in extreme close-up.* Richard III, *directed by Richard Loncraine (top).* © *Richard III Limited 1995. All rights reserved.* Young and Innocent, *directed by Alfred Hitchcock (bottom).* © *General Film Distributors Ltd 1937. All rights reserved. Screen grabs.*

War', seemingly now cleaned up for polite company. Yet the shot's disclosure of the ravages that age, perhaps bruxism, and clearly cigarette-smoking have wrought on Richard's oral cavity is comparable to Hitchcock's revelation of his killer's eye-twitch and flawed make-up, with the disguise unravelling and betraying itself. As a decisive move away from associations of Richard's monstrosity with bodily deformity or Black male otherness, this shot reveals McKellen-as-Richard's English heritage, RP-accented, classically trained Shakespearean voice as the true source of his villainy (Figure 8).

These two subtle moments of cinematic allusion are far from isolated incidents in Loncraine's *Richard III*. Although the rise of fascism in 1930s Europe is the movie's most obvious historical referent, Loncraine's primary focus is not political history itself but political history as mediated through cinematic history. The film's attention to its own medium reveals the chiasmatic ties between cinema and fascism: that the 'Nazi past' is 'as much a part of cinema as cinema is a part of the Nazi past'.[40] But fascist European ideologies of the mid-twentieth century are not the film's only target. They are also synecdoches for the more insidious racist ideologies of both Britain and the United States as mediated, respectively, through Shakespeare's text and allusions to the long history of American cinema. The casting of white actors, both English heritage actors and American stars, are the vehicles through which these ideologies are both conveyed and critiqued. In particular, the 'rudely stamped' body of McKellen's Richard III is the nexus where the tyrant king's metaphorically Black monstrosity, the history of Black Richards in American stage performance, and the racializing imaginary of American movies from the 1920s to the 1950s intersect to provide a new understanding of the ongoing dialectic between race and Shakespeare in history.

White Heat, film noir and Richard III's marked body

At the very moment that the United States sought to differentiate itself from Nazi Europe, the image of an all-white, ethnically uniform America portrayed in gangster films from the mid-1930s through the 1950s was sadly all too similar to the Nazi ideal. By embedding allusions to classic gangster films, especially Raoul Walsh's *White Heat*, into its Nazi-inspired depiction of Shakespeare's humpbacked tyrant, Loncraine's *Richard III* implicates Shakespeare's play in a similar legacy of racism as it also brings the American film industry's racist provenance to light.

The connection between race and the gangster film can be traced to the genre's origins. The foundational trio of American gangster films from the early 1930s – *The Public Enemy, Little Caesar* and *Scarface* – presented antiheroes with defined Irish or Italian ethnicities. Their hyphenated, marginal identities suggest a motivating force for these men's pursuit of the American dream outside the bounds of the law. The actors who took on these roles as well as the films' directors – for example, Paul Muni, Edward E. Robinson and Mervyn Leroy – also demonstrate the increasing presence of immigrant Jews in Hollywood, a development greeted by some Americans with trepidation or frank animosity.[41]

In contrast, the gangster antihero with the closest ties to McKellen's Richard – James Cagney's Cody Jarrett in *White Heat* (1949) – has no clear ethnic identity. This distinction exemplifies a trend resulting from the enforcement of the so-called Hays Code, officially adopted (as the Motion Picture Production Code) to morally regulate the film industry in 1930 but not enforced until four years later. In the Hays Code era of 1934–68, America's cinematic gangsters became whitewashed and vaguely 'WASP' (White Anglo-Saxon Protestant), without any obvious ethnic backgrounds to explain their marginalized status.[42] The temporal link between Hays Code enforcement and the demise of the ethnic gangster is no coincidence; the marginal ethnicity of the early gangster protagonist threatened the WASP ideal of American national identity. The threat heightened after the introduction of sound technology, which by making the gangster's speech audible 'emphasised both his social class and ethnicity'.[43] Hearing these outsiders' voices was especially dangerous during the Great Depression, when 'the ethnic gangster's struggles with economic and cultural disenfranchisement resonated with a growing national condition'.[44]

The identification between McKellen's Richard and Cagney's Cody is most apparent in the film's final moments, when rather than succumb to his enemy's bullets, Richard deliberately plunges into the flames of an exploding Battersea Power Station. As various commentators have observed, this ending mirrors the similarly cataclysmic death of *White Heat*'s antiheroic protagonist. In addition to the visual and thematic parallels of Cody's immolation at the top of a gasworks plant, Cagney's final line – 'Made it, Ma – top of the world!' – is echoed in the concluding soundtrack of Loncraine's *Richard III*, which features Al Jolson's seemingly jubilant 1925 hit, 'I'm Sitting on Top of the World'.[45] Cody's last words voice the commonplace moral lesson of the classic gangster movie regarding overreaching criminal ambition: to gain the whole world is often to forfeit one's soul. The same is true for Richard III, even in an adaptation that mostly does away with the play's Christian providential narrative.

The *White Heat*-inspired demise of McKellen's Richard is the pay-off of a narrative that connects him to Cody not only as an antihero but also based on their respective disabilities and problematic relationships with their mothers. As Loehlin remarks, like Richard, the classic gangster 'antihero is an ambitious man who feels unfairly excluded from society . . . He may be set apart by low or shameful birth, but his marginality often has a physical manifestation as well, such as Paul Muni's disfiguration in *Scarface* or James Cagney's mental illness in *White Heat*'.[46] Although as Tony Camonte Paul Muni's scar is a relatively minor affair, in *White Heat* Cody Jarrett's disability – recurrent migraines that accompany this undefined mental illness – is more pronounced, supplanting ethnicity or class as the source of his marginalized status.[47] His chief legal antagonist, US Treasury investigator Phillip Evans, suggests that Cody's headaches are due to a condition he inherited from his father who 'died in an institution'. Yet the disabling condition is also tied to Cody's relationship with his mother, to whom he has a 'psychopathic devotion'. Not only does the gangster depend upon his mother to soothe him out of his spells and maintain his facade of sanity but also, as Evans suggests, the headaches developed in the first place as a bid to 'get his mother's attention'. The line 'Made it, Ma – top of the world!' highlights this unhealthy attachment.

Similarly, physical deformity and concomitant moral evil are the primary motivating forces for the monstrous behaviour of Shakespeare's Richard III, who hails from the highest of medieval England's bloodlines. Locraine's film emphasizes this parallel between Cody and Richard by also stressing the maternal origins of Richard's moral as well as physical monstrosity. As Loehlin observes, 'Like Cagney's Cody Jarrett in *White Heat*, McKellen's Richard is obsessed with his mother, and his criminal career is linked to a childhood rejection'.[48] McKellen's introduction to and notes on his screenplay attribute Richard's evil to a deprivation of maternal affection: 'verbal and emotional abuse which from infancy has formed' his 'character and behavior'.[49] This interpretation not only coheres with Shakespeare's play, in which Richard traces his deformity to his *in utero* relationship with the Duchess, but relies, like *White Heat*, upon a psychoanalytic interpretation of a villain's motivation. According to Janet Adelman's influential reading of the character, Richard himself locates 'the origin of his aggression in the problematic maternal body' starting with a key line in his first soliloquy in *3 Henry VI*: 'Why, love forswore me in my mother's womb' (3.1.153). Moreover, this 'fantasy emerges only after his father's death, as though that death had deprived Richard of his father's protection and thrust him back toward his mother'.[50] *White Heat*'s parallel representation of Cody, who has also lost his father and is excessively close to his mother, draws on a similar reading of the gangster's psyche.

Equally significant to the link between these antiheroic characters is the status of racial or ethnic difference as an underlying source of their villainy. Although seemingly erased, this difference is nevertheless inscribed into these men's respective narratives of maternally mediated disability. As Urvashi Chakravarty argues, early modern understandings of somatic difference conceived of bodily deformation and racial Blackness as different types of monstrous births, both traceable to impressions upon the maternal imagination.[51] To superimpose this understanding upon Adelman's psychoanalytic reading of *Richard III* is to suggest that Richard's status as 'hell's black intelligencer' is itself a 'fantasy of maternal origin', legible, as Chakravarty asserts, in the play's fascination with mirrors as a metaphor for both 'reproductive futurity' and 'the felicity and integrity of those lineal reflections'. In particular, Richard's speech after successfully wooing Lady Anne – 'Shine out, fair sun, till I have bought a glass, / That I may see my shadow as I pass' (1.2.265–66) – 'refracts Richard's spectacular "deformity" (1.1.27) into a display of darkness'. This form of monstrous, ungenerative birth ultimately underwrites the play's narrative of generative whiteness.[52]

Correspondingly, in *White Heat*, the colour reference of the film's title encodes the racializing metaphor implicit in the term 'film noir', a cinematic mode that achieved its height of popularity during the Second World War and its immediate aftermath. Although *White Heat* lacks the chiaroscuro lighting and dark interiors that characterize the visual style of much film noir, it does display the classic psychologically complex antihero in Cody and the typical femme fatale in his murderous wife Verna. For many scholars, film noir's popularity in the 1940s and 1950s indicates America's identity crisis after the Second World War, when the style 'held up a dark mirror to postwar America and reflected its moral anarchy'.[53]

A term coined by French critics in 1946, 'film noir', of course, literally means 'black film'. Film noir's visual preoccupation with shadow parallels and expresses its examination of metaphysical and metaphorical darkness. Produced during the Cold War years, films of this type reveal the anxieties of an America 'dealing with threats from both inside and outside the country and in need of redefining both a sense of nationhood and citizenship'.[54] The post-war period in which these films proliferated was also an era of increasing agitation for civil rights. As Eric Lott argues, 'At a moment when bold new forms of black, Latino, and Asian activism and visibility are confronting resurgent white revanchism and vigilantism, film noir's relentless cinematography of chiaroscuro and moral focus on the rotten souls of white folks . . . invoke the racial dimension of this play of light against dark'. Even more pointedly, Lott asserts that 'the troping of white darkness in noir has a racial source that is all the more insistent for seeming off to the side. . . . Film noir rescues with racial idioms the whites whose moral and social boundaries seem in doubt. "Black film" is the refuge of whiteness'.[55] Or, as E. Ann Kaplan pronounces with unmincing Freudian profundity, 'Race is film noir's repressed unconscious Signifier'.[56]

The cataclysmic death of a film noir antihero like Cody Jarrett, in other words, functions as a racialized conscience-cleansing. Loehlin writes of the classic gangster film narrative, which he sees Loncraine's *Richard III* as closely following, 'Once the viewer's transgressive desire is vicariously satisfied – when the gangster reaches the "top of the world" – he may be safely rejected, and his fall and destruction assuage the viewer's guilty conscience.'[57] In the post-war United States, film noir sought in part to redress the country's collective guilt. In the wake of the Nazi Holocaust,

> a steady stream of scholarly studies now explained how ethnic and religious (but not class) prejudice led to negative stereotyping and hatred. Writers were quick to point out that elements of such intolerance existed in the United States and had the potential to lead to the type of ethnic violence that had beset Nazi Germany if they were not eliminated.[58]

At the same time that films starring Black protagonists such as *The Home of the Brave* and *Pinky* (both, like *White Heat*, released in 1949) began to confront their culture's racial prejudice head-on, the sacrificial deaths of white film noir antiheroes like Cody Jarrett compartmentalized and symbolically eradicated the 'dark' interiors of white minds.

To my reading, the 'White' in the title *White Heat* is no more a coincidence than the 'noir' in film noir – and likewise relates to racializing metaphors. Notably, the phrase 'white heat' is not used anywhere in the film itself; Cody describes the pain he suffers with each migraine spell as 'like having a red-hot buzz saw inside my head'. But both phrases, 'white heat' and 'red-hot', allude to the same scientific phenomenon. When subjected to high temperatures, metals initially glow red. They turn white when, as the temperature increases further, 'the intensities of all of the visible wavelengths become appreciable'.[59] That the 'white heat' of the film's title replaces Cody's description of his 'red-hot' pain signals the escalation of the emotional, physical and moral drama beyond Cody's first-person perspective as the immediate victim of suffering, providing an external view of Cody himself as an adverse force of which the larger community must be cleansed.

The symbolism of Cody's moral evil, in fact, extends well outside the film's frame of reference. The title *White Heat* resonates not only with Cody's own final fiery end in a veritable mushroom cloud and the various explosions of his rage that precede it but also with the facial steam burns sustained by the ill-fated gang member Zuckie in an earlier train robbery, the similarly mushroom-shaped puff of steam that rises from that train in the film's opening shot and, by extension, the genuine atomic explosions experienced by residents of Hiroshima and Nagasaki four years prior to the film's release.[60]

From a historical perspective, *White Heat* demonstrates how, in the aftermath of the Second World War, American film was preoccupied with the 'destructive passions' that 'rule the very hearts and souls of average Americans' and dramatized those passions' potentially broad and devastating consequences.[61] What remains ambiguous is whether whiteness, rather than its binary opposite, is implicated in those nefarious and cataclysmic desires, or if 'white heat' is the cleansing force that successfully rids the world of Cody's implicitly 'noir' moral evil.

Loncraine's references to *White Heat* in its adaptation of *Richard III* further add to the stakes of this question. It thereby builds upon Shakespeare adaptation's long relationship with film noir in films from Ken Hughes's *Joe Macbeth* (1955) to Michael Almereyda's *Hamlet* (2000).[62] In picking up on the parallels between Shakespeare's *Richard III* and film noir as well as gangster elements of *White Heat*, Loncraine's film also pays subtle homage to Olivier's *Richard III*, released in 1955 during the peak of film noir dominance, and which surrounds its own Richard with a good deal of literal shadow-play.[63] Even a decade after the war's conclusion, 'Richard's shadow is paralleled by the shadow that World War II cast over Europe and the United States'.[64]

In *White Heat*, however, the shadows are internal. In their concluding invocation of this classic film noir, in the final moments of a *Richard III* inspired by the same dark period of world history, Loncraine and McKellen raise this shadow almost to the surface. The death of their own white 'noir' antihero takes place to a swinging tune – the musical version of 'Made it, Ma – top of the world!' – sung by the icon of American blackface performance who was also a proud, public Jew. Al Jolson in blackface, I would like to suggest, may be the repressed unconscious signifier of Loncraine's *Richard III*.

From blackface to Nazi-face

Fully explaining Loncraine's reference to Jolson's 'I'm Sitting on Top of the World' requires a brief exploration of the singer's relevant oeuvre in the context of race and American cinema in the first decades of the twentieth century. As Michael Rogin has demonstrated, Alan Crosland's *The Jazz Singer* (1927), starring Al

Jolson, is one of 'four race movies' which 'provide the scaffolding for' the entirety of 'American film history'.[65] Both *The Jazz Singer* and Jolson's second 'talkie', *The Singing Fool*, which features the song in question, use blackface to present their protagonists in emotionally extreme situations. Although Jolson continued to produce blackface movies through the 1930s, the first two were the most popular and influential – perhaps because, Arthur Knight suggests, 'they revealed, without resolving, the American racial tensions and contradictions exposed by blackface'.[66]

The Jazz Singer is based on a short story-turned-play by Samuel Raphaelson, which is based, in turn, on Jolson's life. It is about a young Jewish boy, Jakie Rabinowitz, who is disowned by his father because of his desire to be a jazz singer instead of, like his father, a cantor in the synagogue. Eventually Jakie achieves his American dream of career success and cultural assimilation. Like Jolson himself, both the film's director and the men behind its eponymous production company, the Warner Brothers, were the sons of immigrant Jews who 'Americanized themselves by interpreting gentile dreams'. Therefore, according to Rogin, '*The Jazz Singer* is less Jolson's individual biography . . . than the collective autobiography of the men who made Hollywood'.[67]

At stake in this story and in Jolson's application of blackface is how Jews, once catalogued with Asians and Blacks as 'Orientals' as in the United States's 1924 Immigration Restriction Act, eventually became 'white'.[68] In 1927, jazz was a musical genre pejoratively identified with Black Americans. *The Jazz Singer*'s shooting script used a racial slur to describe the young Jakie's musical preferences, although it later replaced that slur with the term 'raggy-time songs'. Actual jazz music, however, much like actual Black singers, does not, in fact, appear in the film.[69] Instead, blackface becomes a mechanism for Jolson to transform his Jewish otherness into full-fledged American whiteness.

Towards the end of *The Jazz Singer*, the adult Jakie (now with the stage name Jack Robin) is faced with the impossible choice between his family and religion, on the one hand, and success in his chosen career on the other. His dying father calls upon him to sing the service in his stead on the eve of Yom Kippur, the Jewish Day of Atonement, when Jack is already scheduled to perform in his New York stage debut. As he contemplates this choice, a climactic scene depicts Jack's transformation into his blackface stage persona through the application of burnt cork and a black wool wig. He then sings a tearful rendition of the Irish ballad 'Mother of Mine', which speaks of the son's desire to do right by his self-sacrificing mother. Jack's own mother, as he well knows, is watching from backstage, having come to the theatre to convince her son to come home. But the performance convinces her that Jakie/Jack has made the right choice: 'He doesn't belong to us anymore. He belongs to the world.'[70]

In the end Jack chooses family and sings 'Kol Nidre' – a chant traditionally sung on Yom Kippur eve – in his father's stead. His father, therefore, dies content, convinced of his son's return to the fold. Yet in the aftermath of seemingly making the choice to sacrifice career for family, the rising star nonetheless achieves a Hollywood-style happy ending, not present in the original short story or play, which signifies his genuine assimilation. The film concludes with Jolson's iconic blackface rendition of the more obviously racializing song 'Mammy' while his mother, down in the front row of a large theatre, again worshipfully watches her son perform – as does his shiksa girlfriend from the wings. For Rogin, blackface allows Jolson as 'Jack Robin' to achieve a twofold elevation from his ethnic roots to become a full-fledged American success story: 'by giving Jack his own voice, blackface propels him above both his father and African Americans into the American melting pot.'[71] Both 'Kol Nidre' and 'Mammy' are racialized masks of, respectively, Jewishness and Blackness that the assimilated Jack Robin, now fully white, can put on and off at will.

Yet his ending is not entirely happy. Rather than presenting Jakie/Jack as entirely embracing his cultural assimilation, Linda Williams argues, the song 'Mammy' exposes 'a despairing fear of loss' that is especially palpable when 'Jakie grows anxious and cries, rather than sings, "Mammy I'm a comin', I hope I didn't make you wait! / Mammy I'm a comin', Oh God I hope I'm not late! / Mammy, look at me! Don't you know me? I'm your little baby!"'.[72] Jack's whiteness is therefore incomplete due to his reliance on his mother and his fear of transforming beyond her recognition. Blackface, moreover, becomes a vehicle for emotional expression allied with femininity as well as Blackness. In the protagonist's potentially blackening as well as feminizing relationship with a maternal figure, resonances between *The Jazz Singer*'s use of blackface and both *White Heat* and Loncraine's *Richard III* emerge.

In *The Singing Fool* (1928), the source movie for Jolson's 'I'm Sitting on Top of the World', the gendered component of blackface is more pronounced, while the protagonist's not-fully-white ethnic identity undergoes a partial erasure. In this film Jolson plays another singer, Al Stone, who gets his start as a waiter and comic in a speakeasy cabaret run by the white proprietor suggestively named 'Blackie Joe'. While Al Stone has no explicit immigrant backstory like Jakie Rabinowitz, at one point Al cracks a joke about a cut of meat being 'kosher'.[73] The line calls attention to his Jewish heritage but only at an oblique distance; apparently this performer has already undergone the transformation into whiteness achieved by Jakie/Jack at the end of *The Jazz Singer* – or, for that matter, by Al Jolson himself, with whom the character tellingly shares a first name.

However, that transformation is highly unstable and is ultimately undone by, rather than mediated through, blackface performance. The song 'I'm Sitting on Top of the World' itself foreshadows this eventuality. Towards the beginning of the film, Al sings the song while *not* in blackface, after achieving his initial success as a singer and songwriter. Despite its jaunty tune, the seemingly triumphant song sung by a white man fully confident in his whiteness is really about tragedy waiting to happen – although the singer is apparently too gleeful, and perhaps too white, to care. The second half of the chorus irreverently proclaims, 'Glory hallelujah, I just told the parson / Hey, par, get ready to call / Just like Humpty Dumpty, / I'm going to fall'. The fall in question is the result of familial drama catalysed by Al's wife, the less successful singer Molly, who abandons both her husband and their three-year-old child Sonny, indirectly leading to the boy's death.[74]

Jolson's one and only blackface performance in *The Singing Fool* occurs at the end of the film in a reprise of what would become the real-life singer's most popular song: 'Sonny Boy'. Immediately after Al privately sings 'Sonny Boy' while holding his dying three-year-old in his arms, his callous stage manager forces him to perform the same song in front of an audience. The grief-stricken singer receives a standing ovation before collapsing backstage. The final scene of *The Singing Fool* relies on the 'feminization of the black man' to 'celebrat[e] performance as a vehicle for emotional intensity. . . . Blackface gives full expression' to otherwise intolerable feelings. In this role, moreover, Al's character himself becomes the 'Mammy' figure, since as the sole loving parent, he is both mother and father to young Sonny.[75]

When Al revives from his collapse backstage, the stage manager apologizes for forcing him to perform. But Al, sitting propped between this white man and a white woman named Grace, states that he is glad he did. His final act after declaring to Grace that 'everything is going to be all right' is to kiss her. This visually interracial kiss tellingly lands somewhere behind Grace's neck rather than squarely on her lips. With Al in this compromised position – not fully erect, kiss incomplete, still in blackface – the screen fades to credits as the chords of 'Sonny Boy' continue to swell. The film thus concludes with Al's return to white masculinity optimistically forecast but not fully realized, and, moreover, dependent on the whims of yet another woman.

As a tongue-in-cheek anthem to white, masculine success, 'I'm Sitting on Top of the World' finally reveals the dependency of both whiteness and masculinity upon performative constructions of Blackness and femininity – and hence their inherent trajectory towards a 'fall'. In Loncraine's 1995 *Richard III*, setting both the literal and figurative fall of McKellen's king to Jolson's song makes audible, if not directly visible, the invisible racialized interior of *White Heat*'s fallen antihero as well as that of Richard himself.

Blackface, of course, long predated American cinema. White performers conveyed Blackness using 'natural oils like bitumen, soot from coal, and black clothes' even before members of Shakespeare's own company 'blacked up' to play Aaron the Moor, the Prince of Morocco, Othello or Cleopatra.[76] As early as the medieval miracle and mystery plays, 'the souls of the damned were represented by actors painted black or in black costumes', while 'in the plays of the Fall . . . Lucifer and his confederate rebels, after having sinned, turned black'.[77] Blackness in these instances was a direct signifier of evil. The symbolic presence of blackface in Loncraine's *Richard III* is thus also traceable back to the culture in which the play was originally staged, featuring Richard as what Robert Weiman and Douglas Bruster argue is a simultaneously tragic and farcical version of the medieval Vice figure.[78]

In Loncraine's *Richard III*, while such a visual signification of Blackness persists in the black uniforms of Richard's bodyguards and later of Richard himself – both in turn inspired by real-life SS uniforms – the choice leans more towards farce than tragedy.[79] McKellen's final hellish fall to the tune of Jolson's jaunty song is, moreover, an over-the-top moment of parody. At this instance he is simultaneously a wickedly grinning Vice figure falling into the flames of his originary pit; the film noir sociopath Cody Jarrett expunging his dark insanity, criminality and mommy issues in a burst of white heat; and, most ludicrously yet pointedly of all, a Hitler figure donning the temporary white mask of a Jewish singer headed for a fall into blackface.

Rising to the surface with this mix of early modern and contemporary allusions is the artificial, constructed nature of both whiteness and its Black other. McKellen's Richard III is not, to use Chakravarty's terms, a metaphorically Black, monstrous, improperly queer terrorist properly sacrificed to allow fair futurity to emerge. Rather, he is one acknowledged artificially white villain passing the baton to another. As many commentators have noticed, right after he shoots Richard, Richmond (Dominic West) looks directly into the camera and provides a far-from-heroic smirk. In his commentary on the script McKellen observes that 'Richmond's grin is unsettling' and, moreover, that 'the future is a question mark'. McKellen also recalls, during his view of the film's first cut with Loncraine, having 'relished the double irony of the Al Jolson song which he had overlaid on the final frames of his film. In the moment when their fates collide, Richmond and Richard both feel that they are sitting on top of the world'.[80] They do so, however, not via the blackening signifiers of the early modern Vice figure but rather through the ironized masks of white identity.

The once and future queen

The uncertainty of the future in Loncraine's *Richard III* is perhaps most bluntly signalled by the absence of one significant voice from the past: that of Margaret of Anjou, who is cut from McKellen and Loncraine's script. Although many of Margaret's lines are divided up and assigned to various other female characters, the religious framework of Margaret's accusations and prophecies, as Saskia Kossak notes, is largely eliminated in this mostly areligious film.[81]

Also at stake in Margaret's absence is the film's vision of history as well as the relationship between past and future. McKellen himself explains Margaret's excision as, first, a matter of expediency:

> She haunts *Richard III* like a living ghost, referring back to the recent and distant past. Yet, even theatre audiences are confused

by her persistent litany of revenge. In the film, her powerful presence would not compensate for the time spent in explaining clearly who she is and has been.

The decision also involved 'a change in emphasis'. The result was a more forward-oriented vision 'underlined by bringing to life Princess Elizabeth, who in the play is an offstage character', as well as by 'expand[ing] the presence of Richmond, her husband-to-be'.[82]

The replacement of the 'foul wrinkled witch' and 'hateful, withered hag' with the amplified presence of the much prettier, younger, distinctly white Richmond and Elizabeth of York (Kate Steavenson-Payne) in one sense emphasizes England's fair futurity (1.3.163, 214).[83] Richmond's final speech is displaced from the end of the play to a pre-battle wedding, with the key line apotheosizing the royal couple's marriage as 'God's fair ordinance' uttered by the officiating priest (5.4.31). The scene, which ends with Richmond's pre-battle prayer, takes the place of his textual visitation by the ghosts of Richard's victims.

Substituting for Richard's own ghost scene is a nightmare sequence. The sweating tyrant tosses and turns in his sleep as voices from the past – not all of them characters Richard has slain – replay from elsewhere on the film's soundtrack. Prominent among them are the Duchess's barking insults: 'Are you my son? You toad! . . . Bloody you are, bloody will be your end!' The parallel scenes draw a pronounced contrast between the happy heterosexual match between Richmond and the young Elizabeth versus what is presented as Richard's depraved, lonely homosexuality. When McKellen awakens from his nightmare, he first follows the text by comforting himself with what might be described as extravagantly 'homo' self-love: 'Richard loves Richard; that is, I am I' (5.3.184). When subsequently he falls into doubt, concluding that 'when I die, no soul will pity me', a hand creeps in from the left side of the frame. The camera pulls back to reveal Richard's 'faithful batman' Ratcliffe, who rocks the distraught king back and forth as Richard clutches him and sobs (202).[84] Counterposing their dark, nocturnal embrace is a subsequent interpolated scene depicting the similarly blocked but far brighter, daybreak exchange of caresses and sweet words between Elizabeth and Richmond, who awaken in bed together. As Richmond describes his own 'fairestboding dreams' to his new wife, the camera pulls back to reveal the couple's tastefully nude marital embrace (228). In these paired scenes, the contrast between fair futurity and the queer death drive directly displaces the textual contrast between heavenly and hellish visitations.

Yet even with Margaret and her haunting prophecies erased along with the ghosts, the future orientation of Loncraine's *Richard III* is – as West's final smirk suggests – not only not fully 'fair' but also not fully forward-looking. Replacing Margaret as a ghostly reminder of past events in Shakespeare's first tetralogy are the film's references to its own, equally troubled cinematic past. In a previously quoted line from Shakespeare's *Richard III* that is cut in Loncraine's film, Margaret invokes the religious forebears of film noir's secular light/dark imagery when she calls Richard 'hell's black intelligencer'. The line also alludes to one early modern explanatory model of dark skin colour, tracing its origins to God's curse upon the sinful Ham and his progeny, as well as the popular understanding of the devil in his true form as black.

The context of the line is the 'three queens' scene, in which the former Queen Margaret, current Queen Elizabeth and would-be queen Duchess of York collectively and chorus-like mourn the losses they have suffered at Richard's hands. After providing a long list of the dead, Margaret intones, 'Richard yet lives, hell's black intelligencer, / Only reserved their factor to buy souls / And send them thither. But at hand, at hand / Ensues his piteous and unpitied end' (4.4.71–4). She describes Richard as Satan's spy, allowed temporarily to live as the devil's 'factor', or agent, to send other souls to hell before he is quite deservedly sent there himself. As I discuss in Chapter 1, the line epitomizes Margaret's status as what is often seen as a proponent of the Tudor myth, affirming Richmond's eventual defeat of Richard and establishment of the Tudor line as divine providence.

The residue of this voice in Loncraine's film is most directly found in the character of the Duchess of York. Maggie Smith's Duchess takes several of Margaret's lines in Loncraine's highly abbreviated version of the three queens scene, which here features the Duchess, Queen Elizabeth and the young Princess Elizabeth. All references to God and hell are cut, however. If the spirit of Margaret's prophecy regarding Richard's flame-bound fate as 'hell's black intelligencer' is retained at all in Loncraine's film – and I am suggesting that it is – that retention happens symbolically through the parodic hellfire that swallows McKellen's plummeting, grinning, single-black-gloved Richard at the film's conclusion to the ebullient soundtrack of Al Jolson's *Singing Fool*.

As a result, a connection emerges between Loncraine's *Richard III* and *The Hollow Crown*'s adaptation of the same play two decades later. In this final scene, the 'Margaret function' in Loncraine's adaptation undergoes a paradigm shift from England's chronicle history to American film history, and from biblical to cinematic intertextuality. Margaret's providential prophecy of a sinner's damnation thereby becomes the cataclysmic end of a film noir antihero as well as that antihero's fall into blackface. By invoking the racially loaded heritage of both blackface drama and film noir, Loncraine's *Richard III* anticipates *The Hollow Crown*'s use of a Black Margaret not only to speak for the sins of England's past but to reveal the shadow subsequently cast by twentieth-century history. For both Cooke's and Loncraine's screen versions of *Richard III* end, in some sense, in a holocaust: the former with a panoramic vision of war's tragic outcome, the latter in a tongue-in-cheek moment of black comedy. Both invisible and visible constructions of race are crucial aspects of both final moments and demand, in each case, to be thoroughly recognized.

So, to return to the question with which this chapter began, what is a song by a Jewish-American blackface singer doing in a 1995 retelling of *Richard III* in a hypothetical fascist Britain? The answer is inextricably linked to the question I address in Chapter 1: namely, what is the significance of a Jewish-Nigerian Brit playing Margaret of Anjou in *The Hollow Crown*'s 2016 version of the same play? Both details epitomize the evolving relationship among adaptation, race and intersectionality in Shakespeare's histories on screen. As the product of the evolution of our increasingly interconnected world, the contemporary Shakespeare history adaptation resists circumscription by any singular vision of history. Rather, it is defined by intersections across media, through time and among multiple facets of human identity. Through the ongoing reception of the persistent form of the screen adaptation, moreover, these intersections themselves undergo a continuous process of change.

My exploration of these developments has thus far taken us back in time, from *The Hollow Crown*'s 2016 second season to the 1990s renaissance of Shakespearean cinema. In the conclusion to follow, I take us briefly forward to consider the future ramifications of the racially conscious Shakespeare adaptation. I examine a production that is, at first glance, not Shakespearean at all, although it is clearly focused on race: Netflix's popular serial drama, *Bridgerton*.

Conclusion

Swinging the lens: *Bridgerton* as Shakespearean history in digital cultures

This conclusion investigates the Shakespearean resonances of a production that has become a cultural touchstone for considerations of nontraditional casting in historical serial drama writ large. That is Netflix's Regency-set romance *Bridgerton*, which is based on a popular book series by American novelist, Julia Quinn.[1] While Quinn's novels concern only presumptively white characters, Netflix's *Bridgerton* – like other creations of African American television producer Shonda Rhimes's eponymous production company, Shondaland – deliberately populates its cast with racially and ethnically diverse actors. Moreover, like several Shondaland productions, from ABC's long-running political drama *Scandal* (2012–18) to the short-lived sequel to *Romeo and Juliet, Still Star-Crossed* (2017), *Bridgerton* is part of Shakespeare's inescapable presence, both direct and indirect, acknowledged and unacknowledged, in contemporary TV.[2] This globally popular streaming series is a vital site for considering both the immediate consequences of the adaptations discussed throughout this book, as well as future directions and possibilities for what it means to adapt Shakespeare's histories.

Alongside *Bridgerton*'s more period-appropriate Jane Austen associations, its Shakespearean connections are many and varied. Several involve the show's content in an instance of what Elisabeth Bronfen describes as contemporary serial television's 'mutable process of disseminating and reassembling the Bard's work'.[3] In the following discussion, I demonstrate how references to the comedies in the *Bridgerton* novels shift in the direction of history in the Netflix series – both via the addition of a historical character, Queen Charlotte, and by appropriating aspects of the Henriad as romance. First, however, I examine a crucial context for these elements of *Bridgerton*: what Romano Mullin and Anna Blackwell have shown is the status of the internet, especially social media, as the site of the production of new 'digital Shakespearean objects'.[4] Numerous viewers who have commented on *Bridgerton* in such venues have invoked the Bard's name as a metonym for various aspects of the show's approach to history, including nontraditional casting. This response to *Bridgerton* epitomizes one potentially radical downstream effect of what I have argued throughout this book is the integral role of race in contemporary Shakespeare adaptation. While some commentators invoke the bedrock of Shakespearean theatrical practice to justify nontraditional casting in contemporary period drama, a more subversive reverse alchemy also takes place. Nontraditional casting becomes through *Bridgerton* and its internet remediations the hallmark of what it means to be Shakespeare.

Tweeting the Bard in #*Bridgerton*

As digital technologies continue to transform the ways audiences experience on-screen media, adaptation studies have begun to assess how social networking platforms and other online public discussion spaces not only might contribute to our understanding of the reception of Shakespeare screen adaptations but also undermine the very distinction between production and reception. Regarding the Twitter group @HollowCrownfans, Romano Mullin notes that the platform enables users 'to share their own iterations of Shakespeare within an online context in which the line between producer and consumer has become increasingly blurred'. Despite Twitter's theoretical potential for global connectivity, Mullin also highlights its limitations for producing 'a truly egalitarian, twenty-first century Shakespeare'. The @HollowCrownfans group is primarily white and Anglophone and promotes 'relatively conservative takes on the Bard'. The intervention of alternative perspectives is circumscribed by what Mullin describes as Twitter's 'echo chamber effect', in which 'users often find themselves engaging with people who are just like them and share their views'.[5]

But what happens when Shakespeare is re-mediated through productions that, like *Bridgerton*, do not directly present themselves as either adaptations or citations of his work? I propose that consideration of these 'other' Shakespeares might broaden our understanding of both how Shakespeare signifies in today's digital world and how Shakespeare is both received and constructed by more diverse audiences. Rather than examine a single group's response to *Bridgerton*, I instead have employed the methodology of various Twitter searches using key terms such as 'Bridgerton' and 'Shakespeare' to investigate how these terms intersect across a variety of public Twitter feeds. While this method limits the consideration of crosstalk among Twitter users, it allows for greater breadth in considering how Shakespeare as a cultural object is being constructed by viewers of *Bridgerton*, which as of the last quarter of 2021 was 'the most watched original series' on the world's most popular streaming video platform.[6]

A few more statistics are necessary for context. As of 2022 Twitter had 396.5 million active users worldwide, with the largest number, 77.5 million, in the United States and the second largest, 19.05 million, in the United Kingdom. The other top-five countries were Japan, India and Brazil.[7] In the United States, Twitter has been found to be a racially diverse site overall, with a 2018 survey reporting 35 per cent of Asian, 31 per cent of LatinX, 30 per cent of non-LatinX white and 28 per cent of Black respondents using the social media platform daily.[8]

One component of *Bridgerton*'s Shakespearean pedigree referenced on Twitter involves the show's cast members, many of whom have appeared on the Shakespearean stage. This roster includes several prominent Black actors: Golda Rosheuvel, who plays Queen Charlotte – a historical figure with (as I discuss later) possible African ancestry; Adjoa Andoh, who plays Lady Danbury, a wealthy widow and confidant of the queen; and Regé-Jean Page, whose recent breakout celebrity status emerged from his role in Season One as the rakish but sensitive Simon Basset, newly named Duke of Hastings. For *Bridgerton* audience members familiar with their stage careers, these actors carry a Shakespearean residue through the process that Marvin Carlson has dubbed 'ghosting'.[9]

Twitter users in this group tend to be in the older range and more frequently identify themselves by profession. For example, shortly after *Bridgerton*'s initial season aired, writer Mike McClelland posted, 'I just watched the first episode of Bridgerton with my mom and when I saw the glorious @goldarosh was the Queen I immediately remembered seeing her onstage with the Royal Shakespeare Company 15 years ago when I was a college student in England! What presence!'[10] Publicist Zoë Miller similarly tweeted, 'I realized today that I saw Regé-Jean Page (the Duke of Hastings) in The Merchant of Venice in 2015.'[11] In the case of Page, for some users 'ghosting' extends to another Black actor in another time and medium, in one of the first instances of nontraditional casting in Shakespeare on screen. As marketer Sara Toussaint wrote, '@Jackie531 said that @regejean in #Bridgerton reminds her of Denzel Washington in "Much Ado About Nothing" and I – [emoji indicating coy laughter].'[12] With this double Shakespearean association in hand, Page emerges as a potential contradiction to what Blackwell asserts is the 'implicit whiteness of Shakespearean celebrity'.[13]

The link between *Bridgerton* and Shakespeare is particularly strong in the case of Adjoa Andoh, 'aka Lady Danbury in #Bridgerton'. Andoh's groundbreaking presence as the title character in Shakespeare's Globe Theatre's all-WOC (women-of-colour) production of *Richard II* had editor of *Oprah Mag* Elena Nicolaou wishing she could 'go back in time' to catch a performance.[14] This version of *Richard II*, which I briefly discuss in Chapter 3, emphasizes the often forgotten role in Britain's national story of women and people of colour – a goal that it shares with the Netflix hit drama.[15] It appeared on stage in March and April 2019, just a year before *Bridgerton* dropped on Netflix.

Andoh's ubiquity on social media lends this stage production of *Richard II* a robust digital presence. Prominent on Twitter as well as elsewhere on the internet is the iconic image used to advertise the show, featuring the bare head, neck and upper shoulders of the actress in character as King Richard gazing solemnly outward against the backdrop of St George's flag. In Andoh's own words, this reappropriation of 'the flag of go back where you came from' is a strategic reminder that 'there is no Great Britain without brown bodies'.[16] With the closure of theatres during the Covid-19 pandemic, Andoh's own production company, 'Swinging the Lens', uploaded a filmed performance onto YouTube in April 2020, making the performance itself a component of Andoh's online presence.[17] To 'swing the lens' is, of course, a cinematic metaphor, describing a means of shifting perspective within a continuous shot. With respect to Andoh's venture, the phrase encompasses both the shift from Shakespeare's vision of a white, male English nation to the Globe's BAME female national subjects and the shift in media from the stage to YouTube's digital video platform. Despite a disheartening string of anonymous racist comments posted in response to *Richard II* on YouTube, the production nonetheless defiantly 'exists', in Andoh's words, 'in the world', where it continues to attract online viewers – over sixty-seven thousand of them so far.[18]

In that digital world, Andoh's *Bridgerton* and Shakespearean identities often directly collide. Another frequently appearing image on Twitter is Andoh as Lady Danbury wearing a white satin empire-waist ball gown with a standing collar, elbow-length white gloves and an ornate matching necklace and tiara. It is used, for instance, to advertise Andoh's appearance for a Zoom Q&A and Shakespeare Masterclass at the ICAT acting school in March 2021.[19] Lady Danbury here functions as the literal poster child for masterful Shakespearean acting. Similarly, advertisements for the British Library's April 2021 public online presentation on women in Shakespeare called 'Shakespeare's Sisters' capitalized on Andoh's power as both Shakespearean actor and '#Bridgerton Star'[20](Figure 9).

Alongside invocations of the Shakespearean resumes of individual actors, plot connections between *Bridgerton* and Shakespeare are also a common Twitter theme. Twitter user and *Bridgerton* fan Reggie Graham summarized Season One as follows: 'Bridgerton is literally every Shakespeare play I've ever studied.'[21] Numerous viewers compared the marriage plot of the show's first season involving the reluctant courtship between Simon and the eldest Bridgerton daughter, Daphne (Phoebe Dynevor), to the Beatrice and Benedick plot of *Much Ado about Nothing* – often with direct reference to the 1993 film. 'I see y'all enjoying Bridgerton, please do yourselves a favor and watch Much Ado About Nothing (1993)', tweeted @jen_rizk.[22] Or as Toronto actress Chi-Chi Onuah put the matter: 'I think #Beatrice & #LadyDanbury would get along quite well! Thoughts, @andoh_adjoa?'[23] Similar comparisons have been drawn with respect to the second season's rocky courtship between the womanizing young Viscount Anthony Bridgerton (Jonathan Bailey) and sharp-witted outsider Kate Sharma (Simone

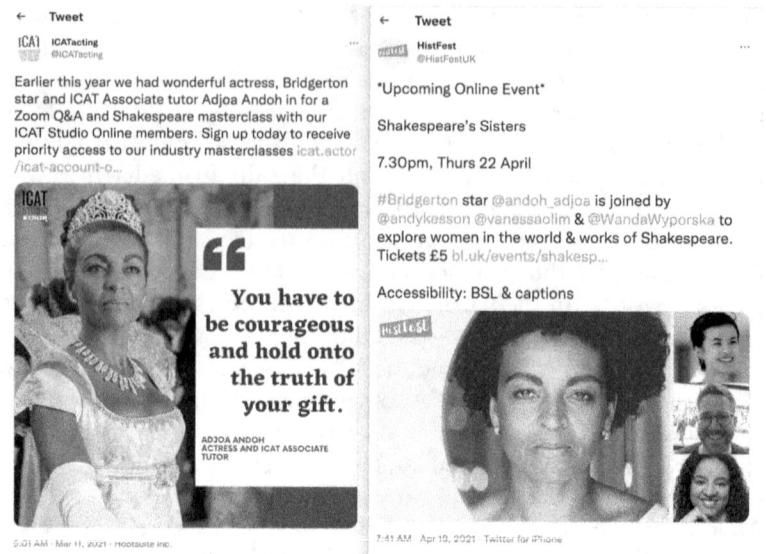

FIGURE 9 Bridgerton *meets Shakespeare: Adjoa Andoh on Twitter. Twitter .com.* https://twitter.com/ICATacting/status/1369951481214930944 *(left) and* https://twitter.com/HistFestUK/status/13841097931581726742 *(right).*

Ashley), where Kate's plot takes on additional resonances with that of her namesake in *The Taming of the Shrew*. On Twitter the latter comparison has gained particular traction, with numerous fans making the connection. The official *Bridgerton* Twitter feed itself pushed the idea. In a copiously 'liked', quoted and re-tweeted reply to one fan asking whether Anthony would be tamed, @Bridgerton responded, 'Dear reader, it still remains to be seen, who shall be taming whom?'[24]

Beyond specific plays and specific actors, digital culture's link between *Bridgerton* and Shakespeare runs deeper still, as a matter of negotiating the representation of the past through the lens of the present. Twitter reactions to *Bridgerton*'s initial appearance on Netflix in December 2020 invoked the Bard in several interrelated ways, many of which deployed the rhetorical device of the metonym. A common theme was the identification of the show's old-fashioned dialogue and historical setting as Shakespeare. @INVISELET wrote, 'they talk about honor so much in bridgerton i'd think this was zuko doing a shakespeare monologue in 5th period drama class'.²⁵ Similarly, @Aliciana posted, 'Bridgerton got me talking like I'm William Shakespeare. Mfs got me out here like "That's preposterous"'.²⁶ For some, this element of the show was frankly off-putting. @kevtahjae, for instance, had to stop watching: '10 minutes into bridgerton and I had to crop out. I can't take the Shakespeare slang.'²⁷ Others, like @KBK_811, found that high school Shakespeare made it 'easier . . . to understand #Bridgerton'.²⁸ Fast-forward to Season Two, and Marnie Wellar exuberantly tweeted, 'Light went on for me today, realized the English teacher's long game, all the painstaking effort over "The Taming of the Shrew" was to prepare us for Bridgerton Season 2; sir, I commend you'.²⁹

Debates about nontraditional casting in *Bridgerton* engage the show's metonymic association with Shakespeare to trouble the distinction between past and present as well as between history and fiction, locating the various iterations of his plays in a contested and shifting middle ground. When, in response to a February 2021 *New York Times* article on *Bridgerton* and period costuming, Victor Coronado from Copenhagen, Denmark, tweeted the standard anti-nontraditional casting logic – 'What's the point of having an inclusive cast in a series that is set in a time and place that (historically) wasn't like that? This is absurd' – several respondents brought up Shakespeare explicitly to reject *Bridgerton*'s historicity. Jassodra from Trinidad answered the tweeter's question directly: 'Because nincompoop, it's a TV hist romance not a hist documentary. The book it's based on is pretty absurd, so a black Duke makes no difference. Ppl probably said little back then when actors black faced Othello.' Romina Ricci offered a list that links *Bridgerton*, Shakespeare, history and fiction: 'First: an inclusive cast is always a positive thing, second Shakespeare's tragedies have black characters too, third Queen Charlotte had black ancestors, fourth it's fiction and it's fascinating. #Bridgerton.'³⁰ Elsewhere on Twitter, in response to an interlocutor's concern that fans of *Bridgerton* might confuse fiction with 'actual history', @wuthering_alice made a direct connection to the history play genre: 'Thing is, I don't think it IS trying to be real history. It says at the start. It just happens to have a character who existed. It's in the same vein as Shakespeare's histories in that respect. And even Queen Charlotte pops up in Bridgerton IIRC [If I Recall Correctly].'³¹

Strikingly, while many individuals alluded to the Bard in relation to nontraditional casting, those perspectives occupy a wide demographic and political range. Kevin L, who identifies himself as 'Christian, husband, dad, anarchist', claimed that while watching *Bridgerton* he 'didn't really think much about it having black actors. It's a historical fiction dramedy and after all Shakespeare used white men and boys for all parts, so whatever'.[32] An apparently Gen-Z 'journalism student' and 'lover of all things cinema', Akshaya Abbina, defended *Bridgerton*'s diverse casting as follows: 'man ... Bridgerton is a fantasy, and the new Macbeth is shakespeare, every person of every race and gender have been Shakespeare since as long as I can remember.'[33]

While the latter post, especially, hints of a dawning 'brave new world' in which Shakespeare is synonymous with casting inclusivity, the association between the Bard and nontraditional casting is not always a progressive one. Lay viewers' invocations of Shakespeare on Twitter in defence of *Bridgerton*'s casting practices are thematically similar to but tonally distinct from more authoritative opinion pieces that appeared around the same time in such places as *The New York Times* and NPR (National Public Radio). At the heart of these articles beat a largely conservative impulse: to link apparently liberal choices in televisual casting to the privileged venues of theatre and, especially, Shakespearean theatre – forms of high culture with authority that transcends considerations of mere historical accuracy. In a July 2021 broadcast of the popular highbrow news programme, *All Things Considered*, NPR's long-standing theatre and film critic Bob Mondello began with a series of rhetorical questions designed to poke fun at the parochial attitudes represented by social media commentators on this topic: 'If *Slumdog Millionaire* star Dev Patel takes a seat at the Round Table in *The Green Knight,* does that mean King Arthur recruited knights of Indian descent in the 12th century?' Those who question 'unconventional casting choices' were presumed to be insufficiently educated in literary and theatrical history, since 'cross-cultural casting is about as old as casting itself'. In his subsequent discussion of the history of nontraditional casting practices in theatre, twentieth-century prejudices against casting Black actors in the title role of Shakespeare's *Othello* featured prominently. Mondello, like @akshayaabbina, concluded with praise for Joel Coen's 2021 *Macbeth*, which stars Denzel Washington in the title role.[34]

In a similar vein, in January 2021 London theatre critic Matt Wolf wrote an article for *The New York Times* designed to educate his largely American audience about the theatrical origins of

Bridgerton's approach to race. Oddly not mentioning the crucial contribution of Joseph Papp in the United States, Wolf traced *Bridgerton*'s progressive casting choices to 'Britain's pioneering interest in colourblind casting'. He went on to observe that many of the same Black actors who appear in *Bridgerton*, most notably Rosheuvel as Queen Charlotte and Andoh as Lady Danbury, are 'regulars on the London stage'.

While Wolf's cited instances of classic British nontraditional casting include both Nicholas Hytner's 2003 *Henry V* and the Globe's 2019 all-WOC *Richard II*, his description of a non-Shakespearean example highlights the particular importance of the Bard to his understanding of the practice. Describing in detail how *Bridgerton* reminded him of Josette Simon's 1990 cross-cast role as the Marilyn Monroe-like 'seductress' Maggie in Arthur Miller's *After the Fall*, Wolf concludes, 'Suddenly, a comparatively minor piece from the playwright seemed both more substantial and more moving, and Simon, who went on to play Cleopatra for the Royal Shakespeare Company just a few years ago, enjoyed a deserved moment of glory'.[35] By linking Simon's role as Maggie with her Shakespearean future as another historically infamous, variably Black femme fatale with a white man as her target, Wolf suggests that this elevation of a minor Miller play – like the upward trajectory of Simon's career, and like the legitimacy of cross-racial casting itself – also fundamentally depends on the power of something beyond them both. That something is Shakespeare, this time as a metonym for British theatre as agent of cultural authority. Yet at the same time, something new is happening, placing the Black female body at the centre of theatrical tradition and, by extension, at the centre of history. Following in the footsteps of Josette Simon is not only Adjoa Andoh but also, as I will now discuss in detail, Golda Rosheuvel as Queen Charlotte, England's first 'Black' queen.

'Was Queen Charlotte real?': Nontraditional casting in/as history

Her 2018 role as a lesbian Othello notwithstanding,[36] Rosheuvel's importance to *Bridgerton* fans appears to have less to do with the actress's resume than with the historical figure she represents on that show. Numerous online articles posted around the release of *Bridgerton*'s first two seasons frame the choice to cast the biracial Guyanese-British actress as Queen Charlotte on the documented likelihood that the historical Charlotte of Mecklenburg-Strelitz, wife of England's King George III, had African ancestry and thus was, in a sense, 'Britain's first biracial royal'.[37]

Even for fans of the *Bridgerton* novels, this was something new. Like the presence of characters of colour, Queen Charlotte's role in the plot is the Netflix series' own addition; she does not appear in Quinn's books. Historians' speculations about the real Charlotte's race in turn provide the groundwork for Shondaland's central historical revision: that a Black reigning queen enabled the rise of Black aristocratic families on equal footing with their white counterparts. Hence the, diegetically speaking, largely unremarked-upon presence of characters of colour in *Bridgerton*'s high society, who mix with white characters in relationships of friendship, courtship, love, sex and marriage.

The idea of a historical Black queen as embodied by Rosheuvel's Charlotte proved to be of almost as much interest to *Bridgerton*'s viewers as the breakout celebrity of Regé-Jean Page. Worldwide Google trends from the period of the show's first Netflix airing in the winter of 2020–1 demonstrate that searches using the topic term 'Charlotte of Mecklenburg-Strelitz' rose dramatically. They peaked at just under half the peak rate of searches for the actor 'Regé-Jean Page', and roughly matched searches for the first season's female lead, Phoebe Dynevor.[38] In the UK during the same period, searches for Queen Charlotte were even more popular, peaking at approximately 70 per cent of the maximum rate of searches for Page.[39] In the United States, where Page was initially less well known, searches for Queen Charlotte came close to matching searches for Page until the latter achieved a second, higher peak later in the spring.[40] In all three localities, all three searches were overwhelmingly more popular than searches for 'Golda Rosheuvel' or other non-lead actors in the series. Similar, if less exuberant trend patterns followed the airing of the second season in March 2022. These data suggest that at least when it comes to a Black queen of England, audience interest in a historical figure can be nearly as strong as audience interest in a sexy, handsome new star.

Bridgerton's premiere episode clearly courts such interest. A scene ostensibly devoted to Daphne Bridgerton's social debut before Queen Charlotte more extravagantly emphasizes the revelation of the queen's Black body before the show's viewers. The series' narrator, Lady Whistledown, prefaces this encounter with a dramatic voiceover: 'Today is a most important day, and for some a terrifying one. For today is the day London's marriage-minded misses are presented to her Majesty the Queen.' With this pronouncement, the scene shifts from the debutantes' flustered preparations to a portrait of James Fleet (who plays George III) and Rosheuvel side-by-side in their royal roles. The image is based on Alan Ramsey's 1761 coronation portrait of the real-life George and Charlotte.[41] While the king's complexion, wig and demeanour are virtually identical to those of the original painting, the queen is altered to display browner skin, higher-piled hair and a sterner facial expression. The camera zooms in on the portraitized Rosheuvel's imperious stare before cutting to a shot of the living actress slumped on her throne, wearing the same wig and a similar glare (Figure 10). Still focusing on the fate of the debutantes about to appear before this surly queen, the voiceover ominously concludes, 'May God have mercy on their souls!'[42] The link between the archivally inspired portrait and the actress's body establishes the historical authenticity of the Black Queen Charlotte at the very moment the show's viewers, along with the terrified young women, first meet her.

FIGURE 10 *Queen Charlotte and her court*. Bridgerton, *Season 1, Ep. 1*. © *Netflix Worldwide Entertainment 2020. All rights reserved. Screen grab.*

Their terror is part of the point: this is not only a Black Queen Charlotte but an empowered Queen Charlotte. Behind the enthroned queen is another portrait that hangs in the room where the scene was filmed in England's Wilton House: Anton Van Dyck's 1635 'Philip Herbert, 4th Earl of Pembroke with His Family'.[43] Its composition and colour scheme emphasize the presence of Lady Anne Clifford, a standing light-skinned female figure in a pale blue gown. From a side-facing posture that situates Lady Anne as less powerful than her husband and male children behind her despite her foregrounded location, she demurely turns her head to face the painting's viewer.

The similarity between the portrait of Rosheuvel as Queen Charlotte and the living body of the actress makes the difference between Rosheuvel's Charlotte and the woman in this background painting even more striking. In direct opposition to the seventeenth-century countess, *Bridgerton*'s Queen Charlotte is brown-skinned, peeved and far-from-demure; her comportment towards her subjects, as the voiceover insists, is a commanding, even threatening one. Her central position, moreover, is not diminished by the presence of husband and sons but amplified by surrounding members of her mostly female court, who represent a diversity of skin tones and ethnicities. Although the historical Queen Charlotte had fifteen children, all but three of whom survived well into adulthood, none of these offspring are mentioned in the show's first two seasons. Most notable is the absence of the eldest son, the eventual George IV, who historically served as Prince Regent during his father's mental incapacity. In *Bridgerton*'s world it is the queen, not Prince George, who is in charge; in this version of Regency England, there is apparently no Regent.

In addition to revising Queen Charlotte's familial role, *Bridgerton* revises her hairstyle. Second only, perhaps, to the queen's real-life snuff habit – a quirk highlighted in Rosheuvel's performance – her ever-changing hairdo is the least demure thing about this character. Across both seasons of *Bridgerton*, the queen's wigs showcase and celebrate her extravagance and her difference. According to Rosheuvel, the lightest of these contraptions weighed upward of thirty pounds; wearing them was a physical feat as well as a decorative endeavour. They are also weighty in a symbolic sense. By repeatedly conveying the message that 'Black hair is beautiful' via the not quite historically authentic accessories of a historically

'Black' queen, *Bridgerton* fashions history to serve a contemporary purpose.⁴⁴ Despite the fact that race is not directly mentioned until the series' fourth episode, both these wigs and the series' use of historical paintings to introduce its Black Queen Charlotte immediately disturb any understanding of *Bridgerton* as an example of truly colourblind casting. As neither modern nor truly 'period' elements of the production's mise en scène, paintings and wigs alike convey a fluid and fantastical approach to historicity in general as well as to race in/as history.

Then, at a key moment in Episode Four, precisely midway through the first season, Lady Danbury (Adjoa Andoh) delivers what has become, in certain internet circles, an oft-cited monologue. 'Look at our queen. Look at our king', the world-wise widow exhorts her young Black mentee Simon, who is dubious about a match with the white heiress Daphne. 'Look at their marriage. Look at everything it is doing for us, allowing us to become. We were two separate societies divided by color, until a king fell in love with one of us. Love, Your Grace, conquers all.'⁴⁵ Lady Danbury's words confirm not only that race indeed exists in this world but that along with race, racism also exists – or at least, has previously existed. However, it has recently been eradicated, fairy-tale style, through love.

And thus a new controversy was born. 'Reader: I yelled', began a recap on Vulture.com by Renaissance cultural historian Tracy E. Robey in response to this declaration. '"An Affair of Honor" finally, conclusively demonstrates the extent to which *Bridgerton* is speculative historical romance. . . . [I]t's such a brilliant way to use love, the bedrock of the story and entire genre, to imagine a more inclusive past that draws on what historians know about Queen Charlotte's Black ancestry.'⁴⁶ But while some celebrated, others saw this revelation of *Bridgerton*'s historically inspired colour-consciousness insufficient against the weight of actual history. Aja Romano wrote for *Vox*, 'It is, in a nutshell, the *Hamilton* question – does historicity matter if the lack of historical accuracy is part of the point? – but this time applied to a story that is much less clear about what it wants to be.'⁴⁷ In a dialogue posted on *Refinery29* journalists Ineye Komonibo and Kathleen Newman-Bremang noted places where acknowledging race might have added psychological depth to *Bridgerton*'s characters. For instance, being Black in a white-privileging world might explain why Simon's father was so hard on his only son, to the point that the young duke had taken a personal vow not to have children in order to stymie his father's dream of carrying on the family name.⁴⁸

These considerations of the plights of individual characters coexist with what multiple commentators agree is a fundamental political problem with the show's selective attention to race. As film critic Carolyn Hinds pointed out in *The Observer*, 'You can't say race isn't of consequence when the world these characters inhabit was created in part through racism. The money to build the show's white row houses in Bath, the grand country estates and the palace came from the slave trade. Yes, slavery exists in this world, so *how* could race not matter?' Moreover, numerous elements of the show's not-quite-colour-conscious-enough world seem designed to court a white supremacist perspective: the entire lack of romance narratives between characters of colour, a preference (in the first season, at least) for light-skinned Black leads⁴⁹ and a tendency to pigeonhole Black characters in stereotypical roles, such as Lady Danbury as a maternal, self-abnegating 'Mammy' or the pregnant teen Marina as a promiscuous, light-skinned 'Jezebel'.⁵⁰ To this list one might also add Queen Charlotte herself as a threateningly assertive 'Sapphire'.⁵¹ With the subsequent introduction of Indian characters without direct acknowledgement of empire, the conversation about Season Two has continued in the same vein, with Isabel Molina-Guzmán, professor of Latina/Latino studies at the University of Illinois, concluding that *Bridgerton* 'keeps white subjectivity and pleasure intact through eliding the lived and fictional racial trauma of the past and present'.⁵²

The primary counterargument to these concerns as presented in public digital conversations privileges the benefits of racial equity in the linked arenas of pleasure and representation over the accurate portrayal of historical racism. As Rosheuvel herself puts the matter:

> I'm biracial. I was brought up in England. My mother was crazy about period dramas, which made me crazy about them. I never thought that I'd be able to be in one. It was something that was far away. I couldn't touch it. Now we can rewrite that story for the little girl who's sitting at home. That cycle is stopping now.⁵³

Part of *Bridgerton*'s pleasure-value is the release it offers Black viewers from the burden of confronting the spectacle of oppression. 'In my 40+ years of life', one viewer commented, 'finally being able to watch a period-show where Black people aren't just slaves and servants is refreshing as hell'.⁵⁴

Digital conversations also insist that historical truth is itself more complicated than the world of white aristocrats and Black slaves and servants often depicted in traditional period drama. Alongside the fantasy, *Bridgerton* also quite intentionally showcases a too-often unacknowledged historical reality. As Black romance novelist Vanessa Riley points out in a 2022 blog post, 'Black People existed in the Regency'; this population included 'over 10,000-20,000 that lived in London during the time of Jane Austen'. Both in England and worldwide, during this period people of colour occupied multiple social ranks, including the aristocracy.⁵⁵

While *Bridgerton* calls attention to this reality, however, reflecting the actual world of Regency England is also clearly not the show's chief aim. Robey's identification of *Bridgerton*'s genre as 'speculative historical romance' is therefore on point, and quite compatible with the show's association with Shakespeare. For Shakespeare functions in contemporary digital culture not only as a metonym for the re-appropriability of historical narratives through time but also as a locus for debates surrounding these reappropriations.

The question of audience is crucial in this regard. *Bridgerton*'s showrunner Chris Van Dusen, himself a white man, has justified the show's inclusive approach to race in terms of its obligation to 'reflect the world that we live in today'.⁵⁶ As I argue in Chapter 1, the adapted Shakespeare's history play must grapple with that genre's long-standing charge to represent 'who we are as a society', and in so doing accommodate as appropriate the 'we' not only of Britain but of digitalized media's global audience. The adapted contemporary period romance novel on a globally streaming platform occupies a similar cultural terrain and thus holds a similar obligation to a diverse viewership. Although the largest subpopulation of Netflix's viewers are white Americans, a fact that is driving its content, that subpopulation is not a majority. Moreover many viewers – especially international viewers – are not white. In the United States, which in the fourth quarter of 2020 comprised 65.3 million of Netflix's 203 million subscribers, 57 per cent identified as white, 22 per cent as LatinX and 15 per cent as Black. The other top-ranking countries for numbers of Netflix subscribers were, in order, Brazil, the UK, France, Germany and Mexico.⁵⁷ In the realm of Shakespeare adaptation and in Netflix's

Bridgerton, nontraditional casting is less about recreating period history in its own time than about reappropriating history in the current historical moment, thereby asserting the belonging of non-white groups not only in modern British or American political culture but within the not-inconsequential global world of televisual pleasure.

Bridgerton, the Henriad and the future of Shakespearean history

Towards the goal of remaking history in the name of both televisual pleasure and political representation, Netflix's *Bridgerton* goes beyond merely depicting England's first 'Black' queen. It also incorporates into her depiction, as well as into its primary romance narrative, elements of Shakespeare's most well-known historical plot. Just as Shakespeare's own histories are never quite free of the spectres of both comedy and tragedy, history hovers around the edges of *Bridgerton*'s citations of *Much Ado about Nothing* and, especially, *The Taming of the Shrew*. Along with Queen Charlotte's explicit presence, the Henriad's implicit presence in Netflix's adaptation shifts the comedic/romantic concerns of Quinn's novels towards the thematic territory of the contemporary adapted Shakespearean history play.

The first two seasons' overarching narrative of Anthony, the eldest Bridgerton son, invokes elements of Prince Hal's story from *1* and *2 Henry IV* as well as his eventual courtship of Katherine in the last act of *Henry V*. Due to the untimely death of his father ten years before the opening events of the series, Anthony became Viscount of Bridgerton at the tender age of eighteen. Although both the novels and the TV series characterize Anthony as what Lady Whistledown calls a 'capital R Rake', only the latter emphasizes his struggles with properly ascending to his role as patriarchal head of the household.[58] Moreover, it does so against the backdrop of a social and political world dominated by Rosheuvel's queen.

As portrayed by Shondaland, Anthony Bridgerton thus functions as a Prince Hal figure – but with a significant twist. For this young, rakish Viscount, the model for successful rule is not that of the properly English, properly masculine, militarily and politically successful usurper Henry IV, but, rather, a relationship of love transcending racial barriers – as represented by Charlotte's own match to the now mentally debilitated King George III. By setting its version of the Henriad story in a Regency England re-imagined as the province of a Black female sovereign for whom interracial love is the chief symbol of her power, *Bridgerton* reappropriates the history play genre as romance. In the process, the show insists upon the central, defining presence of Black women not only in Britain's national story but also in the broader imagined community of the global Netflix audience.

In Season One of Netflix's *Bridgerton*, Anthony's similarity to Prince Hal is immediately signalled by his initial absence from the crucial event of Daphne's royal debut. As the younger Bridgerton family members pile into the carriage bringing Daphne to the queen, their mother, the Viscountess Violet, asks with exasperation, 'Any sign of him yet?' To her second son Benedict she then fumes, 'If your brother wishes to be obeyed as Lord Bridgerton he must act as Lord Bridgerton. Where is he, Benedict?' After Benedict claims ignorance on this topic, the scene cuts to a mid-coitus close-up of Anthony and his mistress, opera singer and sex worker Siena Rosso (Sabrina Bartlett), a character who is mentioned in the novels but does not appear there, as it were, in the flesh. Anthony glances down at a pocket watch and hurries the pace of his thrusting. The watch, we later find out, is an heirloom from his father and thus an important signifier of Anthony's patriarchal duties as reigning Viscount. Apparently he hits the pacing right, because moments later he arrives at the palace gates, flushed and panting but in the nick of time.[59]

The first of these linked scenes parallels Henry IV's query to Humphrey of Gloucester: 'Where is the Prince your brother?' (*2H4* 4.2.13). The second resonates with the introductory conversation between Hal and Falstaff in *1 Henry IV* – which in production often presents one or both characters in bed with a sex worker, and which begins with Falstaff's temporally directed question, 'Now, Hal, what time of day is it, lad?' (1.2.1). Much as Falstaff's question anticipates Hal's subsequent vow about 'Redeeming time when men least think I will' (1.2.209), the pocket watch signifies the looming necessity of Anthony's own redemption of time. Siena is the closest *Bridgerton* gets to a proxy for Falstaff, and Anthony's various attempts to banish her find little success. After numerous twists and turns, at the end of Season One Siena ends up banishing her unreliable high-class suitor instead, and as a result the Viscount Bridgerton swears off love altogether. His reformation is thus put off until Season Two.

Like Siena as 'Falstaff', Anthony's mother functions as a considerably revised female stand-in for Shakespeare's Henry IV. Not only is Violet Bridgerton a woman and an involved parent instead of an emotionally distant father-king, but she also remains stubbornly, persistently alive. In fact, it might be argued that in continuing to claim the status as the head of the Bridgerton family despite her eldest son being of age, Violet is a usurper from whom Anthony must wrest control. In the series premiere, Violet berates her son for failing to take on his father's responsibilities: 'If your father were still here, Daphne would already have been matched. . . . So, you must ask yourself, are you merely an older brother, or are you the man of this house?' Later in the same episode she tells her son, 'I know society has dictated your present role in this family, Anthony, but with Daphne officially out, I assure you, I am more than capable'.[60] In the same conversation, Violet makes a not-so-subtle hint that it is Anthony's duty to find a proper wife and marry and, moreover, that doing so is essential to his ability to properly function as the head of the Bridgerton family.

A flashback scene in Season Two, Episode Three underscores this conflict between mother and son. Like most of their shared scenes, this flashback occurs exclusively in the Netflix version of *Bridgerton*. A few days after his father is killed by an anaphylactic reaction to a bee-sting, the doctor attempting to deliver the eighth Bridgerton child approaches Anthony in the dead of night to ask him, as the new head of household, to make a life-or-death decision involving Violet. A C-section, likely necessary to save the breech-positioned infant, will almost certainly in this pre-antibiotic era result in the mother's death. 'Who would your lordship prefer?' the doctor gravely asks the paralysed teen while his agonized mother shrieks her protests in the background. (Yes, this show is a romance!)

Here again, Violet couches Anthony's failure to measure up to his father in terms of matrimonial love. 'He [Edmund] loved me so much', she moans, 'this wouldn't even be a conversation. Because that kind of love, the answer, this choice, is obvious. I should not have to explain this to anyone! Edmund should be here!' Anthony finally gives up. 'Do what she wants', he tells the doctor. 'Whatever she chooses.' In leaving Violet this choice he also flees, abandoning her. In the end both mother and infant survive. In the adult Anthony's mind, however, the not-choosing was a failure. The camera reveals this point of view with a high-angle shot of the present-day 28-year-old Viscount, staring up at a portrait of his dead father while his mother's wail echo in his ears: 'Don't leave me!'[61]

The scene both parallels and revealingly revises Prince Hal's own crucial filial error in *2 Henry IV* when he mistakes his father's sleep for death and prematurely assumes the crown. What the dying king interprets as his son's rash 'hunger' for kingship was, rather, Hal insists, his chastising stance towards an object '[t]hat had before my face murdered my father' (4.5.225, 298). Accepting this explanation, the king is reconciled with his son before his death. In *Bridgerton*, the childbirth scene presents similar stakes in a similar setting – a potential transfer of power at a parent's bedside and potential deathbed – but with a significantly contrasting outcome. In *Henry IV, Part Two*, by seemingly reluctantly but in fact quite ably assuming the play's most potent symbol of authority, a seemingly 'effeminate', disloyal son and heir proves his filial loyalty, masculinity and kingly savvy all at once, just before his father dies. In *Bridgerton* Season Two, an overwhelmed teenager refuses the mantle of authority – and thus ostensibly fails as both man and household head in the very act that saves his mother's life.

By including Violet's articulate pleas, however, the scene asks the audience to judge Anthony's actions not by the patriarchal standards of either Renaissance or Regency England but by *Bridgerton*'s revised version of those standards. Anthony's failure in this scene is not his refusal to take on his assigned role of patriarchal authority, per se, but his failure in love – or, more precisely, his failure to properly express his position of authority *through* love, as his father so assuredly would have done.

As the remainder of the season reveals, for Anthony successfully to assume his place as Viscount of Bridgerton requires that he not only take on this paternalistic position but also, like Prince Hal, that he outdoes his father in the role. While Prince Hal manages this feat by assuming the crown with a blood claim to the throne that his father lacked, Anthony must do so by accepting a match that not only, like his parents', has love at its basis but that, like the match of Queen Charlotte herself, triumphs over seemingly insurmountable social barriers. I say 'seemingly', because the logic of a series that presents class barriers such as the one between Anthony and Siena as absolute is less consistent, to say the least, in matters of race. What Anthony needs to properly mimic both his father and his queen is a wife who is other in the 'right' way. He ultimately finds that woman in the enigmatic Kate Sharma – after an initial, unsuccessful courtship of her younger half-sister, Edwina.

The opening of Season Two reveals the Sharma family's backstory. Kate has travelled to London from India with her stepmother, Mary (Shelley Conn) and Edwina (Charithra Chandran), under the auspices of Lady Danbury, who is a family friend. Kate's only goal is to find a noble match for her sister in order to secure Edwina's inheritance from her socially conscious grandparents. While Edwina aims to please others, Kate is headstrong, behaviourally nonconformist (the first time we meet her, she is riding a horse on her own, astride!) and rightfully suspicious of the motives of London's marriageable young men. From the start she is especially disdainful of Anthony Bridgerton, whom she overhears early on expressing his contempt for the 'ton's' young women and his determination to acquire a wife for the sole purpose of producing a worthy Bridgerton heir.

With these characterizations in place and the give-away first name of 'Kate', *Bridgerton* viewers on Twitter, as mentioned earlier, immediately picked up on the parallels between the Sharma sisters and Katherine and Bianca in Shakespeare's *The Taming of the Shrew*. And, as per the showrunners' hint on Twitter, both Kate and Anthony undergo a form of 'taming' as the season's plot progresses. While Kate learns a lesson about following her own dreams, Anthony learns that marriage should be a partnership in love. *Bridgerton*'s engagement of this Shakespearean storyline here deliberately revises the original *Shrew*'s considerable misogyny, perhaps most tellingly by making the two sisters close, loving companions instead of hateful, bickering rivals.

While the name 'Kate' and certain *Taming of the Shrew* allusions come from the novel on which this season is based, Kate and Edwina's Indian origins are, like the Queen Charlotte character, a Shondaland innovation. In Quinn's *The Viscount Who Loved Me*, Kate and Edwina Sheffield are the stepdaughter and daughter of the relatively poor but aristocratic widow Mary Sheffield. The family has come to London for the season to find matches for the two girls, the younger of whom, Edwina, is blond and beautiful (underscoring her association with Shakespeare's Bianca), while her sister is darker and plain.⁶² On Netflix, Kate's otherness is represented more starkly. Mary Sharma, née Sheffield, has the scandalous history of having left England as a young woman to marry an Indian commoner who already had a child. The darker-skinned Kate, unlike Edwina, is thus the offspring of two non-ranking Indian parents. The show makes it clear, moreover, that Mary herself is the daughter of a white Englishman and a British-Indian mother, played respectively by Anthony Head and Shobu Kapoor. While this match, like other interracial marriages, does not itself stand out in the *Bridgerton* universe, Kate's simultaneously non-English, non-aristocratic origins, along with her dark skin, mark her as a notable outsider.

In a move that was variously received by British-Indian and Indian viewers, the cultural heritage of the Sharma family permeates *Bridgerton*'s second season. Some of these elements are linguistic. Kate speaks Hindustani to herself when she first meets Anthony, and she and Edwina address one another when speaking in private with Hindi pet names: 'didi', or 'big sister' and 'bon', or 'sister'. Other moments invoke culturally specific objects and/or rituals: Kate's assertion to Lady Danbury that Edwina expertly plays Indian musical instruments as well as the pianoforte, the Haldi ceremony in which the Sharma women apply a turmeric-based paste to the bride the night before the wedding, and the bangles Kate received from her biological mother (now deceased) to wear at her own wedding. There are even intertextual references, such as a prominent musical quotation from Bollywood's *Kabhi Khushi Kabhie Gham* on the series' eclectic soundtrack. Via these details the series implicitly acknowledges not only the colour diversity of its audience but also the more broad-ranging ethnic and cultural diversity of modern British viewers.⁶³ Yet there are inconsistencies throughout these references, which according to one Indian blogger, who also cites the complaints of other Indian viewers on Twitter, tend towards a problematic 'homogenisation of Indian culture'.⁶⁴ Moreover, in inscribing the Sharma women with experiences that differentiate them culturally as well as racially from other members of the 'ton', the show simultaneously gestures towards and holds at arm's length complex questions of race, identity and empire.⁶⁵

The importance of Kate's ethnicity to *Bridgerton*'s Shakespearean references abides most particularly in the use of names. Not only does Quinn's Kate Sheffield become Shondaland's Kate Sharma but in the second season's final episode it is revealed that 'Kate' is short for 'Kathani'. Resonating with the common immigrant experience of changing one's name in order to assimilate, the revelation also recalls the treatment of two famous 'Kates' in Shakespeare's plays. The first is, of course, Kate from *The Taming of the Shrew*. 'Good morrow, Kate, for that's your name, I hear', the brash Petruchio first greets her, to which she replies, 'Well have you heard, but something hard of hearing; / They call me Katherine that do talk of me'. Petruchio then begins the taming process by willfully renaming Katherine in a series of increasingly diminishing puns (2.2.181–8). In Act Five, once her taming is complete, he names her again in the memorable line, 'Come on, and kiss me, Kate', before summoning her 'to bed' (5.2.186, 190).

Concerns of a higher political nature frame the renaming of Shakespeare's other main Kate: the historical Catherine of Valois, aka Princess Katherine of France in *Henry V*, whom the young king forcibly woos and inevitably wins as the spoils of war. 'O fair Katherine', King Henry implores her, 'if you will love me soundly with your French heart I will be glad to hear you confess it brokenly with your English tongue. Do you like me, Kate?' (5.2.104–7). He goes on to repeat this nickname that he himself has invented an additional thirty times as a way of cementing his ownership over his bride.

Via the revelation of Kate Sharma's true name, Netflix's *Bridgerton* suggests a recuperation of both Shakespearean moments – especially the latter. Like Catherine of Valois, Kate Sharma is a foreign national who ends up marrying a high-ranking Englishman. In the climactic scene in which Anthony and Kate mutually declare their love, Anthony reverses King Henry's imposition of a culturally foreign nickname upon his intended spouse:

> ANTHONY   I want a life that suits us both.
> KATE   You know there never will be a day that you do not vex me.
> ANTHONY   Is that a promise, Kathani Sharma?[66]

For one Iranian-Canadian viewer who identified emotionally with this exchange, here Anthony 'embraces the part of [Kate] deemed unpalatable to the rest of society'.[67] Rather than enforce his beloved's English assimilation, Anthony highlights and lovingly accepts her true identity. It bears acknowledgement at this point that *Bridgerton*'s official explanation for the barrier to Anthony's match with Kate is a matter not of race but of social propriety:

the fact that Anthony initially courts, and nearly marries, Kate's sister. By alluding to the final scene of *Henry V* in this moment of acknowledging his fiancée's given name, *Bridgerton* doubly suggests that her Indian heritage does in fact matter.

Adding to the stakes of this subtle connection among race, *Bridgerton* and Shakespeare's histories is Queen Charlotte's own prominent role in resolving the social impasse preventing Anthony and Kate from marrying. Distinct from the plot of Quinn's novel, where Anthony's initial wooing of the younger sister Edwina is only a brief, initial distraction, Shondaland's *Bridgerton* takes the unintended couple all the way to the altar in a magnificent ceremony overseen by the queen herself. The wedding is forestalled when Edwina belatedly realizes that her sister and fiancé are in love with each other. In jilting her groom, she also outrages her queen.

However, that outrage is short-lived. Amidst the chaos that follows the interrupted marriage, an agitated King George emerges from his chambers, having mistaken a blast of fireworks for the celebration of his own long-ago nuptial rites. The disruption wrought by this ailing figure of former monarchical authority stymies everyone but Edwina. Via a soothing monologue, she calms not only the king but the queen as well with a reminder of how the pair 'faced many trials during [their] happy courtship'. She assures George, and with him an uncharacteristically subdued, tearful Charlotte, that 'today will make all of it well worth it' as they go on together to 'rule this kingdom with the kind of love, compassion and kindness the two of [them] undoubtedly share'.[68]

This assertion of love's power to transcend social barriers is also a reminder of love's instrumentality in granting Charlotte the power to rule and enact social change: an encapsulation of the series' central revisionist fantasy. Eventually Edwina's speech convinces the queen to get over her outrage and support the otherwise scandalous love match between Anthony and Kate. When the pair makes waves by dancing together at a subsequent ball, prompting shocked stares and gossip from onlookers, Edwina herself boldly declares, using modern code for describing nontraditional couples, 'I think they look beautiful together'. The queen then proclaims, 'Beautiful indeed', before commanding the rest of her subjects to agree with her.[69]

In the figure of Rosheuvel's Queen Charlotte, the story of a quasi-historical Black woman's life and rule plays out just to the side of the central romantic narratives of *Bridgerton*'s comedically structured, if historically inflected, serial drama. As the ruling Black queen consort of an ineffectual white king, this character is, it should also be noted, a figure potentially very like Okonedo's Queen Margaret in *The Hollow Crown*. While edging *Bridgerton* towards the territory of Shakespearean history, however, Netflix's Charlotte also resists aspects of the genre – especially what Bronfen describes as the essentially villainizing roles of Shakespeare's own 'historically reimagined queens', whose legitimacy not only depends upon their husbands but is constantly called into question by 'internal political battles'.[70] Unlike Okonedo's Margaret – or, for that matter, the character in American serial television whom Bronfen identifies most closely with the French queen consort, First Lady and then President Elizabeth Keane in HBO's *Homeland* – Rosheuvel's Charlotte never takes on Margaret's Shakespearean 'trajectory' of 'assuming the role of tyrant in the face of being slandered as a rogue'.[71] In Shondaland's province of *Bridgerton* – *Scandal*, with its covert *Antony and Cleopatra* associations, is quite another story[72] – that is the power of love.

Yet the histories, both via their content and via their retroactively imposed serial structure, nonetheless continue to inform the unfolding of Charlotte's narrative. Due to public interest in Rosheuvel's character, a *Bridgerton* prequel written by Shonda Rhimes herself is currently in the works. In good Shakespearean serial fashion, this miniseries promises to provide backstory on the event that initially incited the show's alternative racial history: the young Queen Charlotte's ground-shifting romance with the young King George.[73]

This move towards unpacking *Bridgerton*'s past is also a move towards constructing the future of that peculiar genre that Shakespeare helped invent: the English history play. In addition to full-scale adaptations like *The Hollow Crown* and unacknowledged repackagings like *The Wire*, *Homeland* and *Bridgerton* itself, that genre's afterlives are currently reflected in numerous recent serial dramas about England's queens – the BBC's *The White Queen* (2013), ITV's *Victoria* (2016) and *Anne Boleyn* (2021), Starz's *The Spanish Princess* (2019) and *Becoming Elizabeth* (2022) – as well as in HBO's eight-season Wars-of-the Roses-inspired fantasy, now with its own prequel, *Game of Thrones* (2011).[74] Somewhere in between history and fantasy – and with, inevitably, a strong pinch of Shakespeare – lies the origin story of England's first Black queen – coming soon on Netflix and, no doubt, soon to be discussed and debated on Twitter. The lens swings on.

NOTES

Introduction

1 Dimas Sanfiorenz, 'How the Rodney King Beating Became the First Viral Video', *Okayplayer*, accessed 1 April 2022, https://www.okayplayer.com/news/rodney-king-beating-viral.html; David Grossman, 'On This Day 25 Years Ago, the Web Became Public Domain', *Popular Mechanics*, 30 April 2018, https://www.popularmechanics.com/culture/web/a20104417/www-public-domain/.

2 See, for instance, Alliss V. Richardson, *Bearing Witness While Black: African Americans, Smartphones, and the New Protest #Journalism* (Oxford: Oxford University Press, 2020); Lynn Mei Itagaki, *Civil Racism: The 1992 Los Angeles Rebellion and the Crisis of Racial Burnout* (Minneapolis: University of Minnesota Press, 2016).

3 'H4', *Kickstarter*, 16 October 2013, https://www.kickstarter.com/projects/1671808639/h4.

4 Louis Brennan, 'How Netflix Expanded to 190 Countries in 7 Years', *Harvard Business Review*, 12 October 2018, https://hbr.org/2018/10/how-netflix-expanded-to-190-countries-in-7-years; Julia Stoll, 'Number of Netflix Paid Subscribers Worldwide from 3rd Quarter 2011 to 1st Quarter 2022', *Statista*, 22 April 2022, https://www.statista.com/statistics/250934/quarterly-number-of-netflix-streaming-subscribers-worldwide/.

5 Brandi K. Adams, 'The King, and not I: Refusing Neutrality', *The Sundial*, 9 June 2020, https://medium.com/the-sundial-acmrs/the-king-and-not-i-refusing-neutrality-dbab4239e8a9/.

6 Nicholas Watt, 'Cameron Defies Tory Right over Referendum', *The Guardian*, 29 June 2012, https://www.theguardian.com/politics/2012/jun/29/cameron-no-eu-referendum.

7 Satnam Virdee and Brendan McGeever, 'Racism, Crisis, Brexit', *Ethnic and Racial Studies* 41, no. 10 (2018): 1802–19; Tina G. Patel and

Laura Connelly, '"Post-race" Racisms in the Narratives of "Brexit" Voters', *The Sociological Review* 67, no. 5 (2019): 968–84.

8   While the primary focus of this book is on Anglophone productions of the United Kingdom and the United States, *Chimes at Midnight*, as discussed in Chapter 3, was produced in Europe. In that chapter I also briefly consider examples of non-Anglophone, world cinema productions of the histories and related plays – *Faustão* (dir. Eduardo Coutinho, 1971), a Brazilian adaptation of *Henry IV* as well as *As Alegres Comrades/The Merry Wives* (dir. Leila Hipólito, 2003). Another example of a Brazilian adaptation of Shakespeare's histories is *Águia na Cabeça* (dir. Paulo Thiago, 1984), which loosely transposes the plot of *Richard III* to 'the world of the illegal gambling game *Jogo do Bicho*' – mentioned in Paul Heritage and Ilana Strozenberg, eds, *The Art of Cultural Exchange: Translation and Transformation between the UK and Brazil* (Wilmington: Vernon Press, 2019), 156.

9   Courtney Lehman, '"Faux Show": Falling into History in Kenneth Branagh's *Love's Labours Lost*', in *Colorblind Shakespeare: New Perspectives on Race and Performance,* ed. Ayanna Thompson (London and New York: Routledge, 2006), 6.

10 Lynda E. Boose and Richard Burt, 'Totally Clueless: Shakespeare Goes Hollywood in the 1990s', in *Shakespeare the Movie: Popularizing the Plays on Film, TV, and Video,* ed. Boose and Burt (London and New York: Routledge, 1997), 14.

11 Peter Kirwan, *The Hollow Crown: An Introductory Essay* (Bloomsbury Publishing, 2019), https://www.dramaonlinelibrary.com/context-and-criticism/the-hollow-crown-an-introductory-essay-iid-173357/ba-9781474208659-3000012.

12 *Diversity and Inclusion Strategy 2016-20,* 2016, http://downloads.bbc.co.uk/diversity/pdf/diversity-and-inclusion-strategy-2016.pdf.

13 'H4', *Kickstarter.*

14 Urvashi Chakravarty and Ayanna Thompson, 'Race and Periodization: Introduction', *New Literary History* 52, nos. 3–4 (2021): vii.

15 Geraldine Heng, *The Invention of Race in the European Middle Ages* (Cambridge: Cambridge University Press, 2018).

16 Cord J. Whitaker, *Black Metaphors: How Modern Racism Emerged from Medieval Race-Thinking* (Philadelphia: University of Pennsylvania Press, 2019), 3.

17 Ayanna Thompson, 'Did the Concept of Race Exist for Shakespeare and His Contemporaries? An Introduction', in *The Cambridge*

Companion to Shakespeare and Race, ed. Ayanna Thompson (Cambridge: Cambridge University Press, 2021), 6–7.

18 L. Monique Pittman, 'Introduction: Representing the Nation's History', in *Shakespeare's Contested Nations: Race, Gender, and Multicultural Britain in Performances of the History Plays* (London and New York: Routledge, 2022), 6, 9.

19 Barbara Hodgdon, *The Shakespeare Trade: Performances and Appropriations* (Philadelphia: University of Pennsylvania Press, 1998), xii.

20 Ian Smith, 'We Are Othello: Speaking of Race in Early Modern Studies', *Shakespeare Quarterly* 67, no. 1 (2016): 122–3.

21 In addition to Pittman, *Shakespeare's Contested Nations*, see Anna Blackwell, *Shakespearean Celebrity in the Digital Age: Fan Cultures and Remediation* (New York: Palgrave Macmillan, 2018), 172–3; Marina Gerzic, 'Broadcasting the Political Body: *Richard III*, #Brexit and #Libspill', *Shakespeare Bulletin* 39, no. 1 (2021): 109–29; Stephen O'Neill, 'Finding Refuge in *King Lear*: From Brexit to Shakespeare's European Value', *Multicultural Shakespeare: Translation, Appropriation and Performance* 19, no. 34 (2019): 119–38; Emma Smith, 'May as Polonius, Gove as Cassius: is Brexit a Shakespearean Tragedy?', *The Guardian*, 12 April 2019, https://www.theguardian.com/books/2019/apr/12/brexit-tragedy-worthy-of-shakespeare-emma-smith.

22 'intersectional, adj.1', *OED Online* (Oxford University Press, June 2020), https://www.oed.com/view/Entry/98301?rskey=cJiDpP&result=1&isAdvanced=false#eid.

23 Conor Friedersdorf, 'Rodney King's Finest Hour', *The Atlantic*, 30 April 2022, https://www.theatlantic.com/ideas/archive/2022/04/rodney-king-riots-30-year-anniversary/629729/.

24 Nikol G. Alexander-Floyd, 'Disappearing Acts: Reclaiming Intersectionality in the Social Sciences in a Post-Black Feminist Era', *Feminist Formations* 24, no. 1 (2012): 4.

25 E.g. Roland Betancourt, *Byzantine Intersectionalities: Sexuality, Gender, and Race in the Middle Ages* (Princeton: Princeton University Press, 2020); Jyotsna Singh, 'Intersectionalities: Postcoloniality and Difference', in *Shakespeare and Postcolonial Theory* (London and New York: Bloomsbury, 2020); Jennifer Drouin, ed., 'Part Two: Intersectional Sex', in *Shakespeare/Sex: Contemporary Readings in Gender and Sexuality* (London and New York: Bloomsbury, 2020).

26 Quoted in Kimberlé Crenshaw, 'Postscript', in *Framing Intersectionality: Debates on a Multi-Faceted Concept in Gender*

Studies, ed. Helma Lutz, Maria Teresa Herrera Vivar and Linda Supik (Farnham: Ashgate, 2011), 222.

27 Patricia Hill Collins and Sirma Bilge, *Intersectionality*, 2nd edn (Medford: Polity Press, 2016), 2, 64.

28 Sirma Bilge, 'The Fungibility of Intersectionality: an Afropessimist Reading', *Ethnic and Racial Studies* 43, no. 13 (2020): 2298–326.

29 Joyce Green MacDonald, *Shakespeare Adaptation, Race, and Memory in the New World* (New York: Palgrave Macmillan, 2021), 3.

30 Linda Hutcheon, *A Theory of Adaptation*, 2nd edn (London and New York: Routledge, 2013), 6–8.

31 Ibid., 28.

32 For instance, Ayanna Thompson, 'Practicing a Theory/Theorizing a Practice: An Introduction to Shakespearean Colorblind Casting' and Lisa M. Anderson, 'When Race Matters: Reading Race in *Richard III* and *Macbeth*', both in *Colorblind Shakespeare*.

33 Hutcheon, *A Theory of Adaptation*, 6.

34 Elisabeth Bronfen, *Serial Shakespeare: An Infinite Variety of Appropriations in American TV Drama* (Manchester: Manchester University Press, 2020).

35 Ibid., 9, 15. Citing Graham Holderness, *Tales from Shakespeare: Creative Collisions* (Cambridge: Cambridge University Press, 2014); Maurizio Calbi, *Spectral Shakespeares: Media Adaptations in the Twenty-First Century* (New York: Palgrave Macmillan, 2013), 4.

36 Douglas Lanier, 'Shakespearean Rhizomatics: Adaptation, Ethics, Value', in *Shakespeare and the Ethics of Appropriation,* ed. Alexa Huang and Elizabeth Rivlin (New York: Palgrave Macmillan, 2014), 21–41.

37 Bronfen, *Serial Shakespeare,* 8–10. Citing Walter Benjamin, 'The Task of the Translator', in *Selected Writings Volume 1 1913–1926*, ed. Marcus Bullock and Michael W. Jennings (Cambridge, MA: Harvard University Press, 1996), 256.

38 Ibid., 10.

39 Ibid., 5, 11.

40 David Sterling Brown, 'White Hands: Gesturing toward Shakespeare's "*Other* Race Plays"', *Shakespeare Association of America Annual Meeting* (Washington, DC, 19 April 2019).

41 Arthur L. Little, Jr, 'Re-Historicizing Race, White Melancholia, and the Shakespearean Property', *Shakespeare Quarterly* 67, no. 1 (2016): 84n2, 86, 101, 92. Citing Anne Anlin Cheng, *The Melancholy of Race* (Oxford: Oxford University Press), 8.

42 Ambereen Dadabhoy, 'The Unbearable Whiteness of Being (in) Shakespeare', *Postmedieval: A Journal of Medieval Cultural Studies* 11, nos. 2–3 (2020): 230.

43 The Racial Imaginary Institute, *On Whiteness*, SBPH Essays, no. 4 (London: SPBH Editions, 2022), 10.

44 All quotations from Shakespeare's plays are from Richard Proudfoot et al., eds, *The Arden Shakespeare Third Series Complete Works* (London and New York: Bloomsbury, 2021) and are cited parenthetically in the text by act, scene and line number(s).

45 Unless otherwise specified, all references to this film are to *H4*, dir. Paul Quinn (Zelko Films, 2015), DVD.

46 Kevin Jagernauth, 'Joel Edgerton Talks "Game of Thrones" Meets Shakespeare Project with David Michôd', *RadioTimes.com*, 3 February 2016, https://www.indiewire.com/2016/02/joel-edgerton-talks-game-of-thrones-meets-shakespeare-project-with-david-michod-jane-got-a-gun-and-more-83994/.

47 All references to this film are to *The King*, dir. David Michôd (Plan B Entertainment, 2019), Netflix, https://www.netflix.com/title/80182016.

48 Constance Grady, 'Neflix's Timothée Chalamet Vehicle *The King* Is a Humorless Slog on the Inhumanity of War', *Vox*, 7 October 2019, https://www.vox.com/culture/2019/10/7/20891427/king-review-netflix-timothee-chalamet-joel-edgerton-david-Michôd-shakespeare-henriad-henry-v.

49 Spelled 'Catherine' in *The King* versus 'Katherine' in Shakespeare's *Henry V*. On Catherine's 'contemporary feminist sensibility' in *The King*, see Celestino Deleyto, 'Transnational Shakespeare, Feminist Shakespeare: *The King*', *Transnational Screens* 12, no. 1 (2021): 72–4.

50 Benjamin Broadribb, '*The King*: A Shakespeare Film Made for – and by – People Who Don't Like Shakespeare', *'Action is eloquence': (Re)thinking Shakespeare* (blog), 7 November 2019, https://medium.com/action-is-eloquence-re-thinking-shakespeare/the-king-a-shakespeare-film-made-for-and-by-people-who-dont-like-shakespeare-4649253c6755.

51 Adams, 'The King, and not I'.

52 Deleyto, 'Transnational Shakespeare', 63, 71.

53 L. Monique Pittman, 'Colour-Conscious Casting and Multicultural Britain in the BBC's *Henry V* (2012): Historicizing Adaptation in an Age of Digital Placelessness', *Adaptation* 10 (2017): 188.

54 Huw Fullerton, 'Is Netflix's *The King* Shakespeare or Not?', *RadioTimes.com,* 1 November 2019, https://www.radiotimes.com/movies/is-netflixs-the-king-shakespeare-or-not/.

55 Charles Mudede, 'What Netflix's *The King* Tells Us about Brexit and the Defeat of the Labour Party in the UK', *The Stranger*, 16 December 2019, https://www.thestranger.com/slog/2019/12/16/42276340/what-netflixs-the-king-tells-us-about-brexit-and-the-defeat-of-the-labour-party-in-the-uk.

56 Adams, 'The King, and not I'.

57 Rubin Espinosa, *Shakespeare on the Shades of Racism* (London and New York: Routledge, 2021), 49.

58 Virdee and McGeever, 'Racism, Crisis, Brexit', 1802–6.

59 Adams, 'The King, and not I'.

Chapter 1

1 An earlier version of this chapter appeared as 'Through a Glass Darkly: Sophie Okonedo's Margaret as Racial Other in *The Hollow Crown: The Wars of the Roses*', *Shakespeare Survey 73* (Cambridge: Cambridge University Press, 2020): 170–83.

2 In the use of this phrase, I follow Benedict Anderson, *Imagined Communities: Reflections on the Origin and Spread of Nationalism* (London and New York: Verso, 1983).

3 Thompson, 'Practicing a Theory', 17.

4 Jami Rogers, 'The Shakespearean Glass Ceiling: The State of Colorblind Casting in Contemporary British Theatre', *Shakespeare Bulletin* 31, no. 3 (2013): 418–24.

5 Hugh Quarshie, 'Black Kings Are Old Hat', *The Guardian*, 20 September 2000, https://www.theguardian.com/world/2000/sep/20/race.uk.

6 August Wilson, 'The Ground on Which I Stand', *Callaloo* 20 (Summer 1997): 498.

7 Anderson, 'When Race Matters', 91.

8 Ayanna Thompson, *Passing Strange: Shakespeare, Race, and Contemporary America* (Oxford: Oxford University Press, 2011), 77.

9 Ibid., 94.

10 For instance, L. Monique Pittman (2016, 2017, 2022) and Eleanor Rycroft, 'Hair in the BBC's *The Hollow Crown: The Wars of the Roses*: Class, Nation, Gender, Race, and Difference', *Shakespeare* 17, no. 1 (2021): 29–48.

11 Ramona Wray, 'Shakespeare and the New Discourses of Television: Quality, Aesthetics, and *The Hollow Crown*', *Cahiers Élisabéthains* 105, no. 1 (2021): 80. Citing Jason Mittell, *Complex TV: The Poetics*

of *Contemporary Television Storytelling* (New York and London: New York University Press, 2015).

12 Wray, 'Shakespeare and the New Discourses of Television', 79–80.

13 Jean E. Howard and Phyllis Rackin, *Engendering a Nation: A Feminist Account of Shakespeare's English Histories* (London and New York: Routledge, 1997), 10, 14. See also Richard Helgerson, *Forms of Nationhood: The Elizabethan Writing of England* (Chicago: University of Chicago Press, 1994) and Claire McEachern, *The Poetics of English Nationhood: 1590-1612* (Cambridge: Cambridge University Press, 1997).

14 Francesca Royster, 'The Chicago Shakespeare Theater's *Rose Rage*: Whiteness, Terror, and the Fleshwork of Theatre in a Post-Colorblind Age', in *Colorblind Shakespeare*, 221.

15 Arthur L. Little, Jr, *Shakespeare Jungle Fever* (Stanford: Stanford University Press, 2000), 1.

16 Karen Newman, *Fashioning Femininity and English Renaissance Drama* (Chicago: University of Chicago Press, 1991), 71–93, 75, 88; Lara Bovilsky, *Barbarous Play: Race on the English Renaissance Stage* (Minneapolis: University of Minnesota Press, 2008), 37–65.

17 Alyssa Klein, 'Sophie Okonedo Looks Absolutely Boss as Queen Margaret in "The Hollow Crown: The Wars of the Roses"', *okayafrica*, 18 November 2016, https://www.okayafrica.com/sophie-okonedo-queen-margaret-the-hollow-crown-the-war-of-the-roses/.

18 Bethan McKernan, 'Ukip Councillor Attempts to Blast BBC for "Historical Inaccuracy", Gets Destroyed by Actual Historian', *Indy100*, 16 May 2016, https://www.indy100.com/article/ukip-councillor-attempts-to-blast-bbc-for-historical-inaccuracy-gets-destroyed-by-actual-historian--ZyZAasU2fb.

19 Klein, 'Sophie Okonedo Looks Absolutely Boss'.

20 Neela Debnath, 'Sophie Okonedo Was the "Best Actress" to Play White Shakespeare Role in *The Hollow Crown*', 6 May 2016, https://www.express.co.uk/showbiz/tv-radio/667894/Sophie-Okonedo-Undercover-The-Hollow-Crown-Benedict-Cumberbatch-Dominic-Cooke.

21 See, for instance, the diverse cast of the RSC's 2022 *Henry VI* trilogy, *The Wars of the Roses*, accessed 22 August 2022, https://www.rsc.org.uk/henry-vi-wars-of-the-roses/cast-and-creatives.

22 Urvashi Chakravarty, 'Actors of Color in the UK', in *The Cambridge Companion to Shakespeare and Race*, 204–5.

23 Stuart Hampton-Reeves and Carol Chillington Rutter, *The Henry VI Plays*, Shakespeare in Performance (Manchester: Manchester University Press, 2007), 60.

24 'The Making of *The Hollow Crown*', in *The Hollow Crown: The Wars of the Roses,* dir. Dominic Cooke (Universal City: Universal Pictures, 2016), DVD.

25 All references to this series are to *The Hollow Crown: The Wars of the Roses*, dir. Dominic Cooke (Universal City: Universal Pictures, 2016), DVD.

26 Carole Levin and John Watkins, *Shakespeare's Foreign Worlds: National and Transnational Identities in the Elizabethan Age* (Ithaca: Cornell University Press, 2012), 62.

27 L. Monique Pittman, '*Hollow* Refuge: The BBC's *The Wars of the Roses* and This Fortress Built by Nature', in *Shakespeare's Contested Nations*, 128–56.

28 Peter Kirwan, '*The Hollow Crown: Henry VI Part 1* @ The BBC' (blog), 9 May 2016, http://blogs.nottingham.ac.uk/bardathon/2016/05/09/hollow-crown-henry-vi-part-1-bbc/.

29 Phyllis Rackin, 'History into Tragedy: The Case of *Richard III*', in *Shakespearean Tragedy and Gender*, ed. Shirley Nelson Garner and Madelon G. Sprengnether (Bloomington: Indiana University Press, 1996), 37.

30 Phyllis Rackin, 'Anti-Historians: Women's Roles in Shakespeare's Histories', *Theatre Journal* 27 (1985): 332.

31 Katherine Schwarz, 'Fearful Simile: Stealing the Breech in Shakespeare's Chronicle Plays', *Shakespeare Quarterly* 49 (1998): 141.

32 Hampton-Reeves and Rutter, *The Henry VI Plays*, 75–6.

33 Edward Burns, 'Introduction', in *King Henry VI, Part 1*, ed. Burns (London: Bloomsbury, 2000), 26.

34 As Rycroft notes, however, Margaret's hair remains long and can be seen under her armour after her final battle, 'reminding us that she is still a woman underneath it all'. 'Hair in the BBC's *The Hollow Crown*', 40.

35 Little, Jr, 'Re-Historicizing Race', 91.

36 Kathryn Schwarz, 'Amazon Reflections in the Jacobean Queen's Masque', *Studies in English Literature, 1500–1900* 35, no. 2 (1995): 303.

37 Pittman, '*Hollow* Refuge', 137. See also Kirsten Mendoza's reading of this scene in '"I am Content": Race, Seduction, and the Performances of Consent in *The Hollow Crown*', *Shakespeare Bulletin* 39, no. 4 (2021): 619–23.

38 Rycroft, 'Hair in the BBC's *The Hollow Crown*', 32, 36, 40–1.

39 Kim F. Hall, '"These bastard signs of fair": Literary Whiteness in Shakespeare's Sonnets', in *Postcolonial Shakespeares*, ed. Ania Loomba and Martin Orkin (London and New York: Routledge, 1998), 68–9.

40 Mendoza, '"I am Content"', 624.
41 See also Pittman's discussion of this word choice in 'Hollow Refuge', 140.
42 Joyce Green MacDonald, *Women and Race in Early Modern Texts* (Cambridge: Cambridge University Press, 2002), 80–98.
43 Little, 'Re-Historicizing Race', 91–2.
44 Whitaker, *Black Metaphors*, 54. Whitaker borrows the term 'shimmering' from Michelle R. Warren's 'notion of "shimmering philology"', which is used 'to explore . . . the nexus of relations that allows whiteness to be invisible sometimes and visible at others' (4–5). Citing Warren, 'Shimmering Philology', *Postmedieval: A Journal of Medieval Cultural Studies* 5, no. 4 (2014): 389–97.
45 'The Making of *The Hollow Crown*'.
46 Mary Floyd-Wilson, *English Ethnicity and Race in Early Modern Drama* (Cambridge: Cambridge University Press, 2003), 39–40, quoting Raymond Klibanksy et al., *Saturn and Melancholy* (New York: Basic Books, 1964), 61–2 and Thomas Walkington, *The Opticke Glasse of Humors* (London, 1607), 112–13.
47 Sujata Iyengar, *Shades of Difference: Mythologies of Skin Color in Early Modern England* (Philadelphia: University of Pennsylvania Press, 2004), 103, 107.
48 Carolyn M. West, 'Mammy, Sapphire, and Jezebel: Historical Images of Black Women and their Implications for Psychotherapy', *Psychotherapy: Theory, Research, Practice, Training* 32, no. 3 (1995): 462–3. L. Monique Pittman notes that domination of her 'inept' husband also codes Okonedo's Margaret as a version of the '"shrill, loud, argumentative"' 'Sapphire' stereotype ('Hollow Refuge' 139).
49 Sandra Logan, *Shakespeare's Foreign Queens: Drama, Politics, and the Enemy Within* (New York: Palgrave Macmillan, 2018), 214.
50 Pittman, 'Hollow Refuge', 142.
51 Nina Levine, *Women's Matters: Politics, Gender, and Nation in Shakespeare's Early History Plays* (Newark: University of Delaware Press, 1998), 89–90. Quoting Emrys Jones, *The Origins of Shakespeare* (Oxford: Oxford University Press, 1977), 278.
52 Pittman, 'Hollow Refuge', 143–4.
53 Levine, *Women's Matters*, 68.
54 Howard and Rackin, *Engendering a Nation*, 85.
55 Ibid., 98.

56 Rycroft, 'Hair in the BBC's *The Hollow Crown*', 40.

57 Thompson, 'Practicing a Theory', 15. Quoting E. Patrick Johnson, *Appropriating Blackness: Performance and the Politics of Authenticity* (Durham: Duke University Press, 2003), 40.

58 Elizabeth E. Tavares, '*The Hollow Crown*'s "Richard III": the Affective Failure of Direct Address', *In the Glassy Margents*, 2 January 2018, https://glassymargents.com/2018/01/02/the-hollow-crowns-richard-iii-the-affective-failure-of-direct-address/.

59 Urvashi Chakravarty, '"Live, and beget a happy race of kings": *Richard III*, Race, and Homonationalism', in *Shakespeare/Sex*, 150.

60 Ian Smith, 'Othello's Black Handkerchief', *Shakespeare Quarterly* 64, no. 1 (2013): 1–25.

61 Chris Hastings, 'Benedict's Really Got the Hump', *Daily Mail*, 14 May 2016, https://www.dailymail.co.uk/news/article-3590907/Benedict-s-really-got-hump-Cumberbatch-dons-prosthetic-hunchback-play-Richard-III-BBC-series.html.

62 Rosemarie Garland-Thomson, *Extraordinary Bodies* (New York: Columbia University Press, 1997), 60.

63 Rosemarie Garland-Thomson, 'The Politics of Staring: Visual Rhetorics of Disability in Popular Photography', in *Disability Studies: Enabling the Humanities*, ed. Sharon L. Snyder et al. (New York: MLA, 2002), 56.

64 See the TV documentary *Richard III: The King in the Carpark*, dir. Louise Osmond and Peter Woods (Darlow Smithson Productions, 2015). See Philip Schwyzer, *Shakespeare and the Remains of Richard III* (Oxford: Oxford University Press, 2013) on Western culture's centuries-long obsession with the 'left-over remnants and traces' of the historical Richard III (5).

65 'Benedict Cumberbatch Plays Richard III', BBC Media Centre, 5 February 2016, https://www.bbc.co.uk/mediacentre/mediapacks/warsoftheroses/benedict.

66 Turi King, 'We're All Related to Richard III – It's Just a Matter of Degree', 26 March 2015, https://theconversation.com/were-all-related-to-richard-iii-its-just-a-matter-of-degree-38862.

67 Blackwell, *Shakespearean Celebrity*, 149–50.

68 Sebastian Shakespeare, 'Old Etonian Barney Harris Is Just the Chap to Cap a VERY High-Class Cast in BBC's *Hollow Crown*', *Daily Mail*, 21 October 2014, https://www.dailymail.co.uk/tvshowbiz/article-2802506/sebastian-shakespeare-old-etonian-barney-harris-just-chap-cap-high-class-cast-bbc-s-hollow-crown.html.

69 See Ayanna Thompson, *Blackface* (London and New York: Bloomsbury, 2021), 36–9 and Dympna Callaghan, *Shakespeare without Women* (London and New York: Routledge, 2000), 77.

70 Rachel O'Connell, '"That Cruel Spectacle": The Extraordinary Body Eroticized in Lucas Malet's *The History of Sir Richard Calmady*', in *Sex and Disability*, ed. Robert McRuer and Anna Mollow (Durham: Duke University Press, 2012), 115.

71 Brown, 'White Hands'.

72 O'Connell, 'That Cruel Spectacle', 115.

73 On the repetition of 'fair' in Richmond's speech, see Chakravarty, '"Live, and beget"', 157–9.

74 'Director's Commentary', *Richard II*, dir. Gregory Doran (London: Opus Arte, 2014), DVD.

75 Serena Davis, 'A Chilling End to *The Hollow Crown*, Series Two', *The Telegraph*, 21 May 2016, https://www.telegraph.co.uk/tv/2016/05/21/a-chilling-end-to-the-hollow-crown-series-two-review/.

Chapter 2

1 Tomas Elliot, 'Shakespearean Seriality: The "Hollow Crown", the "Wooden O", and the "Circle in the Water" of History', *Adaptation* 12, no. 2 (2019): 69–88.

2 Ramona Wray, 'The Shakespearean Auteur and the Televisual Medium', *Shakespeare Bulletin* 34, no. 3 (2016): 472–3.

3 Graham Holderness, *Shakespeare: The Histories* (New York: Palgrave Macmillan, 2000), 1–4.

4 '*The Hollow Crown* (TV Series)', *Wikipedia*, updated 11 July 2022, https://en.wikipedia.org/wiki/The_Hollow_Crown_(TV_series).

5 Bronfen, *Serial Shakespeare* and Elliot, 'Shakespearean Seriality'.

6 Annamarie Jagose, 'Feminism's Queer Theory', *Feminism and Psychology* 19, no. 2 (2009): 158.

7 Lee Edelman, *No Future: Queer Theory and the Death Drive* (Durham: Duke University Press, 2007), 3, 14.

8 Bronfen, *Serial Shakespeare*, 6–7.

9 All references to this series are to *The Hollow Crown: The Complete Series*, dir. Rupert Goold, Richard Eyre and Thea Sharrock (Universal City: Universal Pictures, 2013), DVD.

10 David Livingstone, 'Silenced Voices: A Reactionary Streamlined *Henry V* in *The Hollow Crown*', *Multicultural Shakespeare: Translation, Appropriation, and Performance* 12 (2015): 87–100.
11 Pittman, 'Colour-Conscious Casting', 183, 185.
12 Wray, 'The Shakespearean Auteur', 481.
13 Livingstone, 'Silenced Voices', 92.
14 On the Boy's status as a figure of whiteness, see Anna-Claire Simpson, 'Surrogating Boys and the Performance of Whiteness in *Henry V*', *Shakespeare Studies* 50, no. 63 (2022): 63–72.
15 Simpson, 'Surrogating Boys', 69.
16 Ibid., 64, citing Robin Bernstein, *Racial Innocence: Performing American Childhood from Slavery to Civil Rights* (New York: New York University Press, 2011), 22.
17 See for instance Bruce Smith, *Homosexual Desire in Shakespeare's England: A Cultural Poetics* (Chicago: University of Chicago Press, 1995) and Stephen Orgel, *Impersonations: The Performance of Gender in Shakespeare's England* (Cambridge: Cambridge University Press, 1996).
18 Simpson, 'Surrogating Boys', 68.
19 See also Simpson's reading of this passage, which emphasizes the intersections of class, race and masculinity, in 'Surrogating Boys', 67–8.
20 Sarah Werner, 'Firk and Foot: The Boy Actor in *Henry V*', *Shakespeare Bulletin* 21, no. 4 (2003): 19–27.
21 Simpson, 'Surrogating Boys', 70. See Jean Feerick's discussion of grafting imagery in this scene as racialization in 'The Imperial Graft: Horticulture, Hybridity, and the Art of Mingling Races in *Henry V* and *Cymbeline*', in *The Oxford Handbook of Shakespeare and Embodiment: Gender, Sexuality, and Race*, ed. Valerie Traub (Oxford: Oxford University Press: 2016), 221–2.
22 Werner, 'Firk and Foot', 26.
23 Amanda Zoch, 'Macduff's Son and the Queer Temporality of *Macbeth*', *SEL* 57, no. 2 (2017): 370–1.
24 Simpson, 'Surrogating Boys', 69.
25 All references to this film are to *Henry V*, dir. Laurence Olivier (1944; Irvington: Criterion Collection, 1999).
26 All references to this film are to *Henry V*, dir. Kenneth Branagh (1989; Santa Monica: MGM Home Entertainment, 2000).

27 'Henry V', Peter Babakitis films, accessed 28 October 2022, https://www.babakitisfilms.com/henry-v.html.
28 Sarah Hatchuel, '"Into a thousand parts divide one man": Dehumanised Metafiction and Fragmented Documentary in Peter Babakitis' *Henry V*', in *Screening Shakespeare in the Twenty-First Century*, ed. Mark Thornton Burnett and Ramona Wray (Edinburgh: Edinburgh University Press, 2006), 158–9.
29 *William Shakespeare's Henry V*, dir. Peter Babakitis (Peter Babakitis Films, 2007), Amazon.
30 On the 'social and aesthetic contradictions' of Olivier's use of the 'Globe' setting, see Martin Butler, 'Translating the Elizabethan Theatre: The Politics of Nostalgia in Olivier's *Henry V*', in *Studies in Transpositional Aesthetics*, ed. Shirley Chew and Alistair Stead (Liverpool: Liverpool University Press, 1999), 75–97.
31 Stuart Little, 'Thanks, Palestinians, for St. George', *Palestine Chronicle*, 20 April 2009.
32 Pittman, 'Colour-Conscious Casting', 183.
33 Alan Sinfield, *Faultlines: Cultural Materialism and the Politics of Dissident Reading* (Berkeley: University of California Press, 1992), 136–7.
34 Pittman, 'Colour-Conscious Casting', 185.
35 Ramona Wray, '*Henry V* after the War on Terror', *Shakespeare Survey* 72 (Cambridge University Press, 2019): 14.
36 Kim F. Hall, *Things of Darkness: Economies of Race and Gender in Early Modern England* (Ithaca: Cornell University Press, 1995), 67.
37 See Rubin Espinosa's reading of this line in *Shakespeare and the Shades of Racism*, 51.
38 Elliot, 'Shakespearean Seriality', 5.
39 For a summary see Derrick Higginbotham, 'The Construction of a King: Waste, Effeminacy, and Queerness in Shakespeare's *Richard II*', *Shakespeare in Southern Africa* 26 (2014): 59–73. See also Charles R. Forker, 'Royal Carnality and Illicit Desire in the English History Plays of the 1590s', *Medieval and Renaissance Drama in England* 17 (2005): 115–16.
40 Alan Bray, 'Homosexuality and the Signs of Male Friendship in Elizabethan England', *History Workshop* 29 (1990): 1–19.
41 Quoted in Madhavi Menon, '*Richard II* and the Taint of Metonymy', *ELH* 70, no. 3 (2003): 667.
42 Margaret Shewring, *King Richard II,* Shakespeare in Performance (Manchester: Manchester University Press, 1996), 22–9.

43 Carol Chillington Rutter, 'Fiona Shaw's *Richard II:* The Girl as Player-King as Comic', *Shakespeare Quarterly* 48, no. 3 (1997): 318.

44 *Richard II,* dir. Gregory Doran (Opus Arte, 2014), DVD.

45 'User Reviews', *The Hollow Crown, Richard II, Internet Movie Database,* accessed 12 March 2019, https://www.imdb.com/title/tt1978517/reviews; Peter Kirwan, '*The Hollow Crown: Richard II* @ BBC HD' (blog), 30 June 2012, http://blogs.nottingham.ac.uk/bardathon/2012/06/30/the-hollow-crown-richard-ii-bbc-hd/; Alice Dailey, 'Where Character Is King: Gregory Doran's Henriad', *Critical Survey* 30, no. 1 (2018): 136.

46 Wray, 'Shakespeare and the New Discourses of Television', 84.

47 For instance, Howard and Rackin, *Engendering a Nation,* 142.

48 Tom Sutcliffe, 'The Weekend's Viewing: *The Hollow Crown: Richard II,* Sat, BBC2 Derek Jacobi on *Richard II: Shakespeare Uncovered,* Sat, BBC2', *Independent,* 2 July 2012, https://www.independent.co.uk/arts-entertainment/tv/reviews/the-weekend-s-viewing-the-hollow-crown-richard-ii-sat-bbc2-derek-jacobi-on-richard-ii-shakespeare-uncovered-sat-bbc2-7902671.html.

49 'The Making of *Richard II*', in *The Hollow Crown: The Complete Series,* DVD.

50 Tim Dowling, 'TV review: *The Hollow Crown: Richard II;* Derek Jacobi on *Richard II; Mad Mad World*', *The Guardian,* 1 July 2012, https://www.theguardian.com/tv-and-radio/2012/jul/01/hollow-crown-richard-ii-shakespeare.

51 John Nguyet Erni, 'Queer Figurations in the Media: Critical Reflections on the Michael Jackson Sex Scandal', *Critical Studies in Media Communication* 25, no. 3 (1998): 158–80; Susan Fast, 'Difference that Exceeded Understanding: Remembering Michael Jackson (1958–2009)', *Popular Music Society* 33, no. 2 (2010): 259–66.

52 Michael Mario Albrecht, 'Dead Man in the Mirror: The Performative Aspects of Michael Jackson's Posthumous Body', *The Journal of Popular Culture* 46, no. 4 (2013): 706–7.

53 Attributed to comedian Red Buttons, quoted in Doug Foley, 'I wish I'd said that', *The Spectator,* Ontario, 30 January 2006.

54 Luke Henriques-Gomes, 'Smooth FM Bans Michael Jackson Songs Amid Fresh Abuse Allegations', 7 March 2019, https://www.theguardian.com/music/2019/mar/07/smooth-fm-bans-michael-jackson-songs-amid-fresh-abuse-allegations; Ben Beaumont-Thomas, 'Adverts Declaring Michael Jackson Innocent Taken Off London Buses', 14 March 2019, https://www.theguardian.com/music/2019/

mar/14/adverts-declaring-michael-jackson-innocent-taken-off-london-buses; Salvatore Maicki, 'The Simpsons will Shelve an Early Episode Guest Starring Michael Jackson', 7 March 2019, https://www.thefader.com/2019/03/07/the-simpsons-michael-jackson-episode-pulled-leaving-neverland.

55 Dowling, 'TV Review'.
56 Julian Vigo, 'Metaphor of Hybridity: The Body of Michael Jackson', *The Journal of Pan African Studies* 3, no. 7 (2010): 40.
57 Victor Huertas Martin, 'Rupert Goold's *Richard II* (2012): A Network of Visual Intertextuality', *Romanian Shakespeare Journal* II, no. 2 (2014): 42.
58 Dan Jones, 'The Plantagenets Are All over the Stage and Screen', *Sunday Times, London,* 6 May 2012; Martin (cited earlier) quotes portions of the same interview in his discussion of Goold's Flint Castle scene.
59 Martin, 'Rupert Goold's *Richard II*', 42.
60 Alice Daily, '"Little, Little Graves": Shakespeare's Photographs of Richard II', *Shakespeare Quarterly* 69, no. 3 (2018): 142–3, citing Ernst H. Kantorowicz, *The King's Two Bodies: A Study in Medieval Political Theology* (Princeton: Princeton University Press, 1957), 194–6.
61 Vigo, 'Metaphor of Hybridity', 40.
62 Wray, 'The Shakespearean Auteur', 479.
63 Edward Said, *Orientalism* (New York: Vintage Books, 1979), 138.
64 Wray, 'The Shakespearean Auteur', 478.
65 Kirwan, '*The Hollow Crown: Richard II*'.
66 Higginbotham, 'The Construction of a King', 68.
67 Jerry Brotton, 'Shakespeare's Turks and the Spectre of Ambivalence in the History Plays', *Textual Practice* 28, no. 3 (2014): 528.
68 For example, 'Richard II: Sad Stories of the Death of Kings', *Illuminations* (blog), 7 July 2012, https://www.illuminationsmedia.co.uk/richard-ii-sad-stories-of-the-death-of-kings/; Matthew Lyons, 'Review: The Hollow Crown: Richard II', *Matthew Lyons: Writer & Historian* (blog), 16 July 2012, https://mathewlyons.co.uk/2012/07/16/review-the-hollow-crown-richard-ii; Yevgeny Pavlov, 'The Hollow Crown (BBC, 2012): Richard II', *Perverse Egalitarianism* (blog), 8 July 2012, https://pervegalit.wordpress.com/2012/07/08/the-hollow-crown-bbc-2012/.
69 Richard A. Kaye, 'Losing His Religion: Saint Sebastian as Contemporary Gay Martyr', in *Lesbian and Gay Sexualities and*

Visual Cultures, ed. Peter Horne et al. (London and New York: Routledge, 1996), 86–7.
70 L. Monique Pittman, 'Shakespeare and the Cultural Olympiad: Contesting Gender and the British Nation in the BBC's *The Hollow Crown*', *Borrowers and Lenders: The Journal of Shakespeare and Appropriation* 9 (2016): NP.
71 Dailey, 'Where Character is King', 138.
72 Higginbotham, 'The Construction of a King', 71.
73 Pittman, 'Shakespeare and the Cultural Olympiad'.
74 *Edward II*, dir. Derek Jarman (1991; Burbank: New Line Home Video, 1992), VHS.
75 Thompson, *Passing Strange*, 62.

Chapter 3

1 'H4', *Kickstarter*.
2 Barbara Hodgdon, *Henry IV, Part 2*, Shakespeare in Performance (Manchester: Manchester University of Press, 1993), 17.
3 Scott McMillin, *Henry IV, Part 1*, Shakespeare in Performance (Manchester: Manchester University Press, 1991), 1–7; David Scott Kastan, 'Introduction', in *King Henry IV, Part 1*, ed. Kastan (London: Bloomsbury, 2002), 2–3; James C. Bulman, 'Introduction', in *King Henry IV, Part 2*, ed. Bulman (London: Bloomsbury, 2016), 49.
4 Robert Shaughnessy, 'Falstaff's Belly: Pathos, Prosthetics, and Performance', *Shakespeare Survey 63* (Cambridge: Cambridge University Press, 2010): 73–4; Elena Levy-Navarro, *The Culture of Obesity in Early and Late Modernity* (New York: Palgrave Macmillan, 2008), 69–103.
5 Here forward, casting data from the US and UK from 1970 to 2005 was obtained from J. O'Connor and K. Goodland, *A Directory of Shakespeare in Performance*, vols 1–3 (New York: Palgrave Macmillan, 2011) and the online World Shakespeare Bibliography, ed. Heidi Craig (Oxford: Oxford University Press, 2023), which covers the years 1960 to the present. Specific information on race in these performances was obtained from my own internet searches. Additional information was obtained from Manchester University Press's Shakespeare in Performance series, especially McMillan, *Henry IV, Part 1* and Hodgdon, *Henry IV, Part 2*. While an absence is

notoriously difficult to prove, I find no evidence of a Black American Falstaff before 1991 or any British Falstaffs of colour to date.

6 Bulman, 'Introduction', 64, citing Jonathan Baldo, *Memory in Shakespeare's Histories: Stages of Forgetting in Early Modern England* (London and New York: Routledge, 2011), 83.

7 Baldo, *Memory in Shakespeare's Histories*, 82.

8 Harriet Phillips, 'Late Falstaff, the Merry World, and *The Merry Wives of Windsor*', *Shakespeare* 10, no. 2 (2014): 114.

9 Baldo, *Memory in Shakespeare's Histories*, 51–101.

10 Hodgdon, *Henry IV, Part 2*, 11.

11 McMillan, *Henry IV, Part 1*, 5.

12 Kent Puckett, *War Pictures: Cinema, Violence, and Style in Britain: 1939-1945* (New York: Fordham University Press, 2017), 89–95.

13 Hodgdon, *Henry IV, Part 2*, 15.

14 G. Wilson Knight, *The Olive and the Sword: A Study of England's Shakespeare* (London: Oxford University Press, 1944), quoted in Puckett, *War Pictures*, 88.

15 Puckett, *War Pictures*, 88.

16 Ibid., 110, 116.

17 Shaughnessy, 'Falstaff's Belly', 63.

18 Hodgdon, *Henry IV, Part 2*, 17.

19 Ibid.

20 Romola Nuttall, 'Review of Shakespeare's *Richard II* (Directed by Adjoa Andoh and Lynette Linton) at Shakespeare's Globe, Sam Wanamaker Playhouse, London, 2019, Broadcast by Swinging the Lens on YouTube April 2021', *Shakespeare* 17, no. 3 (2021): 365–9. Quoting Greg Morrison, 'Making Sense of History: Adjoa Andoh on *Richard II*', *Shakespeare's Globe*, 12 September 2019, https://www.shakespearesglobe.com/discover/blogs-and-features/2019/09/12/making-sense-of-history/.

21 Miranda Johnson Haddad, 'The Shakespeare Theatre at the Folger', *Shakespeare Quarterly* 41, no. 4 (1990): 516n1.

22 E.g. Howard and Rackin, *Engendering a Nation*, 163–7; Valerie Traub, *Desire and Anxiety: Circulations of Sexuality in Shakespearean Drama* (London and New York: Routledge, 1992), 55–61.

23 Patricia Parker, *Literary Fat Ladies: Rhetoric, Gender, Property* (London and New York: Routledge, 1988), 20–3.

24 Mark Brown, 'Donmar Warehouse to Build Temporary Theatre for All-Female Shakespeare Trilogy', *The Guardian*, 25 May 2016, https://www.theguardian.com/stage/2016/may/25/donmar-warehouse-temporary-theatre-shakespeare-trilogy-kings-cross-station?CMP=gu_com.

25 E.g. Dominic Cavendish, '*Henry IV*, Donmar Warehouse, Review', *The Telegraph*, 10 October 2014, https://www.telegraph.co.uk/culture/theatre/theatre-reviews/11153732/Henry-IV-Donmar-Warehouse-review.html; Michael Billington, '*Henry IV* Review', *The Guardian*, 10 October 2014, https://www.theguardian.com/stage/2014/oct/10/henry-iv-review-all-female-shakespeare-donmar-warehouse.

26 Bulman, 'Appendix 2: Performing Conflated Texts of *Henry IV*', in *King Henry IV Part 2*, 502.

27 Ghazaleh Golpira, '*Henry IV: Part 1* at Shakespeare' Globe', *The Upcoming*, 20 May 2019, https://www.theupcoming.co.uk/2019/05/11/henry-iv-part-1-at-shakespeares-globe-theatre-review/.

28 Joseph Quincy Adams, 'Shakespeare and American Culture' (1932), in *Shakespeare in America: An Anthology from the Revolution to Now*, ed. James Shapiro (New York: Penguin, 2014), 427.

29 Michael D. Bristol, *Shakespeare's America, America's Shakespeare* (London and New York: Routledge, 1990), 1.

30 Kim C. Sturgess, *Shakespeare and the American Nation* (Cambridge: Cambridge University Press, 2004), 3, 16–18, 33, 38, 56–7, 154, 205.

31 Ibid., 2.

32 Abraham Lincoln, 'Letter to James H. Hackett' (1863), in *Shakespeare in America*, 181–2.

33 Chris Naffziger, 'The History of Falstaff, Part One', *St. Louis Magazine*, 25 March 2015, https://www.stlmag.com/history/the-history-of-falstaff%2C-part-one%3A-founding-a-brewery/.

34 VintageTVCommercials.com, 'Old Falstaff Beer Commercial', YouTube Video, 1:03, 5 March 2009, https://www.youtube.com/watch?v=wrScZdC1yn0.

35 Chris Naffziger, 'The History of Falstaff, Part Four', *St. Louis Magazine*, 15 April 2015, https://www.stlmag.com/history/the-history-of-falstaff-part-four-the-death-of-a-great-american-brewery/.

36 Orlando Shakes, 'The Merry Wives of Windsor – Presenting Falstaff Beer!', YouTube Video, 2:23, 24 February 2015, https://www.youtube.com/watch?v=j916z-NjuVg.

37 Kerry Lengel, 'Review: Shakespeare's "Merry Wives" as '50s sitcom', *azcentral.com*, 20 October 2015, https://www.azcentral.com/story/entertainment/arts/2015/10/20/review-southwest-shakespeare-merry-wives/74080064/.

38 John Ahlin, 'The Glories of Playing Falstaff', *Utah Shakespeare Festival*, 9 June 2015, https://www.bard.org/news/the-glories-of-playing-falstaff-by-john-ahlin.
39 Floyd Gaffney, 'In the Dark: King Henry V; Theatre beyond Color?', Negro Digest 18, no. 6 (1969): 36-41; Dan Hulbert, 'Acting Lives up to Unusual Casting Challenge', *The Atlanta Constitution*, 13 July 1993.
40 John Timpane, '*1 Henry IV* by Peggy Shannon', *Shakespeare Bulletin* 10, no. 4 (1992): 29–30.
41 'Actor Profile: Brandon Carter', *American Shakespeare Center*, 13 January 2019, https://americanshakespearecenter.com/2019/01/actor-profile-brandon-carter/.
42 Sam Hurwitt, 'African-American Shakes Hits Stage with Revamped "Richard II"', *The Mercury News*, 13 April 2022, https://www.mercurynews.com/2022/04/13/african-american-shakes-hits-stage-with-revamped-richard-ii/.
43 Barbara Gamarekian, 'Shakespeare Is Given an Outing in Washington', *The New York Times*, 4 June 1991.
44 'Paul Winfield Finds Shakespeare a Challenge', *New York Amsterdam News*, 9 November 1974.
45 Jacqueline Trescott, 'The Worries of Paul Winfield', *The Washington Post*, 4 June 1991.
46 Bates's performance sparked a local debate about nontraditional casting and stereotyping. Grace Kennedy and Tim D'Aquisto, 'Dissenting Opinions on "Merry Wives"', *The New York Times*, 22 August 1993.
47 'The Merry Wives of Windsor', *St. Louis Shakespeare Festival*, https://stlshakes.org/production/the-merry-wives-of-windsor/.
48 Charles Culbertson, 'Lamentable "Falstaff" Fails to Engage', *The News Leader*, Staunton, 1 July 2004.
49 Michael Scott Moore, 'The Son Also Rises', *San Francisco Weekly*, 21 July 2004.
50 Sam Hurwitt, 'Rush Up Your Shakespeare', *East Bay Express*, Oakland, 21 July 2004.
51 A. A. Kristi, 'Oregon Shakespeare Festival Actor G. Valmont Thomas Dies', *Broadway World,* 18 December 2017, https://www.broadwayworld.com/portland/article/Oregon-Shakespeare-Festival-Actor-G-Valmont-Thomas-Dies-20171218.
52 Ayanna Thompson, '(How) Should We Listen to Audiences?: Race, Reception, and the Audience Survey', in *The Oxford Handbook of*

Shakespeare and Performance, ed. James C. Bulman (Oxford: Oxford University Press, 2020), 162–3.
53 Megan Monson, 'Backstage Business', *Oregon Business* 26, no. 6 (2003): 48.
54 Oregon Shakespeare Festival, 'Director Interview: *Henry IV, Part One*', YouTube Video, 5:12, 31 August 2016, https://www.youtube.com/watch?v=tj8x9d_APms; Oregon Shakespeare Festival, 'Director Interview: *Henry IV, Part Two*', YouTube Video, 8:04, 31 August 2016, https://www.youtube.com/watch?v=da4fe3pJQV0.
55 Hailey Bachrach, 'The Oregon Shakespeare Festival 2017', *Shakespeare Newsletter* 67, no. 1 (2017): 16.
56 Sonja Arsham Kuftinec, 'Oregon Shakespeare Festival', *Theatre Journal* 70, no. 1 (2018): 95.
57 Bachrach, 'The Oregon Shakespeare Festival 2017', 18.
58 Suzi Steffen, 'Five Questions for the Falstaffs', *Oregon ArtsWatch*, 14 June 2017, https://www.orartswatch.org/five-questions-for-the-falstaffs.
59 Kuftinec, 'Oregon Shakespeare Festival', 95.
60 '"Merry Wives" a Raucous Time', *San Francisco Examiner*, 15 May 2013, https://www.sfexaminer.com/entertainment/merry-wives-a-raucous-time; Morgan Woodle, '"Henry IV Part I" at the Baltimore Shakespeare Factory', *DC Theater Arts*, 18 August 2015, https://dctheaterarts.org/2015/08/18/henry-iv-part-i-at-the-baltimore-shakespeare-factory/.
61 Kathy M. Howlett, 'Utopian Revisioning of Falstaff's Tavern World: Orson Welles's *Chimes at Midnight* and Gus Van Sant's *My Own Private Idaho*', in *The Reel Shakespeare: Alternative Cinema and Theory*, ed. Lisa S. Starks and Courtney Lehmann (Madison: Fairleigh Dickinson University Press, 2002), 166–7.
62 For details on the film's production, see Bridget Gellert Lyons, ed., 'Interview with Keith Baxter', in *Chimes at Midnight* (New Brunswick: Rutgers University Press, 1988), 267–83; 'Making *Chimes at Midnight*', accessed 26 March 2022, http://www.janusfilms.com.s3-website-us-east-1.amazonaws.com/chimes/making.html.
63 Bridget Gellert Lyons, ed., 'The Greatest Good Man', in *Chimes at Midnight* (New Brunswick: Rutgers University Press, 1988), 261–2.
64 Howlett, 'Utopian Revisioning', 170.
65 Andrew Dickson, 'Richard Eyre on the *Hollow Crown*'s *Henry IV*: From the Pub to the Battlefield', *The Guardian*, 2 May 2016, https://www.theguardian.com/stage/2016/may/02/richard-eyre-henry-iv-plays-bbc-hollow-crown-tom-hiddleston-falstaff-hal.

66 Bulman, 'Introduction', 46. Height information obtained from CelebHeights.com, accessed 11 May 2019, https://www.celebheights.com/.
67 Shaughnessy, 'Falstaff's Belly'.
68 'The Making of *Henry IV*', in *The Hollow Crown: The Complete Series*, DVD.
69 Shaughnessy, 'Falstaff's Belly', 74.
70 'The Making of *Henry IV*'.
71 Levy-Navarro, *The Culture of Obesity*, 71, 74, 81.
72 'The Making of *Henry IV*'.
73 See also Maya Mathur's brief analysis in '"I Know Thee Not, Old Man": Using Film and Television to Teach *1* and *2 Henry IV*', in *Approaches to Teaching Shakespeare's English History Plays*, ed. Laurie Ellinghausen (New York: MLA, 2017), 157.
74 Anna Mollow, 'Disability Studies Gets Fat', *Hypatia* 30, no. 1 (2015): 201.
75 Sally Bayley, 'The Shakespeare Tragedy that Truly Speaks to Us Now', *BBC.com*, 21 April 2021, https://www.bbc.com/culture/article/20210421-the-shakespeare-tragedy-that-truly-speaks-to-us-now.
76 All references to this film are to *Chimes at Midnight*, dir. Orson Welles (1965; Baker City: Nostalgia Family Video, 2008), DVD.
77 McMillan, *Henry IV, Part 1*, 97.
78 'H4', *Kickstarter*.
79 Bulman, 'Appendix 2', 496–7.
80 Marilyn Ferdinand, 'Review of *H4* for the Chicago International Film Festival (CIFF) 2013', 17 October 2013, http://www.ferdyonfilms.com/2013/ciff-2013-h4-2014/19767/.
81 'Angus Macfadyen', *imdb.com*, accessed 1 May 2019, https://www.imdb.com/name/nm0005171/.
82 For a variety of potential reasons involving both gender and American political institutions, *H4* drops the 'Lord' in 'Lord Chief Justice'.
83 'Helping Hands', *Improv Help Desk*, accessed 1 May 2019, http://www.improvhd.com/helping-hands.
84 'Victoria Gabrielle Platt', imdb.com, accessed 1 May 2019, https://www.imdb.com/name/nm0686911/bio?ref_=nm_ov_bio_sm.
85 'Filmmakers' Commentary', in *H4*, DVD.
86 Parker, *Literary Fat Ladies*, 20.

87 Ibid., 20.
88 Ferdinand, 'Review'.
89 Stephen Greenblatt, 'Invisible Bullets: Renaissance Authority and Its Subversion, *Henry IV* and *Henry V*', in *Political Shakespeare: New Essays in Cultural Materialism*, ed. Jonathan Dollimore and Alan Sinfield (Ithaca: Cornell University Press, 1985), 32.
90 Bulman, 'Appendix 2', 497.
91 *H4* Film Screening, Shakespeare Association of America Annual Meeting (Boston, 6 April 2012).
92 'Filmmakers' Commentary'.
93 Bulman, 'Appendix 2', 498.
94 Ibid., 498–9.
95 '*H4*', *Kickstarter*.
96 *Faustão*, dir. Eduardo Coutinho (1971), YouTube Video, 1:41:20, 13 February 2012, https://www.youtube.com/watch?v=utFklgmhs0I.
97 Peter Singelmann, 'Political Structure and Social Banditry in Northeast Brazil', *Journal of Latin American Studies* 7, no. 1(1975): 59.
98 Robert Stam, *Tropical Multiculturalism: A Comparative History of Race in Brazilian Cinema and Culture* (Durham: Duke University Press, 1997), 274–7.
99 Ibid., 275.
100 Ibid., 277.
101 Mark Thornton Burnett, *Shakespeare and World Cinema* (Cambridge: Cambridge University Press, 2012), 114–15.
102 MacDonald, *Shakespeare Adaptation*, 2.

Chapter 4

1 Harold Bloom, *Shakespeare: The Invention of the Human* (New York: Riverhead Books, 1998), 4, 8, 279.
2 Vanessa I. Corredera, '"How Dey Goin' to Kill Othello?!": Key & Peele and Shakespearean Universality', *Journal of American Studies* 54 (2020): 28.
3 Xaque Gruber, 'The Many Faces of Harry Lennix', *Huffington Post*, updated 6 December 2017, https://www.huffpost.com/entry/the-many-faces-of-harry-l_b_3677457.

4 Thompson, *Passing Strange*, 22–3.
5 Dennis Overbye, 'Cosmos Controversy: The Universe Is Expanding, but How Fast?', *The New York Times*, 20 February 2017.
6 'Universe, n.', *OED Online* (Oxford University Press, June 2022), https://www.oed.com/view/Entry/214800?redirectedFrom=universe&.
7 Thomas Cartelli similarly engages student voices in his discussion of Peter Greenaway's *Prospero's Books* (1991) in *Reenacting Shakespeare in the Shakespeare Aftermath: The Intermedial Turn and Turn to Embodiment* (New York: Palgrave Macmillan, 2019), 153–82.
8 '*H4*', *Kickstarter*.
9 Jay S. Jacobs, 'Harry Lennix: Exploring *The Blacklist* and the Bard', *Pop Entertainment*, 18 October 2018, https://popentertainment-interviews.tumblr.com/post/86415889404/harry-lennix-exploring-the-blacklist-and-the-bard.
10 Gruber, 'The Many Faces of Harry Lennix'.
11 Marilyn Ferdinand, 'CIFF 2013: Shakespeare and More – A Conversation with Harry Lennix', *Ferdy on Films*, accessed 21 July 2021, https://web.archive.org/web/20140710110316.
12 'Filmmakers' Commentary', *H4*.
13 Jamir Wilson, 'A Close Look at Gang Culture and Shakespeare', essay written for English 235: Shakespearean Literatures, Allegheny College (2 December 2020). Cited with permission from the author.
14 Luci Scott, 'ASU Dean's Screenplay sets "Henry IV" in LA in Black Community', *The Arizona Republic*, 7 September 2011, http://www.azcentral.com/community/tempe/articles/2011/09/07/20110907tempe-shakespeare-asu-dean-screenplay0907.html.
15 'Filmmakers' Commentary'.
16 Tim Brayton, 'Chicago International Film Festival '13: *H4* (Paul Quinn, USA)', *Antagony and Ecstasy*, 20 October 2013, https://web.archive.org/web/20140308185755/http://antagonie.blogspot.com/2013/10/ciff-13-h4.
17 'Filmmakers' Commentary'.
18 '*H4*', *Kickstarter*.
19 'Filmmakers' Commentary'.
20 Ibid.
21 Ibid.
22 KiaJah Rhodes, '*H4*, Blackness and the Contend for Power', essay written for English 235: Shakespearean Literatures, Allegheny College (13 December 2021). Cited with permission from the author.

23 'Filmmakers' Commentary'.
24 *H4* Film Screening, Shakespeare Association of America.
25 'Filmmakers' Commentary'.
26 '*H4*', *Kickstarter*.
27 'Filmmakers' Commentary'.
28 Ibid.
29 Jan Kott, *Shakespeare Our Contemporary*, trans. Boleslaw Taborski (Garden City: Doubleday, 1964).
30 Mike Sonksen, '12 SoCal Public Art Projects That Explore Race and Marginalized Histories', *KCET*, 21 September 2021, https://www.kcet.org/shows/artbound/inclusive-public-art-and-racial-justice.
31 Dave McNary, '"Blacklist" Actor Harry Lennix Launches Movie Production Company', *Variety*, 4 August 2014, https://variety.com/2014/film/news/harry-lennix-exponent-media-movie-production-company-1201273437/.
32 Sibel Kaba and Deniz Özalpman, 'Non-Theatrical Film Experience and Film Collecting Practices in the Digital Age', *Quarterly Review of Film and Video* 38, no. 4 (2021): 354–5.
33 Scott, 'ASU Dean's Screenplay'.
34 Devin Gaffney, '235 Final', essay written for English 235: Shakespearean Literatures, Allegheny College (7 December 2020). Cited with permission from the author.
35 'Filmmakers' Commentary'.
36 Kyle DiPofi, '*H4*: Adapting a History and Building an Identity', essay written for English 235: Shakespearean Literatures, Allegheny College (5 December 2020). Cited with permission from the author.
37 Thompson, *Passing Strange*, 17.
38 Bronfen, *Serial Shakespeare*.
39 He has, however, stated that 'the reason the Shakespeare is in the film is to transcend time, to show that these things have always happened, everywhere'. Gus Van Sant, *Even Cowgirls Get the Blues/My Own Private Idaho* (London and Boston: Faber and Faber, 1993), xlii–xliii.
40 Andrew Barnaby, 'Imitation as Originality in Gus Van Sant's *My Own Private Idaho*', in *Almost Shakespeare: Reinventing His Works for Cinema and Television*, ed. James R. Keller and Leslie Stratyner (Jefferson: McFarland, 2014), 37; Howlett, 'Utopian Revisioning', 180–2; Elizabeth Zeman Kolkovich, 'Queering Poins: Masculinity

and Friendship in *Henry IV, The Hollow Crown*, and the RSC's "King and Country"', *Shakespeare Bulletin* 36, no. 4 (2019): 649–50; Susan Wiseman, 'The Family Tree Motel: Subliming Shakespeare in *My Own Private Idaho*', in *Shakespeare the Movie*, 232; Nemanja Protic, 'Where Is the Bawdy? Falstaffian Politics in Gus Van Sant's *My Own Private Idaho*', *Literature/Film Quarterly* 29, no. 2 (2001): 116–21; Hugh H. Davis, '"Shakespeare, He's in the Alley": *My Own Private Idaho* and Shakespeare in the Streets', *Literature/Film Quarterly* 41, no. 3 (2013): 117–20.

41 Amy Taubin, 'Objects of Desire' (January 1992), *Sight and Sound* 31, no. 6 (2021): 96.

42 David Handelman, 'Gus Van Sant's Northwest Passage', *Rolling Stone*, 31 October 1991, https://www.rollingstone.com/tv-movies/tv-movie-news/gus-van-sants-northwest-passage-199776/.

43 All references to this film are to *My Own Private Idaho*, dir. Gus Van Sant (1991; New York: Criterion Collection, 2005).

44 Howlett, 'Utopian Revisioning', 165–9.

45 Barnaby, 'Imitation as Originality', 38.

46 Curtis Breight, 'Elizabethan World Pictures', in *Shakespeare and National Cultures,* ed. John J. Joughin (Manchester: Manchester University Press, 1997), 299–302.

47 Ibid., 303–16.

48 Van Sant, *Even Cowgirls Get the Blues/My Own Private Idaho*, 125.

49 Handelman, 'Gus Van Sant's Northwest Passage'.

50 Breight, 'Elizabethan World Pictures', 305.

51 Julian Cha, '"There Is No Spoon": Transnationalism and the Coding of Race/Ethnicity in the Science Fiction/Fantasy Cinema of Keanu Reeves', *Studies in Popular Culture* 35, no. 1 (2012): 49. Citing R. L. Rutsky, 'Being Keanu', in *The End of Cinema as We Know It: American Film in the Nineties*, ed. John Lewis (New York: New York University Press, 2001), 191–2, 185.

52 Breight, 'Elizabethan World Pictures', 307–8.

53 Ibid., 301.

54 Van Sant, *Even Cowgirls Get the Blues/My Own Private Idaho*, 113–14.

55 Breight, 'Elizabethan World Pictures', 316.

56 Ibid., 308, 310.

57 David Roman, 'Shakespeare Out in Portland: Gus Van Sant's *My Own Private Idaho*, Homoneurotics, and Boy Actors', *Genders* 19 (1994): 311–33.

58 Breight, 'Elizabethan World Pictures', 304.

59 Van Sant, *Even Cowgirls Get the Blues/My Own Private Idaho*, 159.

60 Ibid., 162.

61 Barbara Hodgdon, *The End Crowns All: Closure and Contradiction in Shakespeare's History* (Princeton: Princeton University Press, 1991), 152–3.

Chapter 5

1 Samuel Crowl, *Shakespeare at the Cineplex* (Athens: Ohio University Press, 2003), 109.

2 Peter Holland, 'Hand in Hand to Hell', *Times Literary Supplement*, 10 May 1996, 19.

3 See Barbara Hodgdon, 'Replicating Richard: Body Doubles, Body Politics', *Theatre Journal* 50, no. 2 (1998): 207–25; Stephen M. Buhler, 'Camp *Richard III* and the Burdens of (Stage/Film) History', in *Shakespeare, Film, Fin de Siècle*, ed. Mark Thornton Burnett and Ramona Wray (New York: Palgrave Macmillan, 2000), 40–57; Michael D. Friedman, 'Horror, Homosexuality, and Homiciphilia in McKellen's "Richard III" and Jarman's "Edward II"', *Shakespeare Bulletin* 27, no. 4 (2009): 567–88; Robert McRuer, 'Fuck the Disabled: The Prequel', *Shakesqueer: A Queer Companion to the Complete Works of Shakespeare*, ed. Madhavi Menon (Durham: Duke University Press, 2011), 294–301.

4 McRuer, 'Fuck the Disabled', 297.

5 Jessica Walker, '"As Crooked in Thy Manners as Thy Shape": Reshaping Deformity in Loncraine's *Richard III*', *Journal of the Wooden O Symposium* 11, no. 2 (2012): 155.

6 Thomas A. Pendleton, 'Shakespeare . . . with Additional Dialog', *Cinéaste* 24, no. 1 (1998): 65.

7 Peter S. Donaldson, 'Cinema and the Kingdom of Death: Loncraine's *Richard III*', *Shakespeare Quarterly* 53, no. 2 (2002): 241–59. See also Kathy M. Howlett, *Framing Shakespeare on Film* (Athens: Ohio University Press, 2000), 128–48; Jared Scott Johnson, 'The Propaganda Imperative: Challenging Mass Media Representations in

McKellen's *Richard III*', *College Literature* 31, no. 4 (2004): 44–59; Holland, 'Hand in Hand to Hell', 19.

8 Chakravarty, 'Live, and beget', 147, 160. The term 'homonationalism' was coined by Jasbir Puar, *Terrorist Assemblanges: Homonationalism in Queer Times* (Durham: Duke University Press, 2007).

9 Anderson, 'When Race Matters', 100.

10 Rebecca Shier, 'African Americans and Shakespeare', *Shakespeare Unlimited*, podcast audio, rebroadcast 18 August 2020, https://www.folger.edu/shakespeare-unlimited/african-americans-shakespeare.

11 Anderson, 'When Race Matters', 98–100.

12 Mel Gussow, 'Denzel Washington Plays Shakespeare's Top Schemer', *The New York Times*. 17 August 1990.

13 'The Tragedy of *Richard III* by William Shakespeare, Original Cast July–December 1990', accessed 18 June 2022, https://mckellen.com/stage/richard90/cast.htm.

14 Kenneth Branagh, *Much Ado about Nothing* (London: Chatto and Windus, 1993), x.

15 L. Monique Pittman, *Authorizing Shakespeare on Film and Television: Gender, Class, and Ethnicity in Adaptation* (New York: Peter Lang Publishing, 2011), 39.

16 Boose and Burt, 'Totally Clueless?', 14, quoting Luhrmann's 'Production Notes', http://web.idirect.com/-claire/rjintor.html, 2.

17 Nicholas Radel, 'The Ethiop's Ear: Race, Sexuality, and Baz Luhrmann's *William Shakespeare's Romeo + Juliet*', *The Upstart Crow* 28 (2009): 17–34; Jennie M. Votava, 'The Ethiop's Jewel Meets *Euphoria's* Jules: Race, Gender, and Sexuality in an HBO Appropriation of Shakespeare', *Shakespeare Bulletin* 38, no. 4 (2020): 593–614.

18 Lehman, '"Faux Show"', 70.

19 Pittman, *Authorizing Shakespeare*, 40.

20 Boose and Burt, 'Totally Clueless?', 14.

21 Neil Taylor, 'National and Racial Stereotypes in Shakespeare Films', in *The Cambridge Companion to Shakespeare on Film*, ed. Russell Jackson (Cambridge: Cambridge University Press, 2000), 264.

22 Lisa Hopkins, '"How very like the home life of our own dear queen": Ian McKellen's *Richard III*', in *Spectacular Shakespeare: Critical Theory and Popular Cinema*, ed. Courtney Lehmann and Lisa S. Starks (Madison: Fairleigh Dickinson University Press, 2002), 50.

23 Anonymous, 'More Fallen Leaders: *Richard III* Directed by Richard Loncraine', *Rolling Stone*, 25 January 1996, 64.

24 Gary Crowdus, 'Richard III Directed by Richard Loncraine and starring Ian McKellen', Cinéaste 22, no. 1 (1996): 34–6.
25 Rick Groen, 'Film Review of Othello', The Globe and Mail, Toronto, Ontario, 29 December 1995.
26 Jay Stone, 'Othello the Movie Just Doesn't Do the Bard Proud', The Ottawa Citizen, 19 January 1996.
27 Hodgdon, The Shakespeare Trade, 57–8.
28 Holland, 'Hand in Hand to Hell'.
29 James N. Loehlin, '"Top of the World, Ma": Richard III and Cinematic Convention', in Shakespeare the Movie, 71.
30 Hopkins, '"How very like the home life"', 48, 50–8.
31 Loehlin, '"Top of the World, Ma"', 72.
32 Ian McKellen, William Shakespeare's Richard III (London: Doubleday, 1996), 7.
33 All references to this film are to Richard III, dir. Richard Loncraine (1995; Santa Monica, CA: MGM Home Entertainment, 2000).
34 Howlett, Framing Shakespeare on Film, 142–3, 139, 133.
35 McKellen, William Shakespeare's Richard III, 150.
36 The 39 Steps, dir. Alfred Hitchcock (1935; Chicago: Criterion Collection, 1999), DVD.
37 Donaldson, 'Cinema and the Kingdom of Death', 248.
38 Young and Innocent, dir. Alfred Hitchcock (1937; Criterion Collection, 2005), DVD.
39 Michael Torrey, '"The Plain Devil and Dissembling Looks": Ambivalent Physiognomy and Shakespeare's Richard III', English Literary Renaissance 30, no. 2 (2000): 133, 139, 143.
40 Howlett, Framing Shakespeare on Film, 129.
41 Michael Rogin, Black Face, White Noise: Jewish Immigrants in the Hollywood Melting Pot (Berkeley: University of California Press, 1996), 77–8, 88–9.
42 Jonathan Munby, Public Heroes: Screening the Gangster from 'Little Caesar' to 'Touch of Evil' (Chicago: University of Chicago Press, 1999), especially 39–65; Ronald Wilson, The Gangster Film: Fatal Success in American Cinema (New York: Wallflower Press, 2015), 28–46, 65–6.
43 Wilson, The Gangster Film, 30.
44 Munby, Public Heroes, 43.
45 White Heat, dir. Raoul Walsh (1949; Burbank: Warner Home Video, 2005), DVD.

46 Loehlin, '"Top of the World, Ma"', 73.
47 John Bodnar, *Blue-Collar Hollywood Liberalism, Democracy, and Working People in American Film* (Baltimore: Johns Hopkins University Press, 2003), 121.
48 Loehlin, '"Top of the World, Ma"', 74.
49 McKellen, *William Shakespeare's Richard III*, 22, 236.
50 Janet Adelman, *Suffocating Mothers: Fantasies of Maternal Origin in Shakespeare's Plays* (London and New York: Routledge, 1992), 2–3.
51 Chakravarty, '"Live, and beget"', 148.
52 Ibid., 149.
53 David Cook, *The History of Narrative Film* (London: W. W. Norton, 1980), 471.
54 Jonathan Auerbach, *Dark Borders: Film Noir and American Citizenship* (Durham: Duke University Press, 2011), cited in Markos Hadjioannou, 'In the Cold Night of Day: On Film Noir, Hitchcock, and Identity', *Cultural Critique* 94 (2016): 139.
55 Eric Lott, 'The Whiteness of Film Noir', in *Whiteness: A Critical Reader*, ed. Mike Hill (New York: New York University Press, 1997), 81–5.
56 E. Ann Kaplan, '"The Dark Continent of Film Noir": Race, Displacement, and Metaphor in Tourneur's *Cat People* (1942) and Welles's *The Lady from Shanghai*', in *Women in Film Noir*, 183.
57 Loehlin, '"Top of the World, Ma"', 73.
58 Bodnar, *Blue-Collar Hollywood Liberalism*, 122.
59 Paul Flowers et al., *Chemistry 2e*, OpenStax, 2019, https://cnx.org/contents/f8zJz5tx@7.1:QepiZWK9@6/6-1-Electromagnetic-Energy.
60 Tom Conley, *Film Hieroglyphs* (Minneapolis: University of Minnesota Press, 2006), 183.
61 Bodnar, *Blue-Collar Hollywood Liberalism*, 121.
62 Douglas Lanier, 'Shakescorp *Noir*', *Shakespeare Quarterly* 53, no. 2 (2002): 170.
63 Saskia Kossak, '*Frame My Face to All Occasions*': *Shakespeare's Richard III on Screen* (Vienna: Braumüller, 2005), 122.
64 Johnson, 'The Propaganda Imperative', 48.
65 Rogin, *Black Face, White Noise*, 73.
66 Arthur Knight, *Disintegrating the Musical: Black Performance and American Musical Film* (Durham: Duke University Press, 2002), 58.
67 Rogin, *Black Face, White Noise*, 84.

68 Ibid., 101. See also Eric Goldstein, *The Price of Whiteness: Jews, Race, and American Identity* (Princeton: Princeton University Press, 2006), esp. 138–64.
69 Rogin, *Black Face, White Noise*, 98, 112.
70 *The Jazz Singer*, dir. Alan Crosland (1927; Burbank: Warner Home Video, 2007), DVD.
71 Rogin, *Black Face, White Noise*, 100.
72 Linda Williams, *Playing the Race Card: Melodrama of Black and White from Uncle Tom to O. J. Simpson* (Princeton: Princeton University Press, 2001), 153–4.
73 *The Singing Fool*, dir. Lloyd Bacon (1928; Burbank: Warner Home Video, 2009), DVD.
74 Rogin, *Black Face, White Noise*, 147.
75 Ibid., 147, 150.
76 Thompson, *Blackface*, 21.
77 Anthony Gerard Barthelmy, *Black Face, Maligned Race* (Baton Rouge and London: Louisiana State University Press, 1987), 3–4.
78 Robert Weimann and Douglas Bruster, 'Performance, Game, and Representation in *Richard III*', in *Shakespeare and the Power of Performance: Stage and Page in the Elizabethan Theatre* (Cambridge: Cambridge University Press, 2018), 42–56.
79 McKellen, *William Shakespeare's Richard III*, 70, 74.
80 Ibid., 286.
81 Kossak, *'Frame My Face to All Occasions'*, 135.
82 McKellen, *William Shakespeare's Richard III*, 17.
83 Elizabeth Zauderer, '"Neither Mother, Wife, nor England's Queen": Re-visioning Queen Margaret of Anjou in Richard Loncraine's Film *Richard III* (1995)', *Literature/Film Quarterly* 43, no. 2 (2015): 148.
84 McKellen, *William Shakespeare's Richard III*, 279.

Conclusion

1 Comparisons between the novels and the TV series reference Julia Quinn, *The Duke and I* (New York: Harper Collins, 2000) and *The Viscount Who Loved Me* (New York: Harper Collins, 2000).
2 See, for instance, Christina Wald, *Shakespeare's Serial Returns in Complex TV* (New York: Palgrave Macmillan, 2020) and Bronfen,

Serial Shakespeare. For an exemplary analysis of the histories' presence in a recent TV series, see also L. Monique Pittman, 'Resisting History and Atoning for Racial Privilege: Shakespeare's Henriad in HBO's *The Wire*', in *The Routledge Handbook of Shakespeare and Global Appropriation*, ed. Christy Desmet, Sujata Iyengar and Miriam Jacobson (London and New York: Routledge, 2019).

3   Bronfen, *Serial Shakespeare*, 5.
4   Romano Mullin, 'Tweeting Television/Broadcasting the Bard @ HollowCrownFans and Digital Shakespeares', in *Broadcast Your Shakespeare*, ed. Stephen O'Neill (London and New York: Bloomsbury, 2017), 208; Blackwell, *Shakespearean Celebrity*.
5   Mullin, 'Tweeting Television', 207–8, 224.
6   'Number of Netflix Subscribers in 2022/2023: Growth, Revenue, and Usage', *Finance Online*, accessed 12 July 2022, https://financesonline.com/number-of-netflix-subscribers/.
7   Jack Shepherd, '22 Essential Twitter Statistics You Need to Know in 2022', *The Social Shepherd*, 16 June 2022, https://thesocialshepherd.com/blog/twitter-statistics#:~:text=Twitter%20Has%20396.5%20Million%20Users,in%20on%20a%20regular%20basis.
8   S. Dixon, 'Daily Twitter Usage in the United States as of August 2018, by Ethnicity', *Statista*, 28 January 2022, https://www.statista.com/statistics/945945/daily-frequency-usage-twitter-usa-ethnicity/#statisticContainer.
9   Marvin Carlson, *The Haunted Stage: The Theatre as Memory Machine* (Ann Arbor: University of Michigan Press, 2003).
10 Mike McClelland (@magicmikewrites), 'I just watched the first episode of Bridgerton with my mom and when I saw the glorious @goldarosh was the Queen I immediately remembered seeing her onstage', Twitter, 16 January 2021, 11:02 a.m., https://twitter.com/magicmikewrites/status/1350473565125148673.
11 Zoë M. Miller (@Zoe_M_Miller), 'I realized today that I saw Regé-Jean Page (the Duke of Hastings) in The Merchant of Venice in 2015', Twitter, 29 December 2020, 8:57 p.m., https://twitter.com/Zoe_M_Miller/status/1344100314199302144.
12 Sara Toussaint (@SaraToussaint), '@Jackie531 said that @regejean in #Bridgerton reminds her of Denzel Washington in "Much Ado About Nothing" and I –', Twitter, 1 January 2021, 8:11 p.m., https://twitter.com/SaraToussaint/status/1345175881682186244.
13 Blackwell, *Shakespearean Celebrity*, 8.
14 Elena Nicolaou (@elenawonders), 'So Adjoa Andoh (aka Lady Danbury in #Bridgerton) starred as Richard II in an all-WOC

Shakespeare production at the Globe in 2019. . . and if I could go back in time, I'd go back to see THAT', Twitter, 27 December 2020, 9:50 a.m., https://twitter.com/elenawonders/status/1343222778816770050.

15 Belinda Otas, 'Adjoa Andoh's *Richard II* Makes Stage History in the UK', *New African* 593 (April 2019): NP.

16 Adjoa Andoh, response to Plenary Panel, 'Fifty Years of Early Modern Critical Race Studies', Shakespeare Association of America Annual Meeting (Jacksonville, 8 April 2022).

17 Swinging the Lens, '*Richard II*–Swinging the Lens', YouTube Video, 2:31:27, 24 April 2020, https://www.youtube.com/watch?v=BHrXAJ93hRU.

18 Farrah Karim-Cooper, interview with Adjoa Andoh, Shakespeare Association of America Annual Meeting (Jacksonville, 8 April 2022).

19 ICATacting (@ICATacting), 'Earlier this year we had wonderful actress, Bridgerton star and ICAT Associate tutor Adjoa Andoh in for a Zoom Q&A and Shakespeare masterclass', Twitter, 11 March 2021, 5:01 a.m., https://twitter.com/ICATacting/status/1369951481214930944.

20 Histfest (@HistfestUK), '#Bridgerton star @adjoa_andoh is joined by @andykesson @vanessaolim & @WandaWyporska to explore women in the world & works of Shakespeare', Twitter, 19 April 2021, 7:41 a.m., https://twitter.com/HistFestUK/status/1384109793158172674.

21 Reggie Graham (@Ziggyfin), 'Bridgerton is literally every Shakespeare play I've studied', Twitter, 27 January 2021, 11:27 p.m., https://twitter.com/Ziggyfin/status/1354647327819001859.

22 J (@jen_rizk), 'Listennnn. Lmao I see y'all enjoying Bridgerton, please do yourselves a favor and watch Much Ado About Nothing (1993)', Twitter, 1 January 2021, 1:39 p.m., https://twitter.com/jen_rizk/status/1345076114272776193.

23 Chi-Chi Onuah (@chichionuah), 'When @bridgerton meets #Shakespeare', Twitter, 10 October 2021, 1:10 p.m., https://twitter.com/chichionuah/status/1447248085516800005.

24 Bridgerton (@bridgerton), 'Dear reader, it still remains to be seen, who shall be taming whom?', Twitter, 24 January 2022, 1:56 p.m., https://twitter.com/bridgerton/status/1485687952424546305.

25 @INVISELET, 'they talk about honor so much in bridgerton i'd think this was zuko doing a shakespeare monologue in 5th period drama class', Twitter, 18 January 2021, 9:30 p.m., https://twitter.com/INVISELET/status/1351356383535497217.

26 Lici (@Aliciana), 'Bridgerton got me talking like I'm William Shakespeare', Twitter, 24 January 2021, 1:10 p.m., https://twitter.com/Aliciana__/status/1353404909647925252.

27 K@kevtahjae, '10 minutes into bridgerton and I had to crop out. I can't take the Shakespeare slang', Twitter, 13 January 2021, 12:10 a.m., https://twitter.com/kevtahjae/status/1349222358771499009.

28 Kabs (@KBK_811), 'Why did they make us read and analyze Shakespeare in high school?', Twitter, 1 February 2021, 2:05 a.m., https://twitter.com/KBK_811/status/1356136544554389505.

29 Marnie Wellar (@NotWatsonClub1), 'Light went on for me today, realized the English teacher's long game, all the painstaking effort over "The Taming of the Shrew" was to prepare us for Bridgerton Season 2', Twitter, 15 April 2022, 8:15 p.m., https://twitter.com/NotWatsonClub1/status/1515121671061004295.

30 Victor Coronado (@vicvicvictorr), 'What's the point of having an inclusive cast in a series that is set in a time and place that (historically) wasn't like that? This is absurd', Twitter, 6 February 2021, 4:40 p.m., https://twitter.com/vicvicvictorr/status/1358168840367144963; Jassodra from Trinidad (@Jlorna1813), 'Because nincompoop, it's a TV hist romance not a hist documentary', Twitter, 7 February 2021, 11:20 p.m., https://twitter.com/JLorna1813/status/1358631851888435201; Romina Ricci, Twitter, 6 February 2021, 7:54 p.m., https://twitter.com/caterita2008/status/1358217498403893248.

31 Steph (@wuthering_alice), 'Thing is, I don't think it IS trying to be real history. It says at the start. It just happens to have a character who existed', Twitter, 25 February 2021, 3:11 a.m., https://twitter.com/wuthering_alice/status/1364850453893287936.

32 Kevin L (@smellslikekev1n), 'Watching Bridgerton n Netflix, and I didn't really think much about it having black actors', Twitter, 29 December 2020, 8:36 a.m., https://twitter.com/smellslikekev1n/status/1343913883178835968.

33 Akshaya Abbina (@akshayabbina), 'man . . . Bridgerton is a fantasy, and the new Macbeth is shakespeare, every person of every race and gender have been Shakespeare since as long as I can remember', Twitter, 27 September 2021, 8:11 p.m., https://twitter.com/akshayaabbina/status/1442643133095989254.

34 Bob Mondello, 'The Only *New* Thing about Cross-Cultural Casting Is Who's Getting the Roles', *NPR*, 15 July 2021, https://www.npr.org/2021/07/15/1016048049/cross-cultural-casting-anne-boleyn-hamilton-othello-green-knight-bridgerton#:~:text=Tiny%20Desk

%20Contest-, The%20Only%20'New'%20Thing%20About%20Cross%2DCultural%20Casting%20Is,its%20roots%20in%20live%20theater.

35 Matt Wolf, '*Bridgerton*'s Approach to Race and Casting has Precedent Onstage', *The New York Times*, 21 January 2021.

36 Lyn Gardner, '*Othello* Review: Lesbian Moor Boldly Puts Gender under Microscope', *The Guardian*, 4 May 2018, https://www.theguardian.com/stage/2018/may/04/othello-review-golda-rosheuvel-everyman-liverpool.

37 Andrea Park, 'What *Bridgerton* Got Right about Queen Charlotte', *Marie Claire*, 30 December 2020, https://www.marieclaire.com/culture/a35092348/queen-charlotte-bridgerton-true-story/. Additional articles range from the *Tatler* (UK) to *Seventeen Magazine* (US): Hope Coke, 'You've Seen Her on Screen in *Bridgerton* – Now Discover the Real Queen Charlotte', *Tatler*, 14 January 2021, https://www.tatler.com/article/queen-charlotte-bridgerton-true-story-history; Jasmine Washington, 'The True Story of Queen Charlotte from "Bridgerton"', *Seventeen Magazine*, 31 March 2022, https://www.seventeen.com/celebrity/movies-tv/a39491418/queen-charlotte-true-story-bridgerton/.

38 Google Trends, https://trends.google.com/trends/explore?date=2020-11-01%202022-06-01&q=%2Fm%2F01dr47,%2Fg%2F11cn5lfrvn,%2Fm%2F09gct0y,%2Fm%2F0zy0j_l.

39 Google Trends, https://trends.google.com/trends/explore?date=2020-11-01%202022-06-01&geo=GB&q=%2Fm%2F01dr47,%2Fg%2F11cn5lfrvn,%2Fm%2F09gct0y,%2Fm%2F0zy0j_l.

40 Google Trends, https://trends.google.com/trends/explore?date=2020-11-01%202022-06-01&geo=US&q=%2Fm%2F01dr47,%2Fg%2F11cn5lfrvn,%2Fm%2F09gct0y,%2Fm%2F0zy0j_l.

41 Allan Ramsay, 'Coronation Portrait of King George III and Queen Charlotte' (1761–2), accessed 17 June 2022, https://en.wikipedia.org/wiki/Coronation_of_George_III_and_Charlotte#/media/File:George_III_and_Charlotte_coronation_portraits_1762.jpg.

42 *Bridgerton*, Season 1, Episode 1, 'Diamond of the First Water', dir. Julie Anne Robinson, 25 December 2020, Netflix, https://www.netflix.com/title/80232398.

43 Katie White, 'The Enchanting New Netflix Series "Bridgerton" Is Bursting with Historical Works of Art', *Artnet*, 18 February 2021, https://news.artnet.com/art-world/bridgerton-artworks-season-one-1944646.

44 Keisha Hatchett, '*Bridgerton*: Queen Charlotte's 25 Royally Fabulous Wigs, Ranked', *TVLine*, 3 April 2022, https://tvline.com/lists/bridgerton-queen-wigs-ranked/.

45 *Bridgerton*, Season 1, Episode 4, 'An Affair of Honor', dir. Sheree Folkson.

46 Tracy Robey, '*Bridgerton* Recap: Garden Body Party', *Vulture*, 25 December 2020, https://www.vulture.com/article/bridgerton-recap-season-1-episode-4-an-affair-of-honor.html.

47 Aja Romano, 'The Debate over *Bridgerton* and Race', *Vox*, 7 January 2021, https://www.vox.com/22215076/bridgerton-race-racism-historical-accuracy-alternate-history.

48 Ineye Komonibo and Kathleen Newman-Bremang, 'A Double Hot Take on *Bridgerton*, Race & Romance', *Refinery29*, 28 December 2020, https://flipboard.com/@Refinery29/a-double-hot-take-on-bridgerton-race-romance/a-v93YBEJPRnGddI0LiUu_AQ%3Aa%3A692913612-4320f3f483%2Frefinery29.com.

49 Carolyn Hinds, '*Bridgerton* Sees Race through a Colorist Lens', *Observer*, 1 January 2021, https://observer.com/2021/01/bridgerton-sees-race-through-a-colorist-lens/.

50 A widely prevalent viewpoint well summarized by Shaun Armistead, 'Blackness, Dehumanized: A Black Feminist Analysis of "Bridgerton"', *Black Perspectives*, 2 February 2021, https://www.aaihs.org/blackness-dehumanized-a-black-feminist-analysis-of-bridgerton/.

51 West, 'Mammy, Sapphire, and Jezebel', 461–2.

52 Isabel Molina-Guzmán, '*Bridgerton's* Romance with Racial Nostalgia', *Flow*, 16 May 2022, https://www.flowjournal.org/2022/05/bridgertons-romance-with-racial-nostalgia/.

53 MacKenzie Jean-Phillipe, '*Bridgerton* Doesn't Need to Elaborate on Its Inclusion of Black Characters', *Oprah Daily*, 20 December 2020, https://www.oprahdaily.com/entertainment/tv-movies/a35083112/bridgerton-race-historical-accuracy/.

54 Nakedab006, comment on Kathryn VanArendonk, '*Bridgerton* Needs to Decide Whose World It's Living In', *Vulture*, 8 April 2022, https://www.vulture.com/article/bridgerton-colonialism-storytelling-logic-season-2.html.

55 Vanessa Riley, 'Black People in the Regency', *Vanessa Riley* (blog), accessed 22 April 2022, https://vanessariley.com/blackpeople.php.

56 Jean-Phillipe, '*Bridgerton* Doesn't Need to Elaborate'.

57 Nielson Company, 'Tailored Content Strategies Are Driving Viewership Growth Among Streaming Platforms', 19 August 2021, https://www.nielsen.com/us/en/insights/article/2021/tailored-content-strategies-are-driving-viewership-growth-among-streaming-platforms/; 'Number of Netflix Subscribers in 2022/2023'.

58 *Bridgerton,* Season 2, Episode 1, 'Capital R Rake', dir. Tricia Brock, 25 March 2022, Netflix, https://www.netflix.com/title/80232398.

59 *Bridgerton*, Season 1, Episode 1.

60 Ibid.

61 *Bridgerton*, Season 2, Episode 3, 'A Bee in Your Bonnet', dir. Alex Pillai.

62 Quinn, *The Viscount Who Loved Me*, 10–13.

63 Meha Razdan, 'Why *Bridgerton*'s Haldi Scene Made Me Cry', *Town & Country*, 27 March 2022, https://www.townandcountrymag.com/leisure/arts-and-culture/a39541314/bridgerton-haldi-scene-meaning-edwina-season-2/.

64 Dhvani Solani, 'As an Indian, I'm so Confused about How to Feel about *Bridgerton*. I'm Not Alone', *Vice*, 1 April 2022, https://www.vice.com/en/article/3abw8k/indians-thoughts-on-netflix-bridgerton-shonda-rhimes-show.

65 Ibid.; Molina-Guzmán, '*Bridgerton's* Romance with Racial Nostalgia'; VanArendonk, '*Bridgerton* Needs to Decide'.

66 *Bridgerton*, Season 2, Episode 10, 'The Viscount Who Loved Me', dir. Cheryl Dunye.

67 Arezou Amin, 'What's in a Name', *The Geeky Waffle* (blog), 27 March 2022, https://thegeekywaffle.com/home/2022/3/27/kate-sharma-whats-in-a-name.

68 *Bridgerton*, Season 2, Episode 6, 'The Choice', dir. Tom Verica.

69 *Bridgerton*, Season 2, Episode 10.

70 Bronfen, *Serial Shakespeare*, 98.

71 Ibid., 133.

72 Ibid, 141–50.

73 Leena Kim, 'Everything We Know about the *Bridgerton* Prequel', *Town & Country*, 8 July 2022, https://www.townandcountrymag.com/leisure/arts-and-culture/a36449511/bridgerton-spinoff-queen-charlotte/.

74 On Shakespeare's influence on HBO's *Game of Thrones* via the histories, see, for instance, Jeffrey R. Wilson, *Shakespeare and* Game of Thrones (London and New York: Routledge, 2020) and Dan Venning, '*Game of Thrones* as *Gesamtkunstwer*k: Adapting Shakespeare and Wagner', in *Vying for the Iron Throne: Essays on Power, Gender, Death and Performance in HBO's* Game of Thrones, ed. Lindsey Mantoan and Sara Brady (Jefferson: McFarland, 2018), 148–58.

SELECT BIBLIOGRAPHY

Adelman, Janet. *Suffocating Mothers: Fantasies of Maternal Origin in Shakespeare's Plays*. London and New York: Routledge, 1992.

Alexander-Floyd, Nikol G. 'Disappearing Acts: Reclaiming Intersectionality in the Social Sciences in a Post-Black Feminist Era'. *Feminist Formations* 24, no. 1 (2012): 1–25.

Anderson, Benedict. *Imagined Communities: Reflections on the Origin and Spread of Nationalism*. London and New York: Verso, 1983.

Auerbach, Jonathan. *Dark Borders: Film Noir and American Citizenship*. Durham: Duke University Press, 2011.

Baldo, Jonathan. *Memory in Shakespeare's Histories: Stages of Forgetting in Early Modern England*. London and New York: Routledge, 2011.

Barnaby, Andrew. 'Imitation as Originality in Gus Van Sant's *My Own Private Idaho*'. In *Almost Shakespeare: Reinventing His Works for Cinema and Television*, edited by James R. Keller and Leslie Stratyner, 22–41. Jefferson, NC: McFarland, 2014.

Barthelmy, Anthony Gerard. *Black Face, Maligned Race*. Baton Rouge and London, Louisiana State University Press, 1987.

Betancourt, Roland. *Byzantine Intersectionalities: Sexuality, Gender, and Race in the Middle Ages*. Princeton: Princeton University Press, 2020.

Bilge, Sirma. 'The Fungibility of Intersectionality: An Afropessimist Reading'. *Ethnic and Racial Studies* 43, no. 13 (2020): 2298–2326.

Blackwell, Anna. *Shakespearean Celebrity in the Digital Age: Fan Cultures and Remediation*. New York: Palgrave Macmillan, 2018.

Bodnar, John. *Blue-Collar Hollywood Liberalism, Democracy, and Working People in American Film*. Baltimore: Johns Hopkins University Press, 2003.

Boose, Lynda E. and Richard Burt, eds. *Shakespeare the Movie: Popularizing the Plays on Film, TV, and Video*. London and New York: Routledge, 1997.

Bovilsky, Lara. *Barbarous Play: Race on the English Renaissance Stage*. Minneapolis, MN: University of Minnesota Press, 2008.

Branagh, Kenneth. *Much Ado About Nothing*. London: Chatto and Windus, 1993.

Bray, Alan. 'Homosexuality and the Signs of Male Friendship in Elizabethan England'. *History Workshop* 29 (1990): 1–19.

Breight, Curtis. 'Elizabethan World Pictures'. In *Shakespeare and National Cultures*, edited by John J. Joughin, 295–325. Manchester: Manchester University Press, 1997.
Bridgerton (TV series). 2020. Netflix.
Bristol, Michael D. *Shakespeare's America, America's Shakespeare*. London and New York: Routledge, 1990.
Bronfen, Elisabeth. *Serial Shakespeare: An Infinite Variety of Appropriations in American TV Drama*. Manchester: Manchester University Press, 2020.
Brotton, Jerry. 'Shakespeare's Turks and the Spectre of Ambivalence in the History Plays'. *Textual Practice* 28, no. 3 (2014): 521–38.
Buhler, Stephen M. 'Camp *Richard III* and the Burdens of (Stage/Film) History'. In *Shakespeare, Film, Fin de Siècle*, edited by Mark Thornton Burnett and Ramona Wray, 40–57. New York: Palgrave Macmillan, 2000.
Bulman, James C., ed. *King Henry IV Part 2*. London: Bloomsbury, 2016.
Burnett, Mark Thornton. *Shakespeare and World Cinema*. Cambridge: Cambridge University Press, 2012.
Butler, Martin. 'Translating the Elizabethan Theatre: The Politics of Nostalgia in Olivier's *Henry V*'. In *Studies in Transpositional Aesthetics*, edited by Shirley Chew and Alistair Stead, 75–97. Liverpool: Liverpool University Press, 1999.
Calbi, Maurizio. *Spectral Shakespeares: Media Adaptations in the Twenty-First Century*. New York: Palgrave Macmillan, 2013.
Callaghan, Dympna. *Shakespeare Without Women: Representing Gender and Race on the Renaissance Stage*. London and New York: Routledge, 1999.
Carlson, Marvin. *The Haunted Stage: The Theatre as Memory Machine*. Ann Arbor: University of Michigan Press, 2003.
Cartelli, Thomas. *Reenacting Shakespeare in the Shakespeare Aftermath: The Intermedial Turn and Turn to Embodiment*. New York: Palgrave Macmillan, 2019.
Cha, Julian. '"There Is No Spoon": Transnationalism and the Coding of Race/Ethnicity in the Science Fiction/Fantasy Cinema of Keanu Reeves'. *Studies in Popular Culture* 35, no. 1 (2012): 47–69.
Chakravarty, Urvashi. '"Live, and beget a happy race of kings": *Richard III*, Race, and Homonationalism'. In *Shakespeare/Sex*, edited by Jennifer Drouin, 147–68. London and New York: Bloomsbury, 2020.
Chakravarty, Urvashi and Ayanna Thompson. 'Race and Periodization: Introduction'. *New Literary History* 52, nos. 3–4 (2021): v–xvi.
Chimes at Midnight. Directed by Orson Welles. 1965; Baker City, OR: Nostalgia Family Video, 2008. DVD.

Collins, Patricia Hill and Sirma Bilge. *Intersectionality*. 2nd edn. Medford, MA: Polity Press, 2016.
Corredera, Vanessa I. '"How Dey Goin' to Kill Othello?!": Key & Peele and Shakespearean Universality'. *Journal of American Studies* 54 (2020): 27–35.
Crenshaw, Kimberlé. 'Postscript'. In *Framing Intersectionality: Debates on a Multi-Faceted Concept in Gender Studies*, edited by Helma Lutz, Maria Teresa Herrera Vivar and Linda Supik, 221–33. Farnham: Ashgate, 2011.
Crowl, Samuel. *Shakespeare at the Cineplex*. Athens: Ohio University Press, 2003.
Dadabhoy, Ambereen. 'The Unbearable Whiteness of Being (in) Shakespeare'. *Postmedieval: A Journal of Medieval Cultural Studies* 11, nos. 2–3 (2020): 228–35.
Deleyto, Celestino. 'Transnational Shakespeare, Feminist Shakespeare: The King'. *Transnational Screens* 12, no. 1 (2021): 62–78.
Donaldson, Peter S. 'Cinema and the Kingdom of Death: Loncraine's *Richard III*'. *Shakespeare Quarterly* 53, no. 2 (2002): 241–59.
Drouin, Jennifer, ed. *Shakespeare/Sex: Contemporary Readings in Gender and Sexuality*. London and New York: Bloomsbury, 2020.
Edelman, Lee. *No Future: Queer Theory and the Death Drive*. Durham: Duke University Press, 2007.
Edward II. Directed by Derek Jarman. 1991; Burbank, CA: New Line Home Video, 1992.VHS.
Elliot, Tomas. 'Shakespearean Seriality: The "Hollow Crown", the "Wooden O", and the "Circle in the Water" of History'. *Adaptation* 12, no. 2 (2019): 69–88.
Espinosa, Rubin. *Shakespeare on the Shades of Racism*. London and New York: Routledge, 2021.
Floyd-Wilson, Mary. *English Ethnicity and Race in Early Modern Drama*. Cambridge: Cambridge University Press, 2003.
Garland-Thomson, Rosemarie. *Extraordinary Bodies*. New York: Columbia University Press, 1997.
Garland-Thomson, Rosemarie. 'The Politics of Staring: Visual Rhetorics of Disability in Popular Photography'. In *Disability Studies: Enabling the Humanities*, edited by Sharon L. Snyder et al., 56–75. New York, Modern Languages Association, 2002.
Greenblatt, Stephen. 'Invisible Bullets: Renaissance Authority and Its Subversion, *Henry IV* and *Henry V*'. In *Political Shakespeare: New Essays in Cultural Materialism*, edited by Jonathan Dollimore and Alan Sinfield, 18–47. Ithaca: Cornell University Press, 1985.
H4. Directed by Paul Quinn. Zelko Films, 2015. DVD.

Hall, Kim F. '"These Bastard Signs of Fair": Literary Whiteness in Shakespeare's Sonnets'. In *Postcolonial Shakespeares*, edited by Ania Loomba and Martin Orkin, 64–83. London and New York: Routledge, 1998.

Hall, Kim F. *Things of Darkness: Economies of Race and Gender in Early Modern England*. Ithaca: Cornell University Press, 1995.

Hampton-Reeves, Stuart and Carol Chillington Rutter. *The Henry VI Plays. Shakespeare in Performance*. Manchester: Manchester University Press, 2007.

Hatchuel, Sarah. '"Into a Thousand Parts Divide One Man": Dehumanised Metafiction and Fragmented Documentary in Peter Babakitis' *Henry V*'. In *Screening Shakespeare in the Twenty-First Century*, edited by Mark Thornton Burnett and Ramona Wray, 146–62. Edinburgh: Edinburgh University Press, 2006.

Helgerson, Richard. *Forms of Nationhood: The Elizabethan Writing of England*. Chicago: University of Chicago Press, 1994.

Hendricks, Margo and Patricia Parker, eds. *Women, 'Race', and Writing in the Early Modern Period*. London and New York: Routledge, 1994.

Heng, Geraldine. *The Invention of Race in the European Middle Ages*. Cambridge: Cambridge University Press, 2018.

Henry V. Directed by Kenneth Branagh. 2000; Santa Monica, CA: MGM Home Entertainment, 1989. DVD.

Henry V. Directed by Laurence Olivier. 1944; Irvington, NY: Criterion Collection, 1999. DVD.

Higginbotham, Derrick. 'The Construction of a King: Waste, Effeminacy, and Queerness in Shakespeare's *Richard II*'. *Shakespeare in Southern Africa* 26 (2014): 59–73.

Hodgdon, Barbara. *The End Crowns All: Closure and Contradiction in Shakespeare's History*. Princeton: Princeton University Press, 1991.

Hodgdon, Barbara. *Henry IV, Part 2. Shakespeare in Performance*. Manchester: Manchester University Press, 1993.

Hodgdon, Barbara. 'Replicating Richard: Body Doubles, Body Politics'. *Theatre Journal* 50, no. 2 (1998): 207–25.

Hodgdon, Barbara. *The Shakespeare Trade: Performances and Appropriations*. Philadelphia: University of Pennsylvania Press, 1998.

Holderness, Graham. *Shakespeare's History*. Dublin: Gill and Macmillan, 1985.

Holderness, Graham. *Shakespeare: The Histories*. New York: Palgrave Macmillan, 2000.

Holderness, Graham. *Tales from Shakespeare: Creative Collisions*. Cambridge:, Cambridge University Press, 2014.

The Hollow Crown: The Complete Series. Directed by Rupert Goold, Richard Eyre and Thea Sharrock. Universal City, CA: Universal Pictures Home Entertainment, 2013. DVD.

The Hollow Crown: The Wars of the Roses. Directed by Dominic Cooke. Universal City, CA: Universal Pictures Home Entertainment, 2016. DVD.

Howard, Jean E. and Phyllis Rackin. *Engendering a Nation: A Feminist Account of Shakespeare's English Histories*. London and New York: Routledge, 1997.

Howlett, Kathy M. *Framing Shakespeare on Film*. Athens: Ohio University Press, 2000.

Hutcheon, Linda. *A Theory of Adaptation*. 2nd edn. London and New York: Routledge, 2013.

Iyengar, Sujata. *Shades of Difference: Mythologies of Skin Color in Early Modern England*. Philadelphia: University of Pennsylvania Press, 2004.

Jagose, Annamarie. 'Feminism's Queer Theory'. *Feminism and Psychology* 19, no. 2 (2009): 157–74.

The Jazz Singer. Directed by Alan Crosland. 1927; Burbank, CA: Warner Home Video, 2007. DVD.

Kaplan, E. Ann. '"The Dark Continent of Film Noir": Race, Displacement, and Metaphor in Tourneur's *Cat People* (1942) and Welles's *The Lady from Shanghai*'. In *Women in Film Noir*, edited by E. Ann Kaplan, 183–201. London: British Film Institute, 1998.

Kastan, David Scott, ed. *King Henry IV, Part 1*. London: Bloomsbury, 2002.

Kaye, Richard A. 'Losing His Religion: Saint Sebastian as Contemporary Gay Martyr'. In *Lesbian and Gay Sexualities and Visual Cultures*, edited by Peter Horne, et al., 86–105. London and New York: Routledge, 1996.

The King. Directed by David Michôd. Plan B Entertainment, 2019. Netflix.

Kirwan, Peter. *The Hollow Crown: An Introductory Essay*. Bloomsbury Publishing, 2019. https://www.dramaonlinelibrary.com/context-and-criticism/the-hollow-crown-an-introductory-essay-iid-173357/ba-9781474208659-3000012.

Knight, Arthur. *Disintegrating the Musical: Black Performance and American Musical Film* Durham: Duke University Press, 2002.

Kossak, Saskia. *'Frame My Face to All Occasions': Shakespeare's Richard III on Screen*. Vienna: Braumüller, 2005.

Kott, Jan. *Shakespeare Our Contemporary*. Translated by Boleslaw Taborski. Garden City: Doubleday, 1964.

Lanier, Douglas. 'Shakescorp *Noir*'. *Shakespeare Quarterly* 53, no. 2 (2002): 157–80.

Lanier, Douglas. 'Shakespearean Rhizomatics: Adaptation, Ethics, Value'. In *Shakespeare and the Ethics of Appropriation*, edited by Alexa Huang and Elizabeth Rivlin, 21–41. New York: Palgrave MacMillan, 2014.

Lehmann, Courtney and Lisa S. Starks, eds. *Spectacular Shakespeare: Critical Theory and Popular Cinema*. Madison, NJ: Fairleigh Dickinson University Press, 2002.

Levine, Nina. *Women's Matters: Politics, Gender, and Nation in Shakespeare's Early History Plays*. Newark: University of Delaware Press, 1998.

Levy-Navarro, Elena. *The Culture of Obesity in Early and Late Modernity: Body Image in Shakespeare, Jonson, Middleton, and Skelton*. New York: Palgrave Macmillan, 2008.

Little, Jr, Arthur L. 'Re-Historicizing Race, White Melancholia, and the Shakespearean Property', *Shakespeare Quarterly* 67, no. 1 (2016): 84–103.

Little, Jr, Arthur L. *Shakespeare Jungle Fever: National-Imperial Re-Visions of Race, Rape, and Sacrifice*. Stanford: Stanford University Press, 2000.

Livingstone, David. 'Silenced Voices: A Reactionary Streamlined *Henry V* in *The Hollow Crown*'. *Multicultural Shakespeare: Translation, Appropriation, and Performance* 12 (2015): 87–100.

Logan, Sandra. *Shakespeare's Foreign Queens: Drama, Politics, and the Enemy Within*. New York: Palgrave MacMillan, 2018.

Loomba, Ania. *Shakespeare, Race, and Colonialism*. Oxford: Oxford University Press, 2002.

Lott, Eric. 'The Whiteness of Film Noir'. In *Whiteness: A Critical Reader*, edited by Mike Hill, 81–101. New York: New York University Press, 1997.

MacDonald, Joyce Green. *Shakespeare Adaptation, Race, and Memory in the New World*. New York: Palgrave MacMillan, 2021.

MacDonald, Joyce Green. *Women and Race in Early Modern Texts*. Cambridge: Cambridge University Press, 2002.

McEachern, Claire. *The Poetics of English Nationhood: 1590–1612*. Cambridge: Cambridge University Press, 1997.

McMillin, Scott. *Henry IV, Part 1. Shakespeare in Performance*. Manchester: Manchester University Press, 1991.

Mendoza, Kirsten N. '"I am Content": Race, Seduction, and the Performances of Consent in *The Hollow Crown*'. *Shakespeare Bulletin* 39, no. 4 (2021): 617–35.

Menon, Madhavi. '*Richard II* and the Taint of Metonymy'. *ELH* 70, no. 3 (2003): 653–75.

Menon, Madhavi, ed. *Shakesqueer: A Queer Companion to the Complete Works of Shakespeare*. Durham: Duke University Press, 2011.

Mollow, Anna. 'Disability Studies Gets Fat'. *Hypatia* 30, no. 1 (2015): 199–216.

Mullin, Romano. 'Tweeting Television/Broadcasting the Bard @ HollowCrownFans and Digital Shakespeares'. In *Broadcast Your Shakespeare: Continuity and Change Across Media*, edited by Stephen O'Neill, 207–26. London and New York: Bloomsbury, 2017.

Munby, Jonathan. *Public Heroes: Screening the Gangster from 'Little Caesar' to 'Touch of Evil'*. Chicago: University of Chicago Press, 1999.

My Own Private Idaho. Directed by Gus Van Sant. 1991; New York: Criterion Collection, 2005. DVD.

Newman, Karen. *Fashioning Femininity and English Renaissance Drama*. Chicago: University of Chicago Press, 1991.

Orgel, Stephen. *Impersonations: The Performance of Gender in Shakespeare's England*. Cambridge: Cambridge University Press, 1996.

Parker, Patricia. *Literary Fat Ladies: Rhetoric, Gender, Property*. London and New York: Routledge, 1988.

Patel, Tina G. and Laura Connelly. '"Post-race" Racisms in the Narratives of "Brexit" Voters'. *The Sociological Review* 67, no. 5 (2019): 968–84.

Pittman, L. Monique. *Authorizing Shakespeare on Film and Television: Gender, Class, and Ethnicity in Adaptation*. New York: Peter Lang Publishing, 2011.

Pittman, L. Monique. 'Colour-Conscious Casting and Multicultural Britain in the BBC's *Henry V* (2012): Historicizing Adaptation in an Age of Digital Placelessness'. *Adaptation* 10 (2017): 176–91.

Pittman, L. Monique. 'Shakespeare and the Cultural Olympiad: Contesting Gender and the British Nation in the BBC's *The Hollow Crown*'. *Borrowers and Lenders: The Journal of Shakespeare and Appropriation* 9 (2016): NP.

Pittman, L. Monique. *Shakespeare's Contested Nations: Race, Gender, and Multicultural Britain in Performances of the History Plays*. London and New York: Routledge, 2022.

Proudfoot, Richard et al., eds. *The Arden Shakespeare Third Series Complete Works*. London and New York: Bloomsbury, 2021.

Puckett, Kent. *War Pictures: Cinema, Violence, and Style in Britain: 1939–1945*. New York: Fordham University Press, 2017.

Quinn, Julia. *The Duke and I*. New York: Harper Collins, 2000.

Quinn, Julia. *The Viscount Who Loved Me*. New York: Harper Collins, 2000.

The Racial Imaginary Institute. *On Whiteness*. SBPH Essays, no. 4. London: SPBH Editions, 2022.

Rackin, Phyllis. 'Anti-Historians: Women's Roles in Shakespeare's Histories'. *Theatre Journal* 27 (1985): 329–44.

Rackin, Phyllis. 'History into Tragedy: The Case of *Richard III*'. In *Shakespearean Tragedy and Gender*, edited by Shirley Nelson

Garner and Madelon G. Sprengnether, 31–53. Bloomington: Indiana University Press, 1996.
Richard II. Directed by Gregory Doran. London: Opus Arte, 2014. DVD.
Richard III. Directed by Richard Loncraine. 1995; Santa Monica, CA: MGM Home Entertainment, 2000. DVD.
Rogers, Jami. 'The Shakespearean Glass Ceiling: The State of Colorblind Casting in Contemporary British Theatre'. *Shakespeare Bulletin* 31, no. 3 (2013): 405–30.
Rogin, Michael. *Black Face, White Noise: Jewish Immigrants in the Hollywood Melting Pot.* Berkeley: University of California Press, 1996.
Roman, David. 'Shakespeare Out in Portland: Gus Van Sant's *My Own Private Idaho*, Homoneurotics, and Boy Actors'. *Genders* 19 (1994): 311–33.
Royster, Francesca. *Becoming Cleopatra: The Shifting Image of an Icon.* New York: Palgrave Macmillan, 2003.
Rutter, Carol Chillington. 'Fiona Shaw's *Richard II:* The Girl as Player-King as Comic'. *Shakespeare Quarterly* 48, no. 3 (1997): 314–24.
Rycroft, Eleanor. 'Hair in the BBC's *The Hollow Crown: The Wars of the Roses:* Class, Nation, Gender, Race, and Difference'. *Shakespeare* 17, no. 1 (2021): 29–48.
Schwarz, Katherine. 'Fearful Simile: Stealing the Breech in Shakespeare's Chronicle Plays'. *Shakespeare Quarterly* 49 (1998): 140–57.
Schwyzer, Philip. *Shakespeare and the Remains of Richard III.* Oxford: Oxford University Press, 2013.
Shapiro, James, ed. *Shakespeare in America: An Anthology from the Revolution to Now.* New York: Penguin, 2014.
Shaughnessy, Robert. 'Falstaff's Belly: Pathos, Prosthetics, and Performance'. *Shakespeare Survey* 63 (Cambridge University Press, 2010): 63–77.
Shewring, Margaret. *King Richard II. Shakespeare in Performance.* Manchester: Manchester University Press, 1996.
Simpson, Anna-Claire. 'Surrogating Boys and the Performance of Whiteness in *Henry V*'. *Shakespeare Studies* 50, no. 63 (2022): 63–72.
Sinfield, Alan. *Faultlines: Cultural Materialism and the Politics of Dissident Reading.* Berkeley: University of California Press, 1992.
Singh, Jyotsna. *Shakespeare and Postcolonial Theory.* London and New York: Bloomsbury, 2020.
The Singing Fool. Directed by Lloyd Bacon. 1928; Burbank, CA: Warner Home Video, 2009. DVD.
Smith, Bruce. *Homosexual Desire in Shakespeare's England: A Cultural Poetics.* Chicago: University of Chicago Press, 1995.
Smith, Ian. 'Othello's Black Handkerchief'. *Shakespeare Quarterly* 64, no. 1 (2013): 1–25.

Smith, Ian. *Race and Rhetoric in the Renaissance: Barbarian Errors*. New York: Palgrave Macmillan, 2009.
Smith, Ian. 'We Are Othello: Speaking of Race in Early Modern Studies'. *Shakespeare Quarterly* 67, no. 1 (2016): 104–24.
Stam, Robert. *Tropical Multiculturalism: A Comparative History of Race in Brazilian Cinema and Culture*. Durham: Duke University Press, 1997.
Starks, Lisa S. and Courtney Lehmann, eds. *The Reel Shakespeare: Alternative Cinema and Theory*. Madison, NJ: Fairleigh Dickinson University Press, 2002.
Sturgess, Kim C. *Shakespeare and the American Nation*. Cambridge: Cambridge University Press, 2004.
Thompson, Ayanna. *Blackface*. London and New York: Bloomsbury, 2021.
Thompson, Ayanna, ed. *The Cambridge Companion to Shakespeare and Race*. Cambridge: Cambridge University Press, 2021.
Thompson, Ayanna, ed. *Colorblind Shakespeare: New Perspectives on Race and Performance* London and New York: Routledge, 2006.
Thompson, Ayanna. '(How) Should We Listen to Audiences?: Race, Reception, and the Audience Survey'. In *The Oxford Handbook of Shakespeare and Performance*, edited by James C. Bulman, 157–69. Oxford: Oxford University Press, 2020.
Thompson, Ayanna. *Passing Strange: Shakespeare, Race, and Contemporary America*. Oxford: Oxford University Press, 2011.
Torrey, Michael. '"The Plain Devil and Dissembling Looks": Ambivalent Physiognomy and Shakespeare's *Richard III*'. *English Literary Renaissance* 30, no. 2 (2000): 123–53.
Traub, Valerie. *Desire and Anxiety: Circulations of Sexuality in Shakespearean Drama*. London and New York: Routledge, 1992.
Traub, Valerie, ed. *The Oxford Handbook of Shakespeare and Embodiment: Gender, Sexuality, and Race*. Oxford: Oxford University Press: 2016.
Van Sant, Gus. *Even Cowgirls Get the Blues / My Own Private Idaho*. London and Boston: Faber and Faber, 1993.
Virdee, Satnam and Brendan McGeever. 'Racism, Crisis, Brexit'. *Ethnic and Racial Studies* 41, no. 10 (2018): 1802–19.
Votava, Jennie M. 'The Ethiop's Jewel meets *Euphoria's* Jules: Race, Gender, and Sexuality in an HBO Appropriation of Shakespeare'. *Shakespeare Bulletin* 38, no. 4 (2020): 593–614.
Votava, Jennie M. 'Through a Glass Darkly: Sophie Okonedo's Margaret as Racial Other in *The Hollow Crown: The Wars of the Roses*'. *Shakespeare Survey* 73 (Cambridge University Press, 2020): 170–83.

Wald, Christina. *Shakespeare's Serial Returns in Complex TV*. New York and London: Palgrave MacMillan, 2020.
Walker, Jessica. '"As Crooked in Thy Manners as Thy Shape": Reshaping Deformity in Loncraine's *Richard III*'. *Journal of the Wooden O Symposium* 11, no. 2 (2012): 155–71.
Werner, Sarah. 'Firk and Foot: The Boy Actor in *Henry V*'. *Shakespeare Bulletin* 21, no. 4 (2003): 19–27.
West, Carolyn M. 'Mammy, Sapphire, and Jezebel: Historical Images of Black Women and Their Implications for Psychotherapy'. *Psychotherapy: Theory, Research, Practice, Training* 32, no. 3 (1995): 458–66.
Whitaker, Cord J. *Black Metaphors: How Modern Racism Emerged from Medieval Race-Thinking*. Philadelphia: University of Pennsylvania Press, 2019.
White Heat. Directed by Raoul Walsh. 1949; Burbank, CA: Warner Home Video, 2005. DVD.
William Shakespeare's Henry V. Directed by Peter Babakitis. Peter Babakitis Films, 2007. Amazon.
Wilson, August. 'The Ground on Which I Stand'. *Callaloo* 20 (Summer 1997): 493–503.
Wilson, Ronald. *The Gangster Film: Fatal Success in American Cinema*. New York: Wallflower Press, 2015.
Wray, Ramona. 'Henry V after the War on Terror'. *Shakespeare Survey* 72 (Cambridge University Press, 2019): 1–15.
Wray, Ramona. 'Shakespeare and the New Discourses of Television: Quality, Aesthetics, and *The Hollow Crown*'. *Cahiers Élisabéthains* 105, no. 1 (2021): 76–92.
Wray, Ramona. 'The Shakespearean Auteur and the Televisual Medium'. *Shakespeare Bulletin* 34, no. 3 (2016): 469–85.
Zauderer, Elizabeth. '"Neither mother, wife, nor England's Queen"': Re-visioning Queen Margaret of Anjou in Richard Loncraine's Film *Richard III* (1995)'. *Literature/Film Quarterly* 43, no. 2 (2015): 146–62.
Zoch, Amanda. 'Macduff's Son and the Queer Temporality of *Macbeth*'. *SEL* 57, no. 2 (2017): 369–88.

INDEX

accents
   African 76, 78
   American 113, 145, 154–6
   British 88, 110
   French 15
   Received Pronunciation 32, 102, 161
   regional English 15, 32, 94
Adams, Brandi K. 15–16, 18–19
Adams, Joseph Quincey 94–5
adaptation
   dialectic between production and reception 8–9, 106, 178
   digital culture and 178
   race, intersectionality and 8–13, 24, 175, 178
   theories of 8–13
   unacknowledged appropriations 10, 179
Adelman, Janet 164
African-American Shakespeare Company 97, 100
African Grove Theatre Company 95, 152
Afropessimism 8
Ahlin, John 96
Aldridge, Ira 152
Alice, Mary 153
Almereyda, Michael 167
Amankwah, Sarah 93
Amazon streaming video 23, 56, 64, 121, 130–131

American actors in cinematic Shakespeare 152–7, 161
American Shakespeare Center 97
Anderson, Benedict 21
Anderson, Lisa M. 22, 152–3
Andoh, Adjoa 92–3, 179–82, 185, 189
Antony and Cleopatra 200
Arneaux, J. A. 152
As Alegres Comadres 118
Ashley, Simone 181–2
As You Like It 154

Babakitis, Peter 63–4
Bachrach, Hailey 99
Bailey, Jonathan 181
Baldo, Jonathan 89–90
Bale, Christian 63
Baltimore Shakespeare Factory 100
Barnaby, Andrew 135–6
Barthelmy, Anthony Gerard 171
Bayley, Sally 105
Bazely, Paul 48
BBC 3, 7, 23–6, 55–6, 72, 105, 200
Beale, Simon Russell 88–9, 101–7, 109–10
Bedi, Sarah and Federay Holmes 93–4
Bening, Annette 154–8
Bilge, Sirma 8

blackface 38, 48, 118, 149, 159–60, 167–72, 175
Black Lives Matter 1–3, 128
Blackness
  affirmative representations of 12, 45–6
  criminality and 142
  curse of Ham as a cause of 174
  deformity and 46–7, 164
  evil and 5, 40–1, 47–8, 171, 174
  femininity and 25, 31, 47, 71–2
  heliosis as a cause of 31
  interior 35, 48, 166–7, 171
  witchcraft and 47, 50
Blackwell, Anna 49, 178, 180
Black/white binary 5, 25, 30, 36, 47, 51–2; *see also* 'shimmering contraries'
Black women
  absence in Shakespeare 8, 26
  adaptation, nontraditional casting and 8, 185, 193
  intersectionality and 7–8
Blain-Cruz, Lileana 99
blank verse/prose binary 123–4
Bloom, Harold 119
blushing, early modern physiology of 38, 40–1
Bodnar, John 166–7
Bonneville, Hugh 40
Bovilsky, Lara 25
Branagh, Kenneth 3, 19, 22, 63, 66, 70, 120, 136, 153–4, 156
Braveheart 109
Bray, Alan 70–1
Breight, Curtis 136–7, 140–4
Brexit 2–3, 5–6, 18–19, 24, 27, 39, 92

Bridgerton
  novel series 177–8, 186, 192–3, 196–7, 199
  TV series 12–13, 176–200
Bristol, Michael D. 95
Broadribb, Benjamin 15–16
Bronfen, Elisabeth 9–10, 57–8, 177
Brotton, Jerry 80
Brown, Carlyle 152
Brown, David Sterling 11, 50
Bulman, James C. 88–9, 101, 109, 113, 115
Burnett, Mark Thornton 118
Bush, George H. W. and George W. 98

Cagney, James 162–4
Calbi, Maurizio 9
California Shakespeare Festival 97–8
Carlson, Marvin 179
Carter, Brandon 97
Cathey, Reg E. 98
celebrity culture 73, 179–80
Cha, Julian 139
Chakravarty, Urvashi 4, 47, 151, 164, 172
Chalamet, Timothée 14, 16–18
Charlotte of Mecklenburg-Strelitz 178–9, 183, 186–9
civil rights 98, 165
class
  'base' as a class and race term 32–3
  Bridgerton 193–6
  classism and intersectionality 7
  Donmar Warehouse *Henry IV* 93–4
  Eyre's *Henry IV* 89, 101–2, 105–7

INDEX

Falstaff and 100–2, 105–6, 110, 117
Falstaff Beer and 96
gangster movie antiheroes 162–3, 166
H4 124–5
Henry V 59, 61
The Hollow Crown, Season Two 27, 32
My Own Private Idaho 134–7, 139–44, 147–8
Cofield, Paul 99
Cold War 165
Collins, Patricia Hill 8
colourblind casting; *see* nontraditional casting
colour-conscious casting; *see* nontraditional casting
comedy 90, 110–15, 117, 171, 175, 178, 192
'complex TV' 23
Cooke, Dominic 24–7
Corbalis, Brendan 153
Corredera, Vanessa 119
Coutinho, Eduardo 117
Covid-19 pandemic 105, 131, 180
Crenshaw, Kimberlé 7–8
critical race theory 5
cross-dressing 64, 100, 118
'crossmapping' 9–10, 57–8
Crowdus, Gary 155
cultural imperialism 22, 156
Cultural Olympiad 24; *see also* London 2012 Summer Olympics
Cumberbatch, Benedict 26–7, 47–50
Cummings, A. Bernard 97

Dadabhoy, Ambereen 11
Deleyto, Celestino 15–16
Dench, Judi 28

Dido 36
digital culture
  Bridgerton as Shakespearean history in 177–200
  ethics in 16
  film culture's 'digital revolution' 131
  global audiences 6, 23, 56, 64, 92, 191–3
  Shakespeare as a digital object 177–85
  Wikipedia and televisual seriality 57
DiPofi, Kyle 133
disability
  Falstaff's fatness as disability 87–9, 102–8, 110, 113, 115 (*see also* obesity)
  My Own Private Idaho 134, 146
  Richard III 46–52, 150–2, 157, 159–61
  White Heat and *Richard III* 163–4, 166
diversity
  audiences 16, 96, 179, 191, 197
  definitions of 15–16
  hiring practices 3, 26, 92, 99
  national 92 (UK), 96, 116–17 (US)
  Twitter 179
divine right 28, 76, 79–80, 174
Donaldson, Peter S. 151, 159
Donmar Warehouse 93–4
Doran, Gregory 52, 71, 77, 83
Dover, white cliffs of 27, 35–6
Dowling, Tim 74
Downey, Jr, Robert 154–7
Dunbar, Adrian 42
Duncan, Lindsay 83

Edelman, Lee   62
Edgerton, Joel   13–17
Edward II   84
Edward VIII   157
Edward of Langley (aka Duke of Aumerle and Duke of York)   56
Elizabeth I of England   5, 29, 71
Elliot, Tomas   55–7, 70
English heritage actors/films   28, 157, 161
Espinosa, Rubin   18
'extraordinary body'   49–52
Eyre, Richard   55, 101, 150, 153

'fair' as a race term   11, 25, 33–5, 51–2, 61–2, 68–9
'fair futurity'; see white futurity
Falstaff (character in the second tetralogy); see Henry IV plays
Falstaff Beer   96, 136
fascism   150–1, 157, 161, 175; *see also* Nazis
Faustão   117–18
feminism   8, 14–16, 23
femme fatale   29, 33, 37, 41, 165
Ferdinand, Marilyn   109, 112
film noir   165–7, 172, 174–5
Fishburne, Laurence   155–6
Floyd-Wilson, Mary   37
Folger Shakespeare Library   94–5
Folio of 1623   56
France and Frenchness
   Henry V   61–2, 198
   Henry VI plays   23, 25, 27, 29–36, 39, 42
   The King   14–15

Gaffney, Devin   131–2
Game of Thrones   13, 200
gangster films   161–7
'Ganymede' as a term for Renaissance boy players   60–2
Garland-Thomson, Rosemarie   49
gender
   blackface and femininity   169–71
   Blackness and femininity   25, 31, 47, 71–2
   Bridgerton   188, 192–6
   Falstaff and   93–4, 96, 98–100, 105, 112, 118
   The Globe's 2019 *Richard II*   92–4, 180–1
   Goold's *Richard II*   70–3, 76, 85
   H4   112, 131–2
   The Hollow Crown, Season Two   23–45, 47
   masculinity and 'feminism' in *The King*   14–15
   maternal relationships and feminization   163–4, 169–70
   My Own Private Idaho   142–3, 146
   opposition between Richard and Bolingbroke in *Richard II*   72
   queerness versus effeminacy in *Richard II*   70–1
   Sharrock's *Henry V*   59–70
   stereotypes of Black masculinity in *Richard III* on stage   152–3
   white masculinity and feminine otherness in Babakitis's *Henry V*   63–4
gender-blind casting   94
George III   186–7

'ghosting' 179–80
The Globe Theatre; see Shakespeare's Globe Theatre
Gomes, Eliezar 117
Gomes, Jorge 117
Goold, Rupert 55, 72, 74–5, 81
Green, Scott Patrick 141–2
Greenblatt, Stephen 112–13

H4 1–4, 7, 12, 87–9, 108–17, 119–36, 141, 148
Hackett, James 95
hair 30, 32, 44, 188–9
Hall, Kim F. 4, 33, 69
Hamlet 104–5, 154–5, 167
Harris, Kamala 131–2
Harris, Pippa 55
Hatchuel, Sarah 63
Hays Code 162
Helgerson, Richard 5
Hendricks, Margo 4
Heng, Geraldine 4–5
Henry IV plays
  Bridgerton as unacknowledged appropriation of 192–6
  Chimes at Midnight 100, 107, 135–6, 143
  Falstaff in 87–118
  Faustão 117–18
  Globe to Globe Festival 88
  H4 1, 87–9, 108–17, 119–34
  The Hollow Crown 55–6, 87–9, 100–8
  The King 13, 17
  My Own Private Idaho 120–1, 134–48
Henry V
  America and 95, 97
  Babakitis's *Henry V* 63–4
  Branagh's *Henry V* 2–3, 19, 63, 66, 70, 120, 136, 153

Bridgerton as unacknowledged appropriation of 192, 198–9
Chimes at Midnight 100, 147
The Globe's 2019 Henriad 93–4
The Hollow Crown 55–70, 80, 108
The King 13–18
National Theatre's 2003 *Henry V* 26, 185
Olivier's *Henry V* 63–4, 66, 69–70, 91
Henry VI plays 21–45, 47, 52, 164
heteronormativity 57, 59–60, 64, 85–6, 143
heterosexuality 134, 150, 173
Hewlett, James 95, 152
Hiddleston, Tom 26, 65, 68, 101–4, 108
Higginbotham, Derrick 78–9, 83
Hipólito, Leila 118
historical accuracy 25, 45, 106, 183–4, 189–92
historical revisionism 89–90, 186, 189, 199
history play
  Brazilian appropriations 117–18
  Bridgerton and 178, 183, 191–200
  chronology and seriality of 56–7, 70
  contemporary American appropriations 120–1, 134
  masculinist genre 29
  national identity and race in 1–7, 13, 24, 91, 117, 175

INDEX

nationalist genre 5, 15, 29, 152
nontraditional casting in 9, 21–4, 26, 88, 92, 96–8, 152–3
  as race plays 11, 151
  'Tudor myth' in 28–9
history play cycles 56, 90–1, 95–6
Hitchcock, Alfred 158–61
Hitler, Adolph; *see* fascism; Nazis
Hodgdon, Barbara 6, 88, 91–2, 148, 156
Holderness, Graham 5, 9, 56
Holinshed's Chronicles 147–8
Holland, Peter 150, 156
The Hollow Crown (as a unit) 2–3, 5, 7, 11–12, 22–4, 26
  Season One (as a unit) 55–8
    Henry IV plays 55–6, 87–9, 101–8, 110
    Henry V 58–71, 77, 86, 106, 108
    Richard II 70–86
  Season Two (*The Wars of the Roses*) 21–53, 84, 86, 175, 200
Hollywood 139, 154, 162, 168–9
The Holocaust 53, 158, 166
homoeroticism 63–4, 66, 71, 78, 82–5, 144
homonationalism 151
homosexuality 71, 81–2, 134–5, 137–40, 150, 173; *see also* queer sexuality
Hooks, Robert 97
Hopkins, Lisa 154, 156
Howard, Jean E. 5, 42–3
Howlett, Kathy 100, 135–6, 157–8, 161
Hughes, Tom 56, 70–1, 76–7, 79

humoral theory 37–8, 40
Hurt, John 58, 68
Hutcheon, Linda 8–9
Hytner, Nicholas 26, 185

immigration 5, 27, 95, 123, 162, 168, 198
imperialism 109, 136–7, 140–1, 157; *see also* cultural imperialism
India and Indian ethnicity 179, 184, 190, 196–9
Indie Memphis Film Festival 121, 131
International Shakespeare Conference 131
intersectionality 7–8, 12–13
Ireland and Irish ethnicity 24, 76, 90, 123, 162, 169
Irons, Jeremy 26, 103–4
Iyengar, Sujata 38

Jackson, Amad 12, 111, 115–16, 122, 133
Jackson, Michael 11, 58, 71–5, 79–82, 86
Jacobi, Derek 70, 72, 74
Jagose, Annamarie 57–8
Jarman, Derek 84
The Jazz Singer 167–70
Jeremiah, Ivanno 45
Jewishness and Judaism 3, 25, 53, 149, 162, 167–70
Joan of Arc 29–34, 39
Jolson, Al 149, 163, 167–72, 175
Jonson, E. Patrick 45
Joseph, Paterson 3, 56, 58–9, 64, 70–1, 77, 85–6

Kaplan, E. Ann 165
Kaye, Richard 81–2
Keaton, Michael 153

The King 1, 2, 7, 13–19
King, Jr, Martin Luther 121–3
King, Rodney 1, 7
King and Country 71, 79
king's two bodies 75
Kinnear, Rory 26, 81, 85
Kirk, Oliver 137
Kirwan, Peter 3, 28, 71
Klein, Alyssa 25
Knight, Arthur 168
Knight, G. Wilson 91
Kossak, Saskia 167, 172
Kott, Jan 128–9
Krishnan, Lijesh 97

Lanier, Douglas 9–10, 167
Leaving Neverland 73
Lehman, Courtney 3, 154
Lennix, Harry 4, 112, 119, 121–4, 126–8, 131–2
Leonard, Robert Sean 153
Lester, Adrian 26
Levine, Nina 41
Levy-Navarro, Elena 102
Lincoln, Abraham 95
Linton, Lynette 92–3
Little, Jr, Arthur L. 4, 11, 25, 31, 36
Little Caesar 162
Livingstone, David 59
Lloyd, Phyllida 93–4
Loehlin, James 156–7, 163–5
Logan, Sandra 39
Loncraine, Richard 150, 172
London 2012 Summer Olympics 24, 131; *see also* Cultural Olympiad
Loomba, Ania 4
Los Angeles (LA) 1–2, 7, 87, 108, 111, 122–9
Los Angeles Police Department (LAPD) 1–2
Los Angeles Uprising 2

Lott, Eric 165
Luhrmann, Baz 154

Macbeth 55, 62, 105, 167, 184
MacDonald, Joyce Green 4, 8, 36, 118
McEachern, Claire 5
Macfadyen, Angus 88–9, 109–10, 112–13, 115–16, 119, 146
McGuire, Ashley 93–4
McKellen, Sir Ian 150–1, 156, 159–64, 167, 171–3, 175
McRuer, Robert 150
'Magical Negro' 59, 65, 68
Margaret of Anjou (character in the first tetralogy) 4, 23, 25, 27, 29, 32–6, 41–4, 46–7, 50, 172–4; *see also* Okonedo, Sophie
Martin, Victor Huertas 74–5
Matthews, Dakin and Mladen Kiselov 98
memory/memorialization and forgetting 63, 68–9, 90, 94
Mendelsohn, Ben 14
Mendes, Sam 55
Mendoza, Kirsten 34
'merry' and 'merrie England' 90, 100, 107–8, 135, 148
The Merry Wives of Windsor 88, 90, 96–100, 118
metatheatricality 100, 124
metonymy 66, 68, 110, 115, 178, 182–5; *see also* synecdoche
Michôd, David 13, 15–17
mirrors, symbolism of 46–8, 50, 52, 164
Mittell, Jason 23
Mollow, Anna 105

Molyneaux, Paul 152
Mondello, Bob 184
Morgan, Laura 30
Morgan, T. S. 97
Morrissey, David 81
Msamati, Lucian 3, 11, 58, 72, 76
Much Ado about Nothing 22, 153–4, 156, 180–1, 192
Mudede, Charles 18
Mullin, Romano 178–9
multiculturalism 23, 39, 53, 59, 97
Muni, Paul 162–3
Muslims, representations of 41, 94, 112; *see also* Turks, representations of
My Own Private Idaho 3, 12, 120, 134–48, 153

national identity
 American 5, 95, 162, 165
 English, British 2, 5, 9, 17, 22–4, 89–92, 180–1
nationalism 5, 15, 29–30, 52, 90–1, 152
National Theatre 26, 55, 71, 150, 153
Native Americans, representations of 137–8, 140, 144–5, 157
Nazis 150, 156–8, 161–2, 166; *see also* fascism
Netflix 2, 15, 23, 191–3, 200
Newman, Karen 25
New York Shakespeare Festival 22, 97, 153
nontraditional casting
 adaptation and 8–9, 11
 avoidance of 13, 56
 Bridgerton as colourblind v. colour-conscious 189–90

 definitions of 8–9, 21
 The Globe's 2019 Henriad as colourblind v. colour-conscious 94
 H4 as color-conscious 12
 history of 22, 26, 88, 92–3, 96–100, 149, 152–5
 Joseph's York in *The Hollow Crown* as color-conscious 69
 metonym for Shakespeare 177–8, 183–5
 Okonedo's Margaret in *The Hollow Crown* 25–6, 43
 Oregon Shakespeare Festival and 98–9
 problems with 22, 24–5, 152–3
 reappropriating history with 192
 reasons for 16, 96
nostalgia 90–1, 96, 108, 135

Obama, Barack 98, 116, 122–3, 128
obesity 88, 102–5, 110; *see also* disability
O'Connell, Rachel 50–1
Okonedo, Sophie 4, 11, 21–3, 25–9, 31–2, 34–6, 39–44, 47, 50, 52–3, 84, 86, 175, 200
Oldcastle, Sir John 89–90
Olivier, Laurence 45, 63–4, 66, 69, 71, 91, 104–5, 167
Oregon Shakespeare Festival (OSF) 97–9
Orientalism 76, 154
Othello 25, 32–3, 65, 155–6, 183–5
Oyelowo, David 22

Page, Regé-Jean 179–80, 186
Papp, Joseph 22, 97, 185
Parker, Michael 141
Parker, Oliver 155
Parker, Patricia 93, 112
performativity 80, 140, 144, 171
period drama 73, 109, 178, 189–91
periodization 4
Phoenix, River 135
Pittman, L. Monique 5, 16, 27, 32, 41, 59, 65, 68, 82–3, 154
Platt, Victoria 112, 131–2
Portland, Oregon 137–8, 141, 145
Power, Ben 27, 41, 52, 58
presidential elections, US 5, 98, 116, 122, 131–2
prosthetics 48–50, 101–2, 104, 115, 118
psychoanalysis 93, 164
The Public Enemy 162

Quander, Eric 98
Quarshie, Hugh 22, 92
queer 'death drive' 57, 62, 174; *see also* queer temporality; reproductive futurity
queer seriality 12, 57–60, 70–1, 86
queer sexuality
  boy actors 60–2, 143
  Goold's *Richard II* 71–3, 75–86
  Loncraine's *Richard III* 3, 150–1, 173–4
  My Own Private Idaho 3, 134–5, 137–44
  Richard II in modern interpretations 70–1

RSC's *King and Country* 71, 77, 79, 83
queer temporality 57, 82; *see also* queer 'death drive'; reproductive futurity
Quinn, Julia 177, 186, 192, 196–7, 199
Quinn, Paul 4

race
  adaptation and 10–13
  Brazilian representations of Falstaff 117–18
  Brexit 2, 18–19
  Bridgerton 177–200
  early American cinema 149, 161–72, 175
  early modern definitions of 25
  early modern studies and 4–6
  Eyre's *Henry IV, Parts 1* and *2* 87–9, 106, 108
  Falstaff on stage in the UK 92–4
  Falstaff on stage in the US 96–100
  Goold's *Richard II* 11–12, 56–8, 70–81, 84–6
  H4 12, 87–9, 108–17, 119–34
  The Hollow Crown: The Wars of the Roses 21–53
  humoral theories of 37
  The King 13, 15–19
  Loncraine's *Richard III* 149–51, 159–62, 164–5, 167, 169, 171–5
  My Own Private Idaho 120, 134, 137–48
  Richard III on stage 152–3
  seeing and visibility of 1–2, 5, 10–11, 19, 23–4, 29, 175
  Sharrock's *Henry V* 56–70

terminology 4
race-blind casting; *see*
    nontraditional casting
Racial Imaginary Institute 11
racial semiotics 9, 21–3, 25, 33,
    47, 53, 67
racial violence 45, 84, 125–9,
    152, 166
racism
    American cinema 149–52,
        161–2
    American legal system 1,
        125–6
    Brexit 2, 19
    Bridgerton 189–90
    coded 156
    colourblind casting 22–3, 42
    intersectionality 7
    My Own Private Idaho 142
    Renaissance 4
    Shakespeare and 11, 128–9,
        152, 161–2
    YouTube comments 181
Rackin, Phyllis 5, 29, 42–3
Radel, Nicholas 154
rape 33–4, 141–2
Raphaelson, Samuel 168
Received Pronunciation; *see*
    accent
'recording' 112–13
Redgrave, Michael 71, 90
Reeves, Keanu 134, 137,
    139–40, 144, 153
Regency England 188, 191
Rehmani, Sabaa 64
reproductive futurity 57, 62–4,
    164; *see also* queer 'death
    drive'; queer temporality
Rhimes, Shonda 177, 200
'rhizomatics' 9–10
Rhodes, KiaJah 125–6
Richard II
    deposition scene 52

The Globe's 2019 *Richard
    II* 26
The Hollow Crown 3, 11,
    55–8, 70–86
National
    Theatre's 2005 *Richard
    II* 71
RSC's *King and Country* 71,
    79, 83
RSC's 1951 *Richard II* 71
Richard III
    early American
        performance 95, 152
    The Hollow Crown 27,
        45–53
    Loncraine's 3, 12, 149–65,
        167, 169, 171–5
    1990s stage
        performances 153
    Olivier's 45, 167
Richard III, remains of 49
Richert, William 134
Rix, Oliver 71, 79
Rogers, Jami 22
Rogin, Michael 162, 167–70
Rolle, John Livingston 97
Roman, David 143
romance 177–8, 183, 189,
    191–4
Romeo and Juliet 154, 177
roses, color symbolism of 27,
    37–9, 41–3, 51–2
Rosheuvel, Golda 179, 185–8,
    190, 192, 199–200
Royal National Theatre; *see*
    National Theatre
Royal Shakespeare Company
    (RSC)
    Falstaff as symbol of 91
    Goold as director 55
    King and Country 71, 77, 79
    nontraditional casting 22, 26,
        92, 180, 185

INDEX 257

Royster, Francesca 4, 24
RSC; *see* Royal Shakespeare Company
Rutsky, R.L. 139
Rutter, Carol Chillington 71
Ryan, Nick 114
Rycroft, Eleanor 32, 44

Said, Edward 76
St George 64–5, 67–8
St George's flag 38–9, 52, 65, 180
St Sebastian 81–2, 84
Scarface 162–3
Schwarz, Katherine 29, 31
Scotland and Scottish ethnicity 24, 88, 109, 123
Second World War 53, 90–1, 165–7; *see also* The Holocaust
seriality 9–10, 55–8, 177, 200; *see also* queer seriality
sex workers, representations of 103, 120, 134–8, 140–3, 193
Shakespeare
   American cultural icon 16, 94–6, 108
   Blackness and 89, 111, 116, 121
   British cultural icon 16
   cultural authority/capital of 3, 89, 118, 123, 140, 142, 184–5
   endurance 9–10
   exclusion of people of colour in 16
   Falstaff as a metonym for 110
   nontraditional casting, association with 178, 182–5

oppression, agent and critic of 111, 117, 141, 148
ubiquity 7, 177
whiteness and 89, 109, 116, 119, 134, 141–6
Shakespeare Association of America (SAA) 121, 131
Shakespeare's Globe Theatre 26, 88, 92–4, 180–1, 185
Shakespeare Uncovered 72
Sharrock, Thea 55
Shaughnessy, Robert 88, 91, 101–2
Shaw, Fiona 71
Shenandoah Shakespeare Company; *see* American Shakespeare Center
'shimmering contraries' 36, 51; *see also* Black/white binary
Simpson, Anna-Claire 60–2
Simpson, Wallis 157
Sinfield, Alan 66
The Singing Fool 168, 170–1, 175
slavery 44–5, 152, 190–1
Smith, Ian 4, 6, 48
Smith, Maggie 157–8, 174
sodomy 60–1, 70–1, 78–9, 83
sonnets 25, 62–3, 69
Stam, Robert 117–18
stereotyping
   Black female stereotypes 37, 39, 190
   Black male stereotypes 142, 152–3
   colourblind casting and 23–4, 37, 109
   film noir and 166
   Luhrmann's *Romeo + Juliet* and 154

streaming video platforms 19, 23, 56, 130–1, 179, 181, 191
Sturgess, Kim C. 95
'surrogation' 60–1, 68–9
synecdoche 50, 148, 161; *see also* metonymy

The Taming of the Shrew 182–3, 192, 196, 198
Tavares, Elizabeth 47
Tennant, David 71, 79
terrorism 27, 41, 151, 172
Thomas, G. Valmont 97–8
Thompson, Ayanna
  H4 4, 123, 131
  nontraditional casting 22, 98
  race in early modernity 4, 6, 85
  Shakespeare in contemporary America 119, 133
Thornton, Jr, Rene 98
Tillyard, E.M.W. 91
timelessness; *see* universality
Titus Andronicus 32
Torrey, Michael 159
tragedy 88, 101, 104–7, 170–1, 192
tragicomedy 146, 171
transnationalism 15, 100, 139
Troilus and Cressida 28
Troughton, Patrick 34
Troupe, Tom 134, 139
Trump, Donald 5, 18, 98–9
Tudor dynasty 5, 28–9, 39, 51–3, 174
Tudor myth 28–9, 52, 174
Turks, representations of 11, 61, 80
Twitter 178–84, 196–7, 200

universality 12, 15, 119–21, 124–6, 128–30, 133–4, 143–4, 148

Van Sant, Gus 134–5, 137
Vogt, K.T. 99

Wales and Welsh ethnicity 24, 76–7, 90, 123
Walker, Jessica 150
Warner, David 91, 102
Warner, Deborah 71
The Warner Brothers 168
War on Terror 5, 24, 27
Wars of the Roses 5, 27
Washington, Denzel 153–4, 180, 184
Waters, Julie 105
Weiman, Robert and Douglas Bruster 171
Welles, Orson 100–1, 107, 109–10, 135–6, 143, 147–8
Werner, Sarah 61–2
West, Dominic 172, 174
Whishaw, Ben 11, 26, 58, 70–5, 77–8, 81
Whitaker, Cord J. 5, 36
white-face 152
white futurity 61–3, 172–4
White Heat 162–7, 169, 171–2
'white history' 59, 85–6, 106
'white melancholia' 11, 36
whiteness; *see also* 'fair'
  American national identity and 162, 168
  blackface enabling 169–72
  The Boy in *Henry V* as a figure of 59–69
  colourblind casting and 22
  English/British national identity and 9, 24, 35–6, 59, 62, 64–6, 80
  Falstaff as a figure of 89, 92–4, 106, 108–9, 111–12, 116–18

film noir as the 'refuge
    of' 165
Henry V as a figure of 64–6,
    69
The King 2, 13–19
lady's 'white hand' as
    synecdoche for 50
My Own Private Idaho 120,
    134, 137–47
privileged invisibility of 2, 11,
    16, 19, 22
purity/truth/innocence/holiness
    and 5, 31, 40, 47
Richard III 151, 164
rose color symbolism 37–9
Shakespearean celebrity
    and 180
Shakespeare scholarship
    and 6
unacknowledged signifier 11

white privilege 11, 35, 37, 94,
    117, 141, 189; *see also*
    whiteness
white supremacy 59, 64, 94,
    190
Wikipedia 57
Williams, Linda 169
Wilson, August 22
Wilson, Jamir 122–3
Windrush 92
Winfield, Paul 97
Wolf, Matt 184–5
Wood, Christopher 25
Wray, Ramona 23, 59, 68, 71,
    76

YouTube 96, 99, 180–1

Zelko, Giovanni 123–4
Zoch, Amanda 62

www.ingramcontent.com/pod-product-compliance
Lightning Source LLC
Chambersburg PA
CBHW071815300426
44116CB00009B/1329